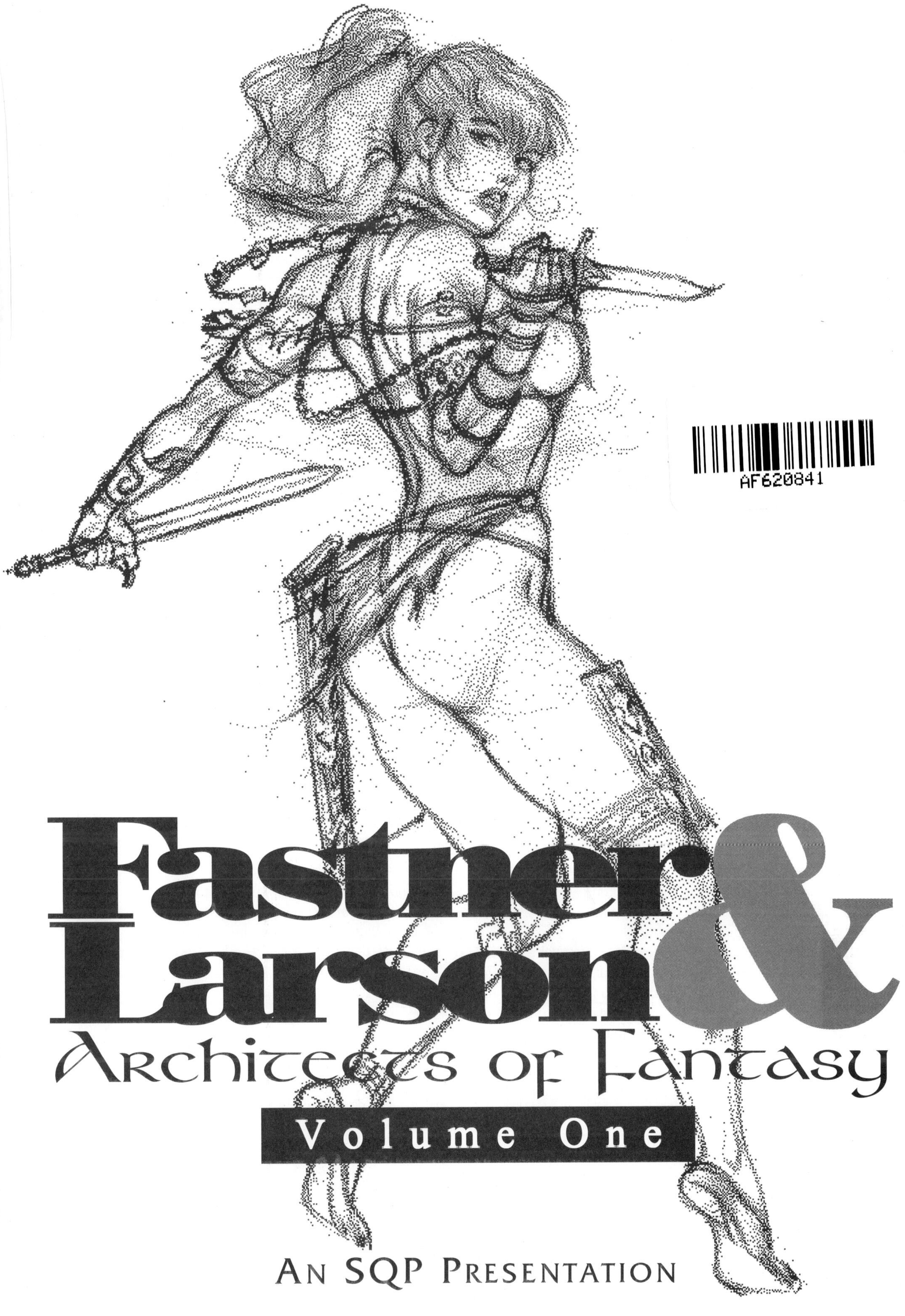

# Fastner & Larson

## Architects of Fantasy

### Volume One



An SQP Presentation

# AN INTRODUCTION BY JIM STERANKO

It was about 18 years ago, amid the chaos of a San Diego comic convention, that I had my first close-up look at their work.

We were all kids then, although I was in my second childhood, having ventured through a number of careers that included music, magic, advertising art, and comics. I'd left my home at Marvel -- somehow Nick Fury and Captain America managed to survive the trauma -- to pursue the ecstasies of publishing, while alternately painting paperback covers and movie posters. Fastner and Larson had just started their journey on a similar Yellow Brick Road a few years earlier.

They were hot shots, fresh and energetic talents capable of charting a number of directions into the fantasy world. Unlike most tyros, however, their portfolio revealed considerable artistic sophistication that surprisingly was matched by their conceptual development. I recommended they concentrate on the material with which they seemed most comfortable: fantastic women in fantastic settings.

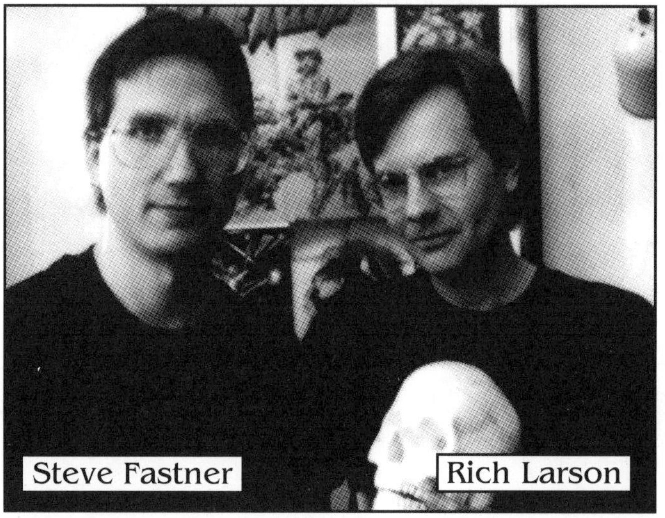

Steve Fastner — Rich Larson

Almost two decades later, I'm pleased to note they agreed with my assessment, having firmly established their collaboration in the pantheon of modern fantasists who specialize in uniting the timeless elements of beauty and bizarre. (In an occasional self-indulgent moment, however, they will lower their standards to simple sex and violence.)

Historically, their roots are in the pulp tradition of Margaret Brundage, Virgil Finlay, Earle Bergey, Allen Anderson and others, whose evocative visions of slave girls and space maidens energized the pages of Weird Tales, Famous Fantastic Mysteries, Startling Stories and a galaxy of SF and fantasy magazines which thrived from the late '20s to the mid-'50s.

Although Fastner and Larson absorbed the pulps slightly after the fact, they compensated by layering over that foundation with a lifetime of film and TV viewing, plus an obvious influence from cartoons and comic books. The resulting amalgam has produced a unique style that even the most indiscriminating eye cannot fail to identify.

Certainly Frazetta paints with more passion. Whelan's works have more sensitivity. Boris renders more realistically. The Hildebrandts are more romantic. None of them, however, embrace the wit and humor glazed into every Fastner and Larson creation. Whether it's the hyper-melodramatic glint in a monster's gaze or the placement of a few decorative baubles, the collaborators inevitably make their artistic statements fun.

Conversely, by today's standards, their work is flawed, seriously lacking some of the most important elements of contemporary fantasy art, all aspects that most of their brotherhood abundantly mix with their paint like matte medium or linseed oil: cynicism, pretension, nihilism, and contempt.

So? Nobody's perfect.

What the team's work may lack in psychopolitical subtlety and sexist grace is more than compensated for by cacophonous compositions that are dense with metaphoric devices, and often basic bad taste, all which reaffirms our darker dreams -- without the annoying pain of anxiety and guilt.

My personal barometer when viewing art, especially fantasy art, evaluates its capability to surprise. Far too many artists who have been sainted by aesthetically illiterate fans are nothing more than anthropomorphic xerox machines, painting predictable cliches by recycling models, palletes, and ideas that were barren decades ago. Those who have maintained the burden of visual surprise are among my favorites.

Fastner and Larson are high on that list.

The latter's prop and costume design is a perfect example of his virtuosity; often similar, yes; alike, no. His characters are equally as varied, particularly the women. Larson knows that feminine beauty is infinite, and explores the concept in most of his efforts.

Fastner, more often than not painting with minimal model reference, pulls the viewer into his make-believe world (where light and shadow sometimes refuse to obey the laws of physics) by a bold -- often outrageous -- use of color, superb draftsmanship, and a command of mixed media that is eclipsed only by a killer airbrush technique.

As collaborators, their work epitomizes the male fantasy, while adding a capricious touch of Mad Magazine-type whimsy, like Robert E. Howard out of Harvey Kurtzman. Their world is one of magic, myth, and menace, of malevolent beasts, bio-mechanical monsters, and beautiful maidens. As storytellers, they open the door to a dimension of split-second action, epic splendor, and fantastic heroism.

Their drawing board is illuminated by imagination.

They are architects of fantasy.

This is their blueprint.

Jim Steranko

Jim Steranko is a pop-culture historian whose two volumes of THE HISTORY OF COMICS have become the definitive works on the subject. As an award-winning artist with more than 160 international exhibitions to his credit, he has influenced several generations of illustrators. As a filmmaker, he has collaborated with Steven Spielberg on *Raiders of the Lost Ark* and, more recently, with Francis Ford Coppola as the Project Conceptualist on *Dracula*. Steranko currently publishes the entertainment magazine PREVUE.

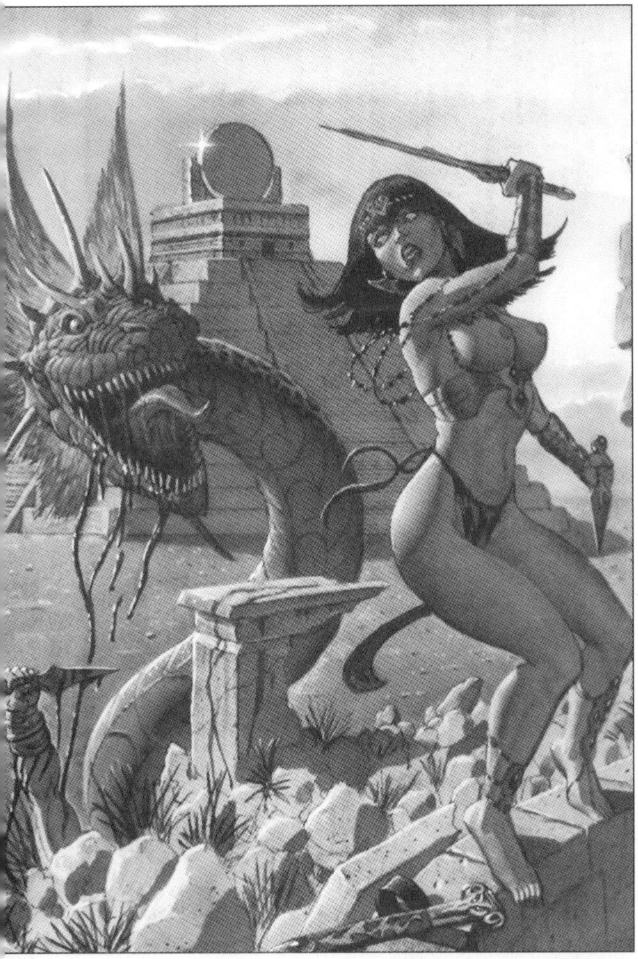

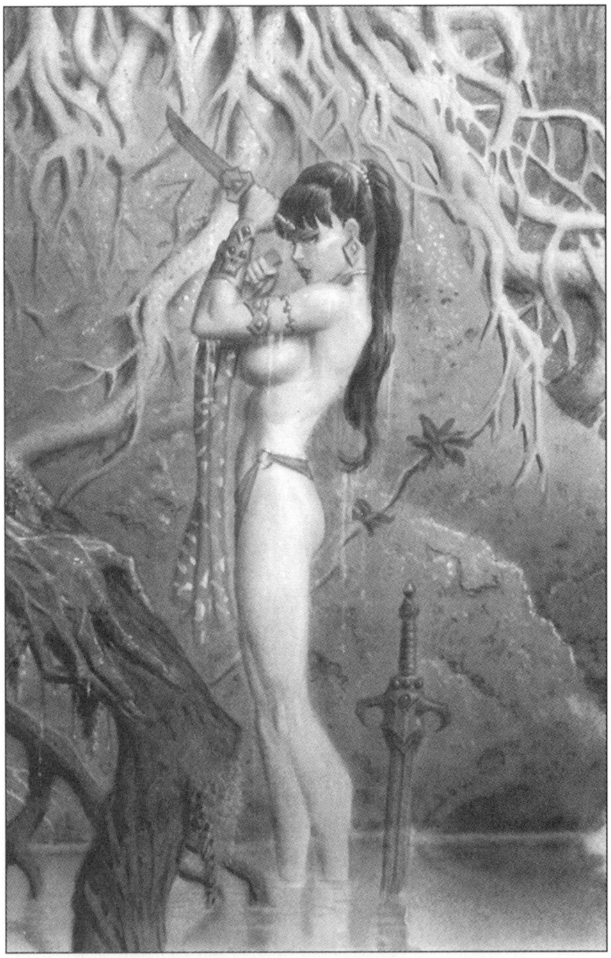

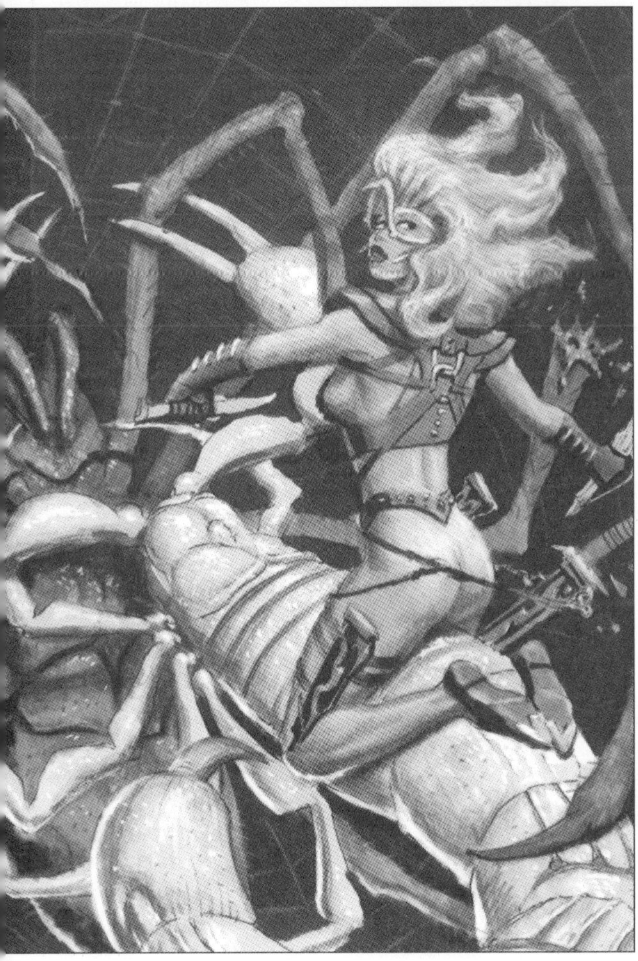

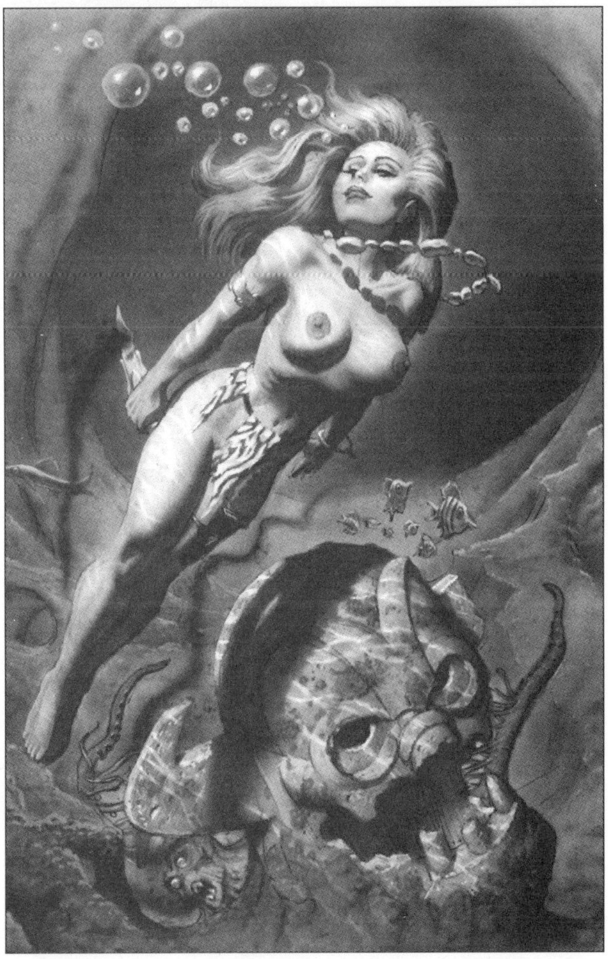

CLOCKWISE FROM TOP LEFT:

COLOR ROUGHS FROM THE PORTFOLIO **NAKED STEEL**

TONE STUDY FOR A PLATE FROM THE PORTFOLIO **NIGHTSLAYERS**

**STEVE:**

*"I try to get the most dramatic lighting possible, often testing three or four different schemes"*

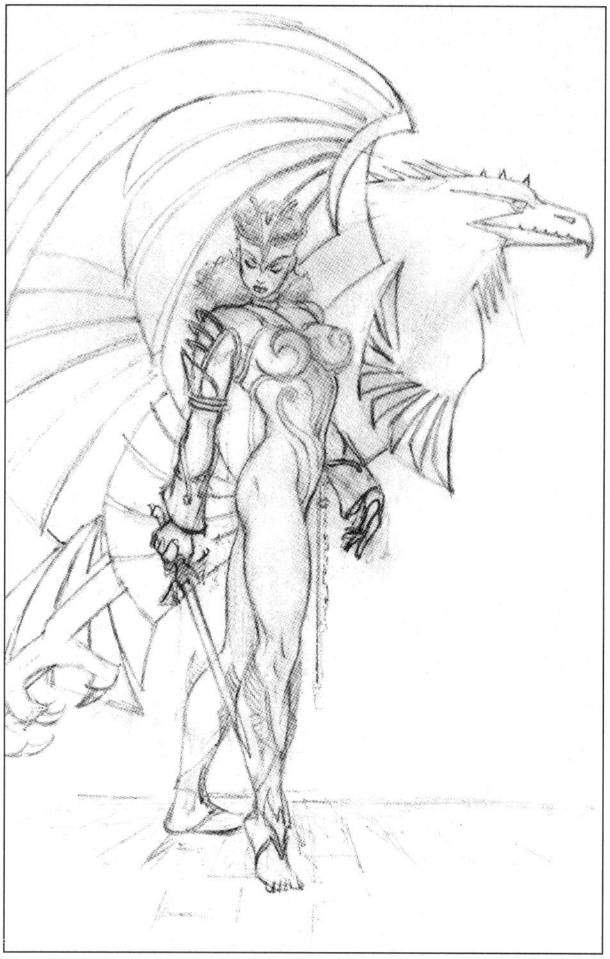

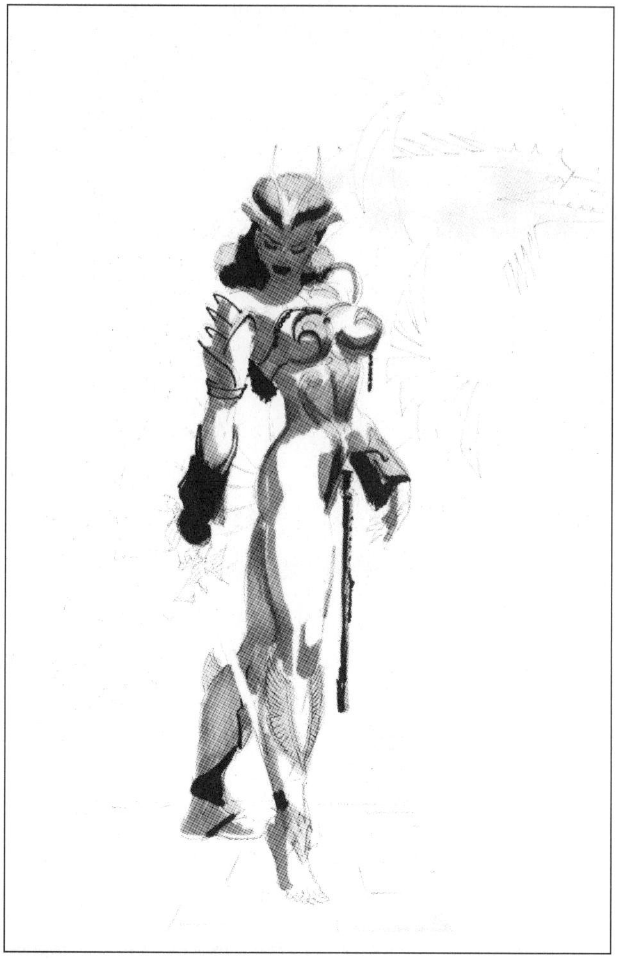

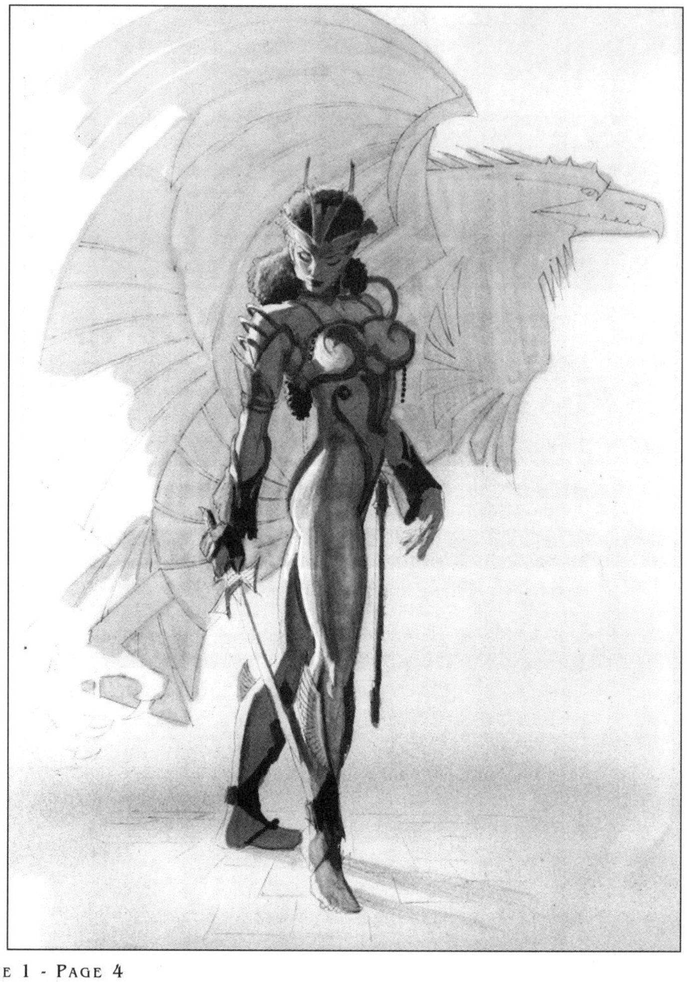

Clockwise from top left:

Initial pencil rough for plate in portfolio **Flesh & Blood Set 2**

Preliminary light study for same

Final light study

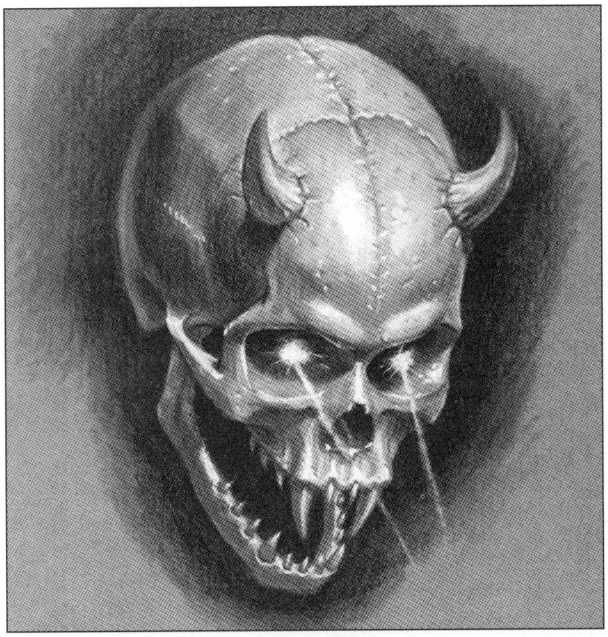

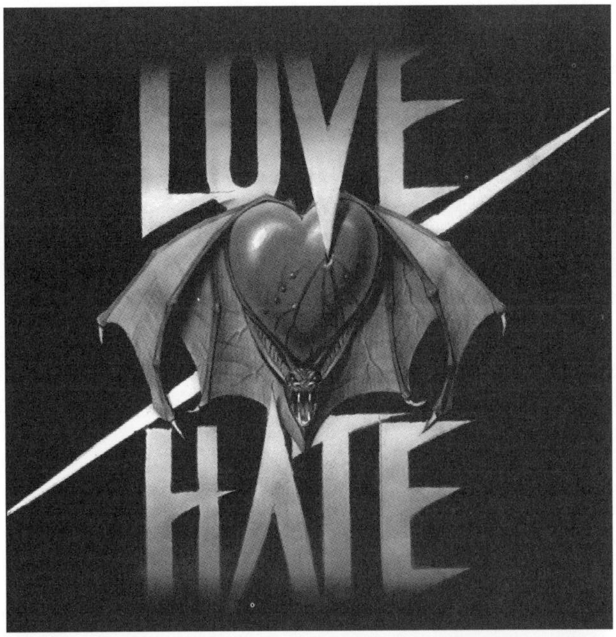


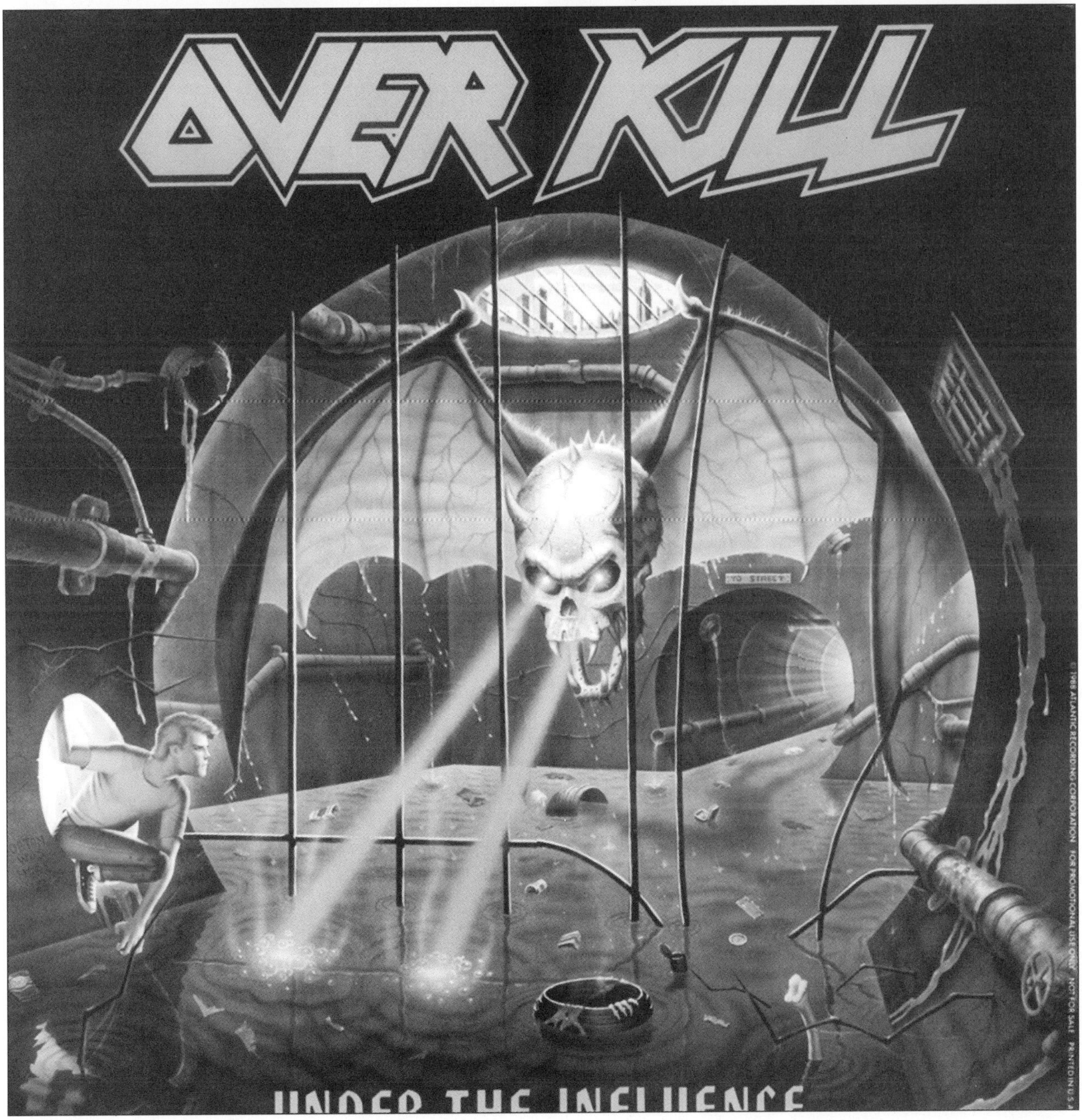


CLOCKWISE FROM LEFT:

DETAILED STUDY FOR **OVERKILL** SKULL

PROPOSED T-SHIRT DESIGN FOR AN L.A. ROCK BAND

**OVERKILL'S** "UNDER THE INFLUENCE" COVER FINISHED PIECE

FOLLOWING PAGE: TONE STUDY FOR A **JUDGE DREDD** COVER

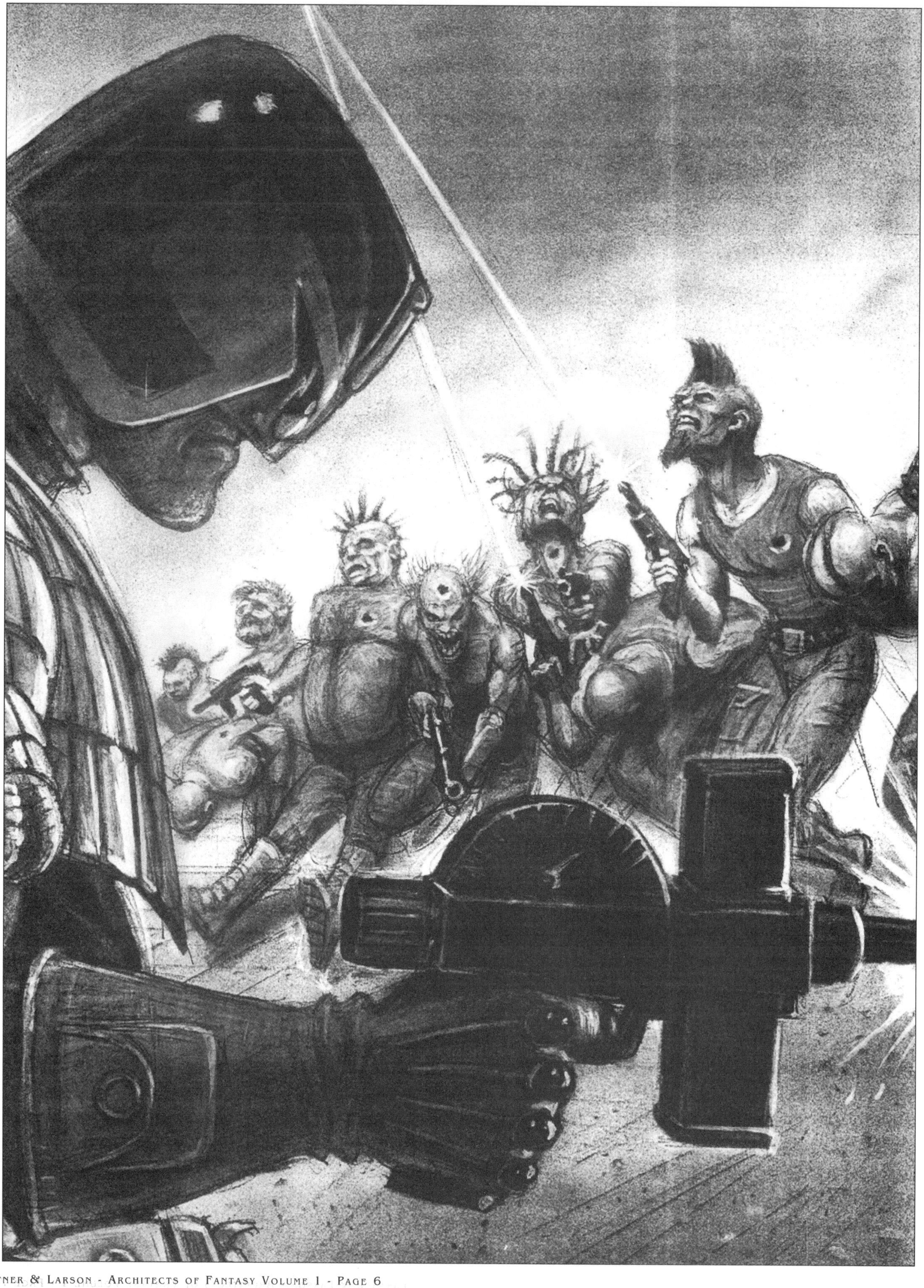

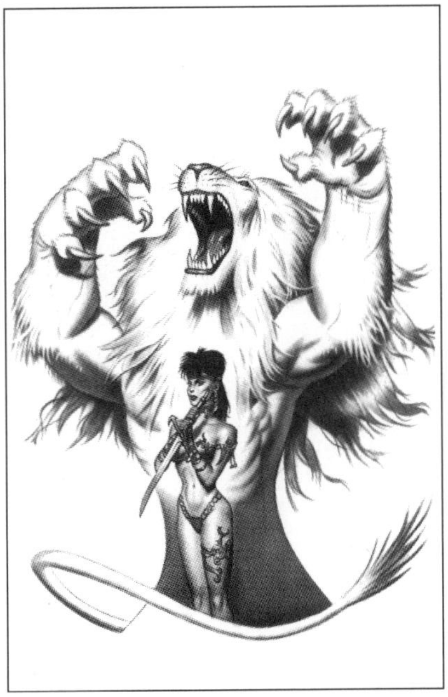

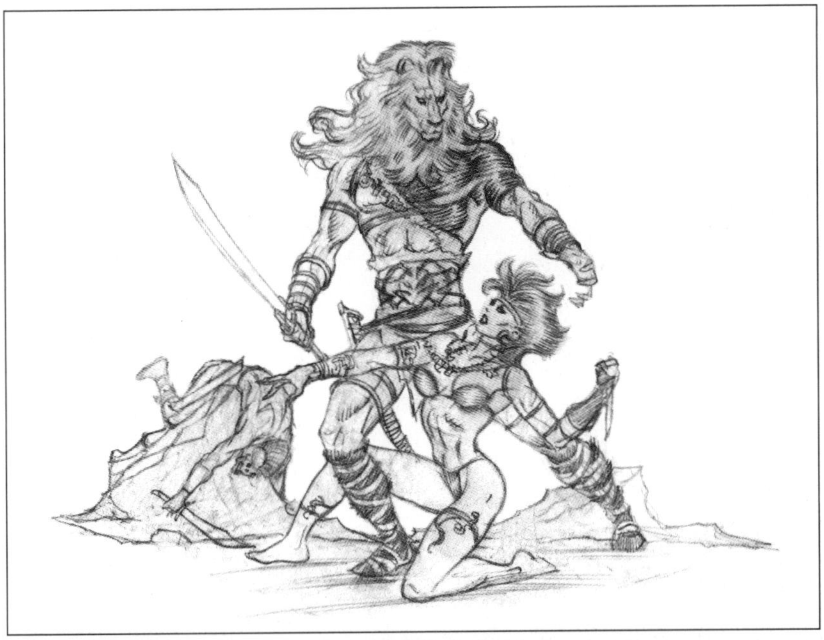

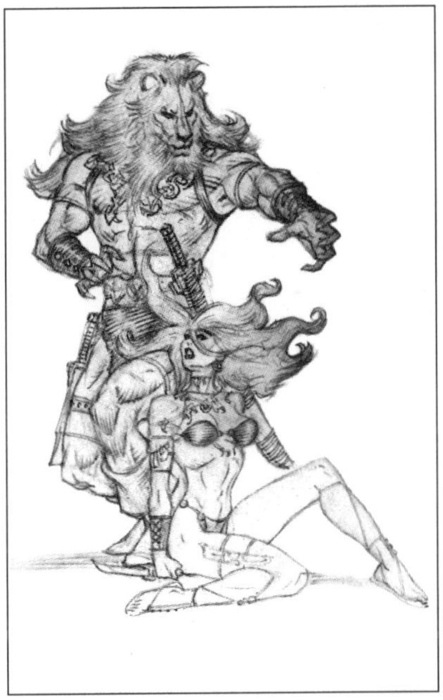

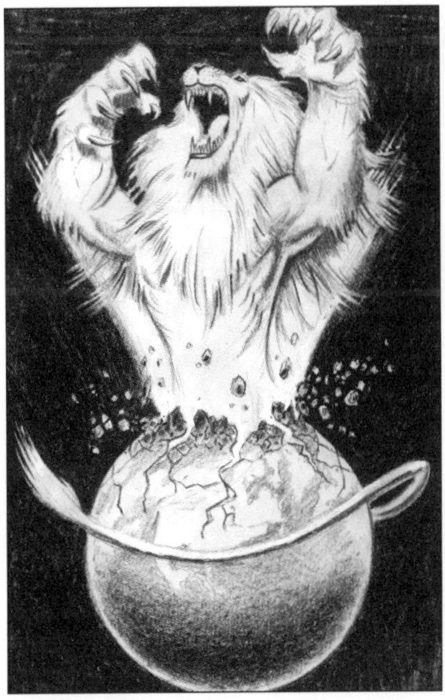

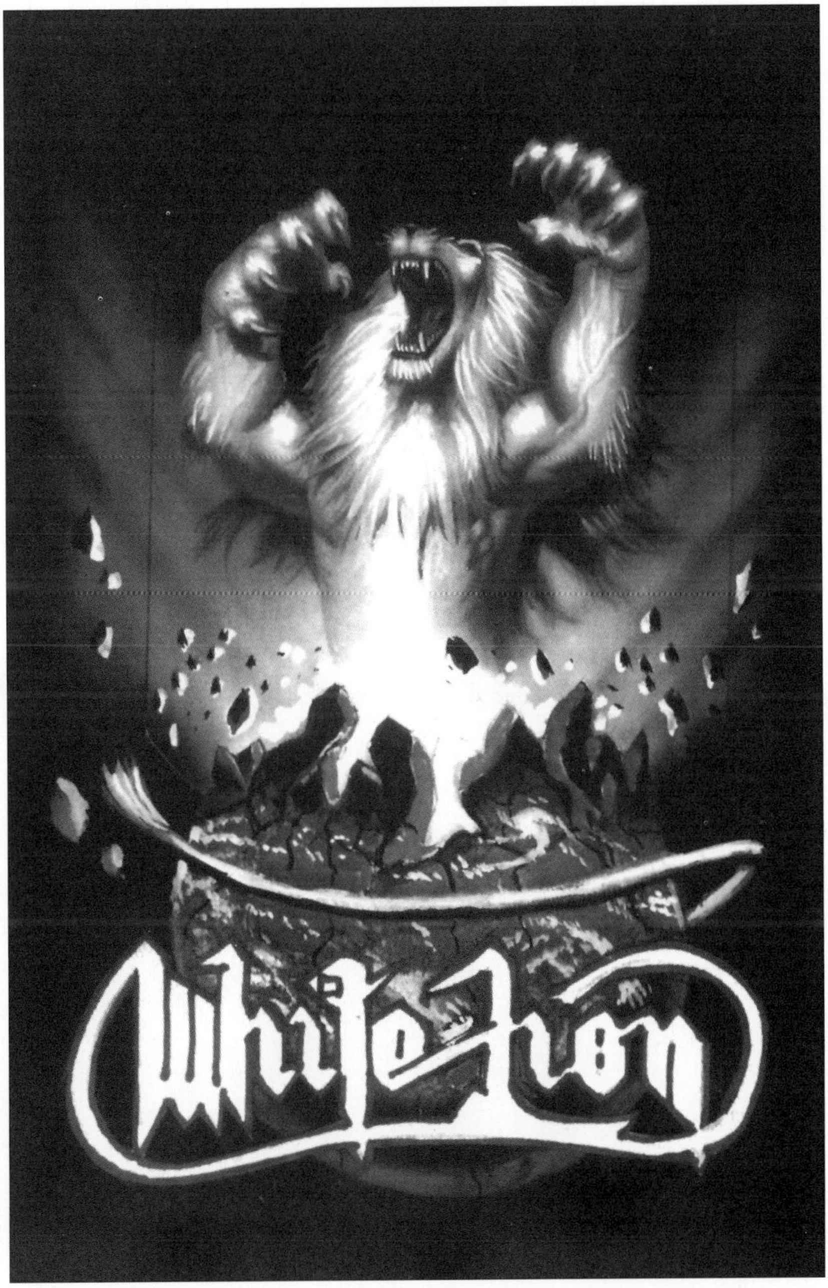


Various stages of T-Shirt concept sketches for the band **White Lion**

Bottom left: Approved pencils

Bottom right: Final color study

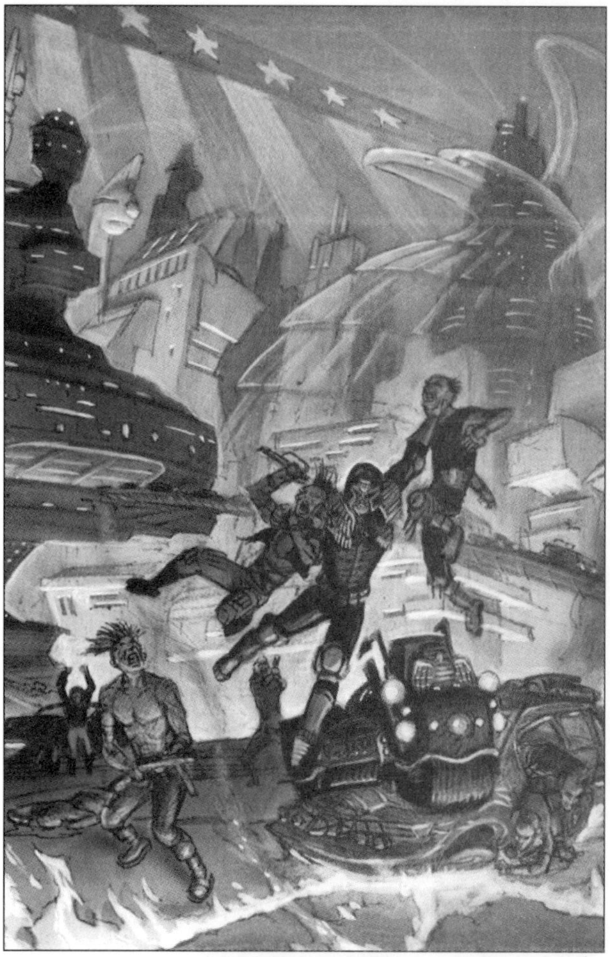

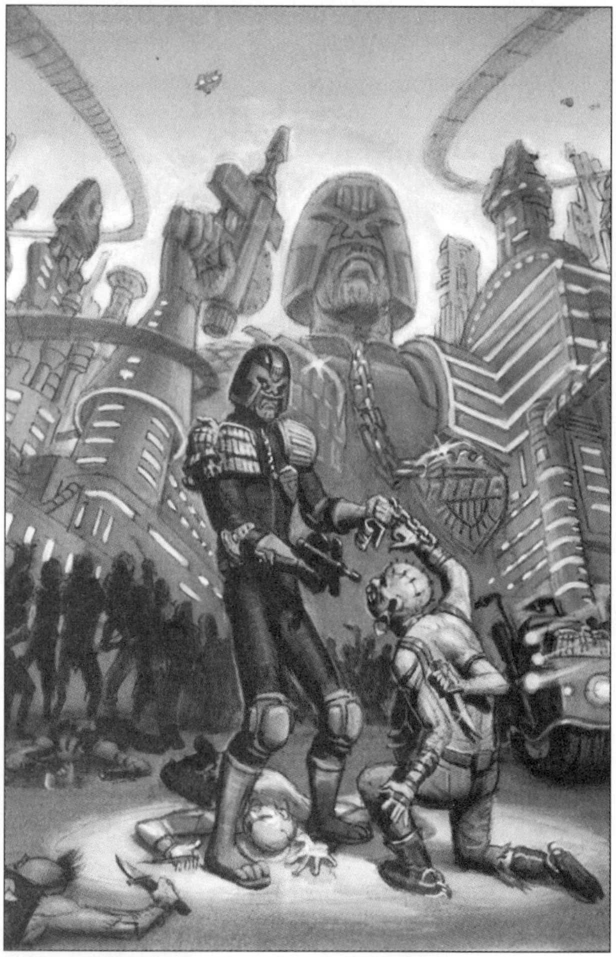

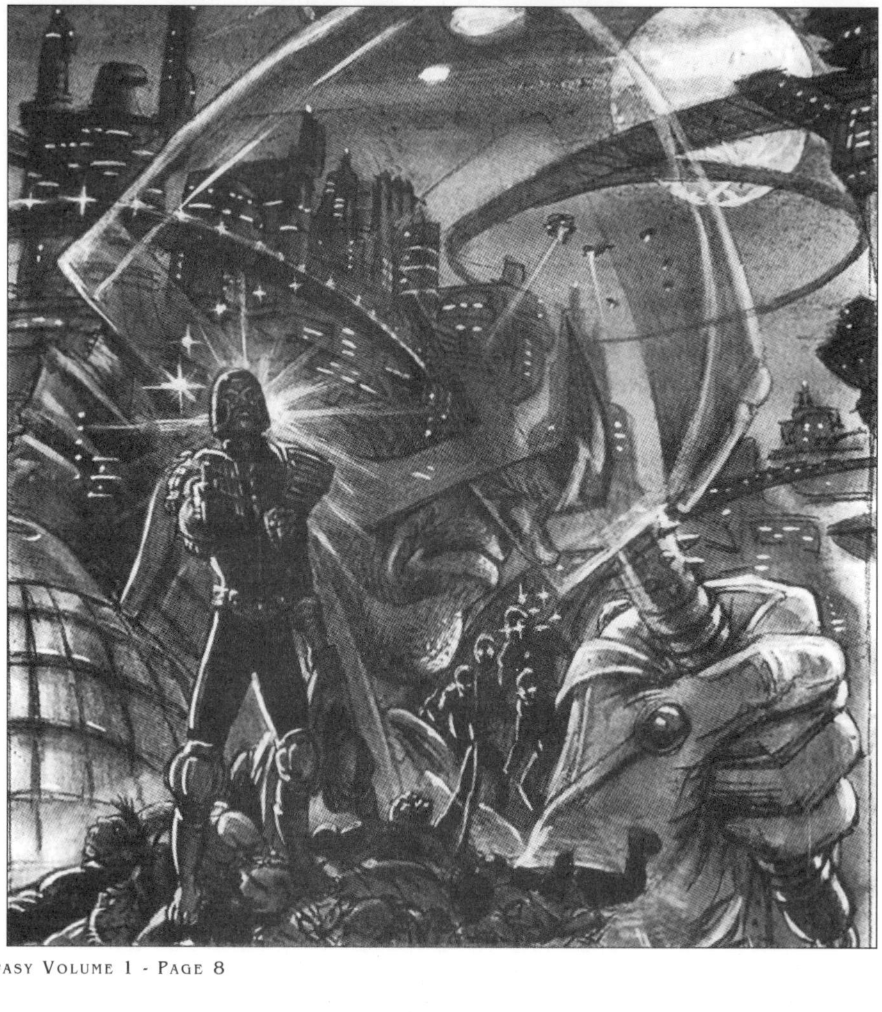

Tone studies for cover of **Judge Dredd's** "Hall of Justice" collection.

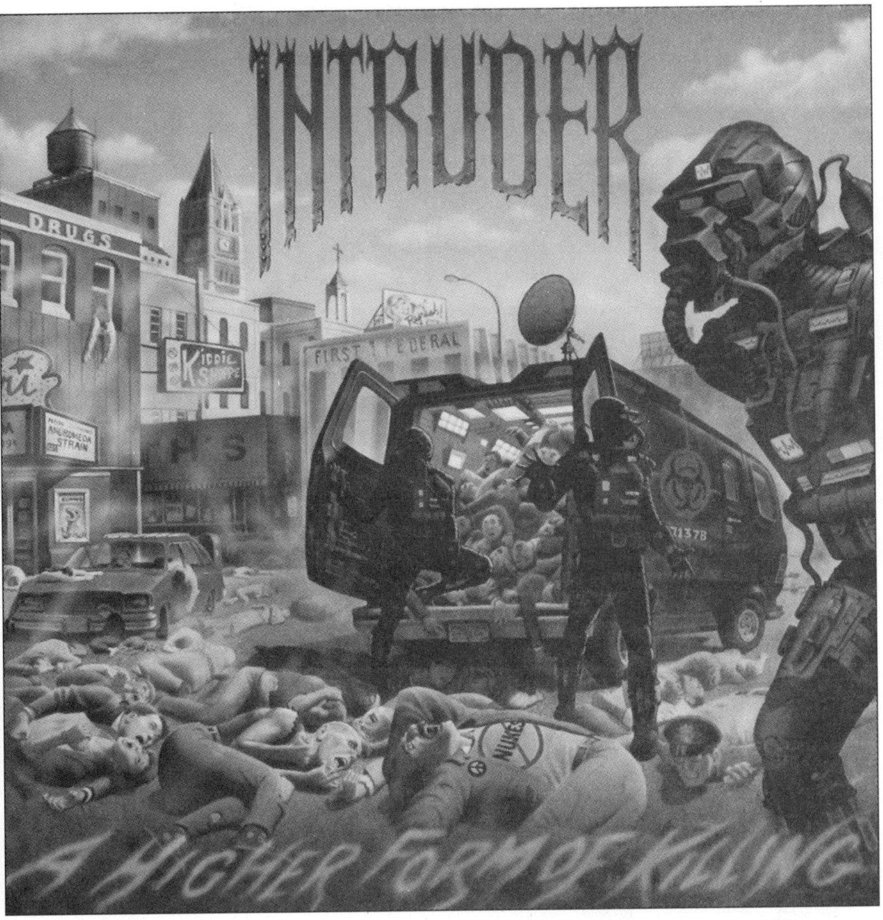


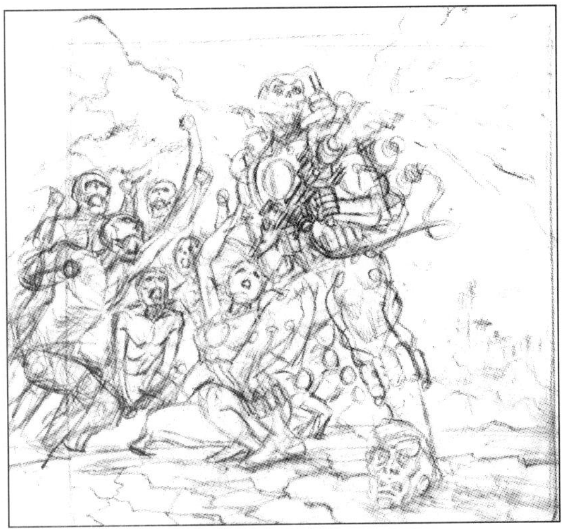

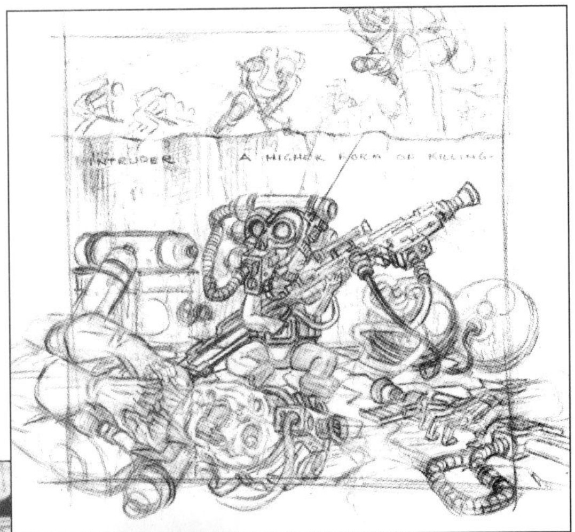


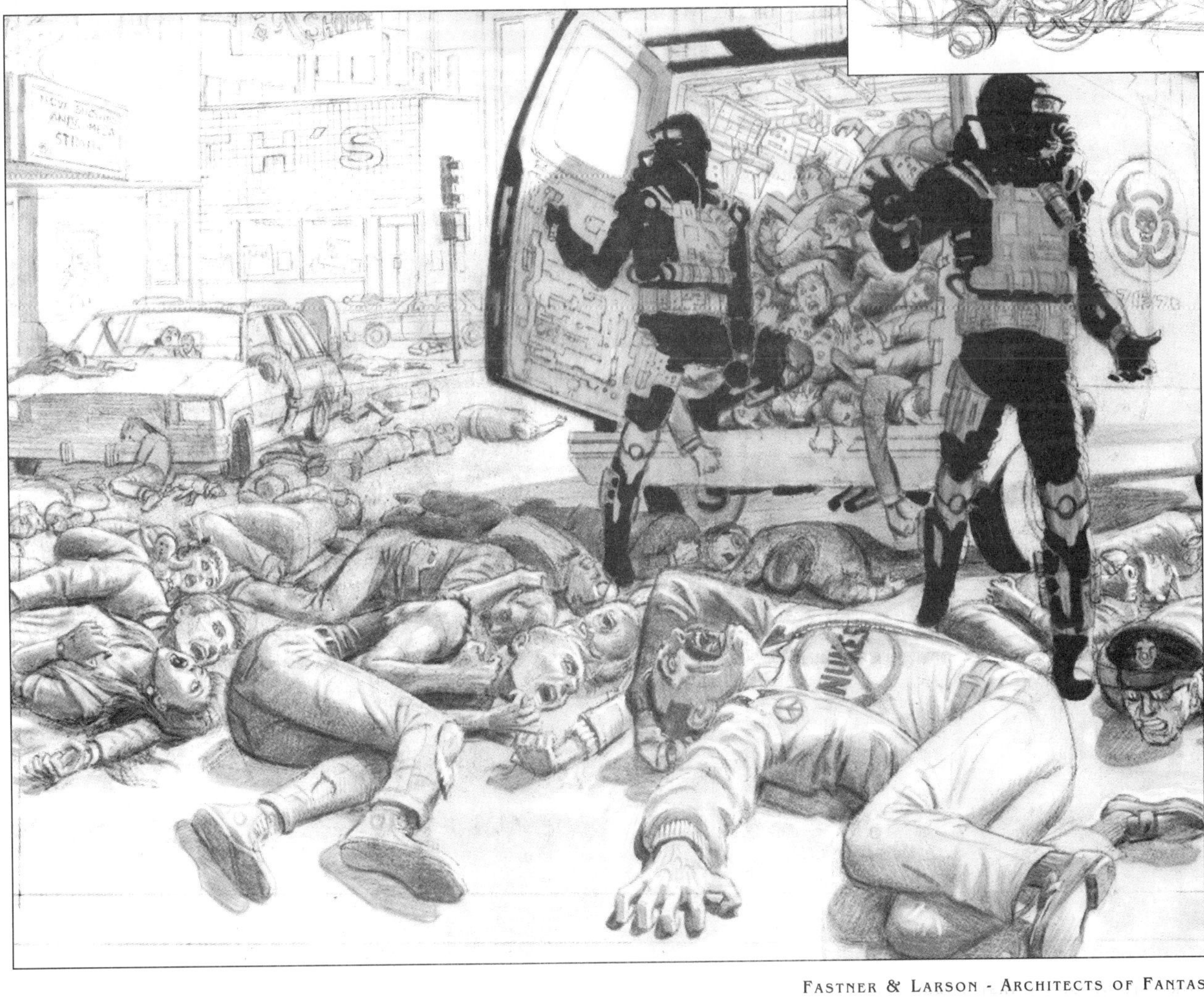

CLOCKWISE FROM TOP LEFT:

FINAL PRINTED FORM OF **INTRUDER'S** "A HIGHER FORM OF KILLING"

FIRST CONCEPT

SECOND CONCEPT

DETAIL FROM TONE STUDY OF FINAL DESIGN

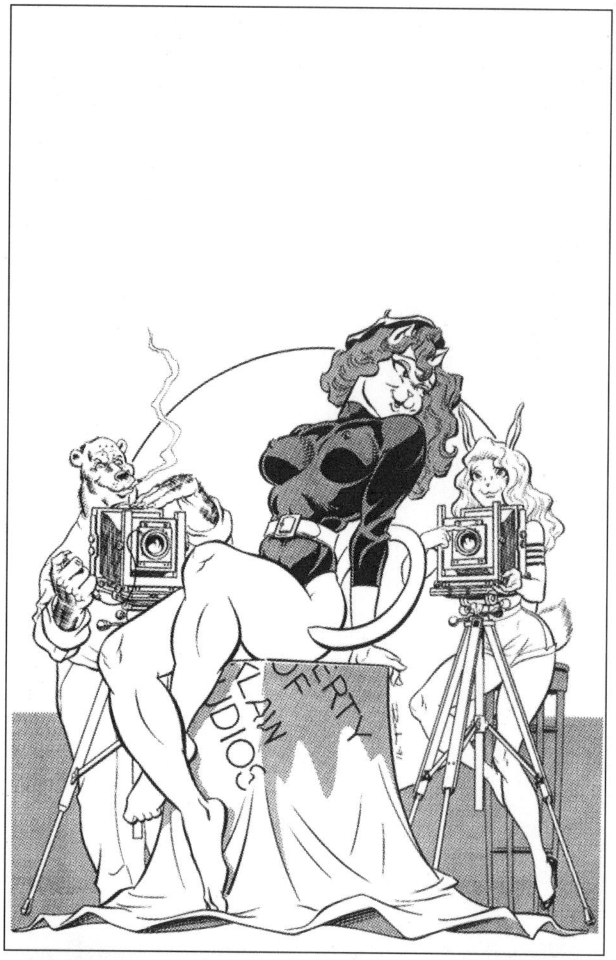

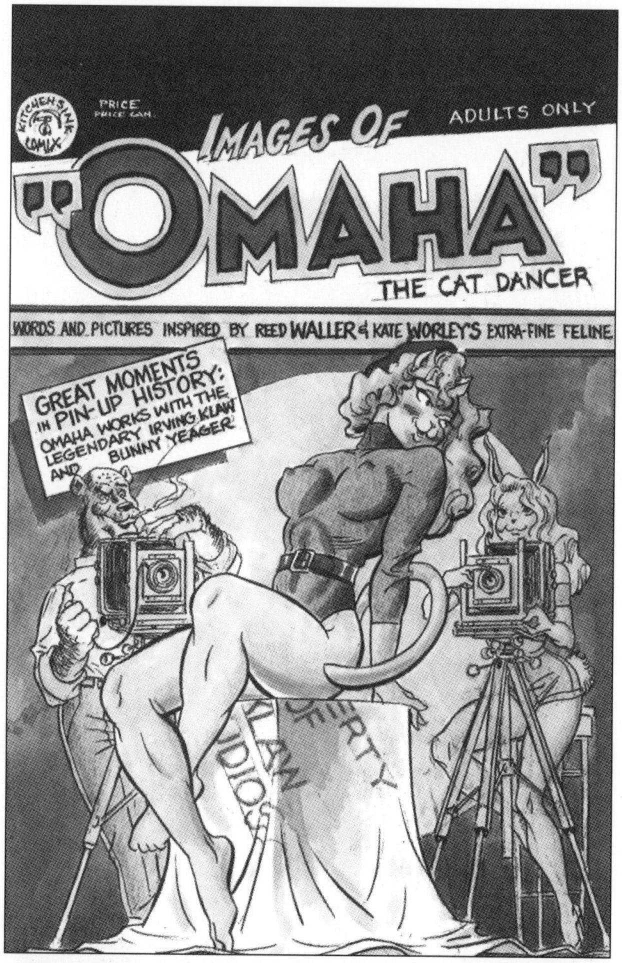


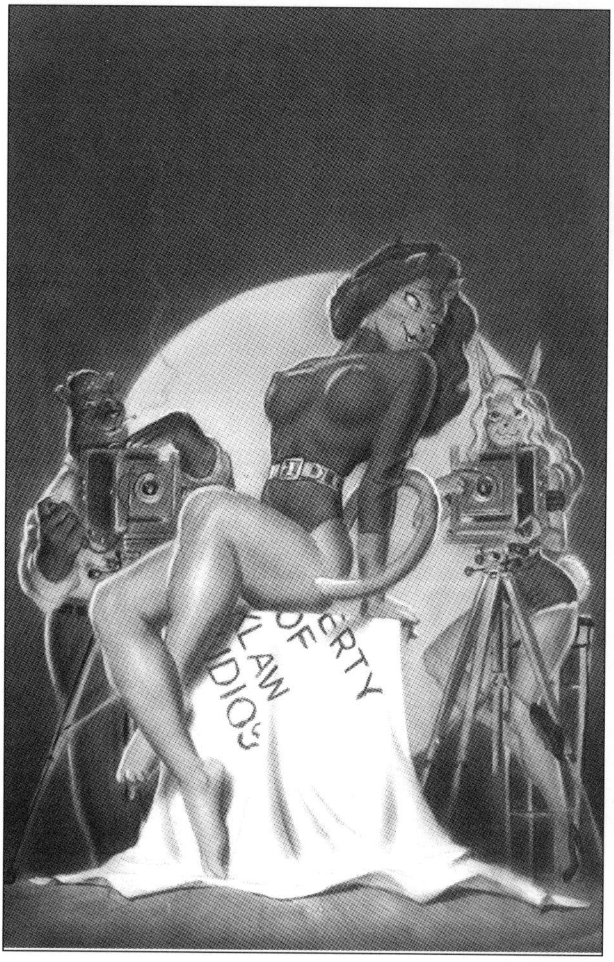

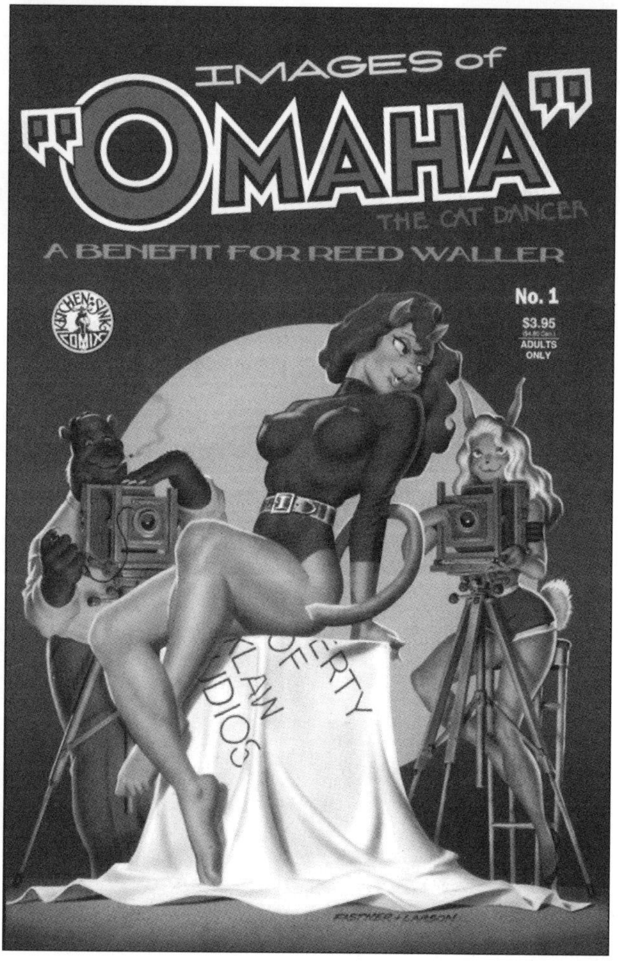


Various stages for the cover of Kitchen Sink's benefit issue for **Omaha** creator Reed Waller

Clockwise from top left:

Black & white advertising

Suggested cover layout

Finished cover

Color study

Opposite page: Tone study for the box cover of the role-playing game, **Mutant**

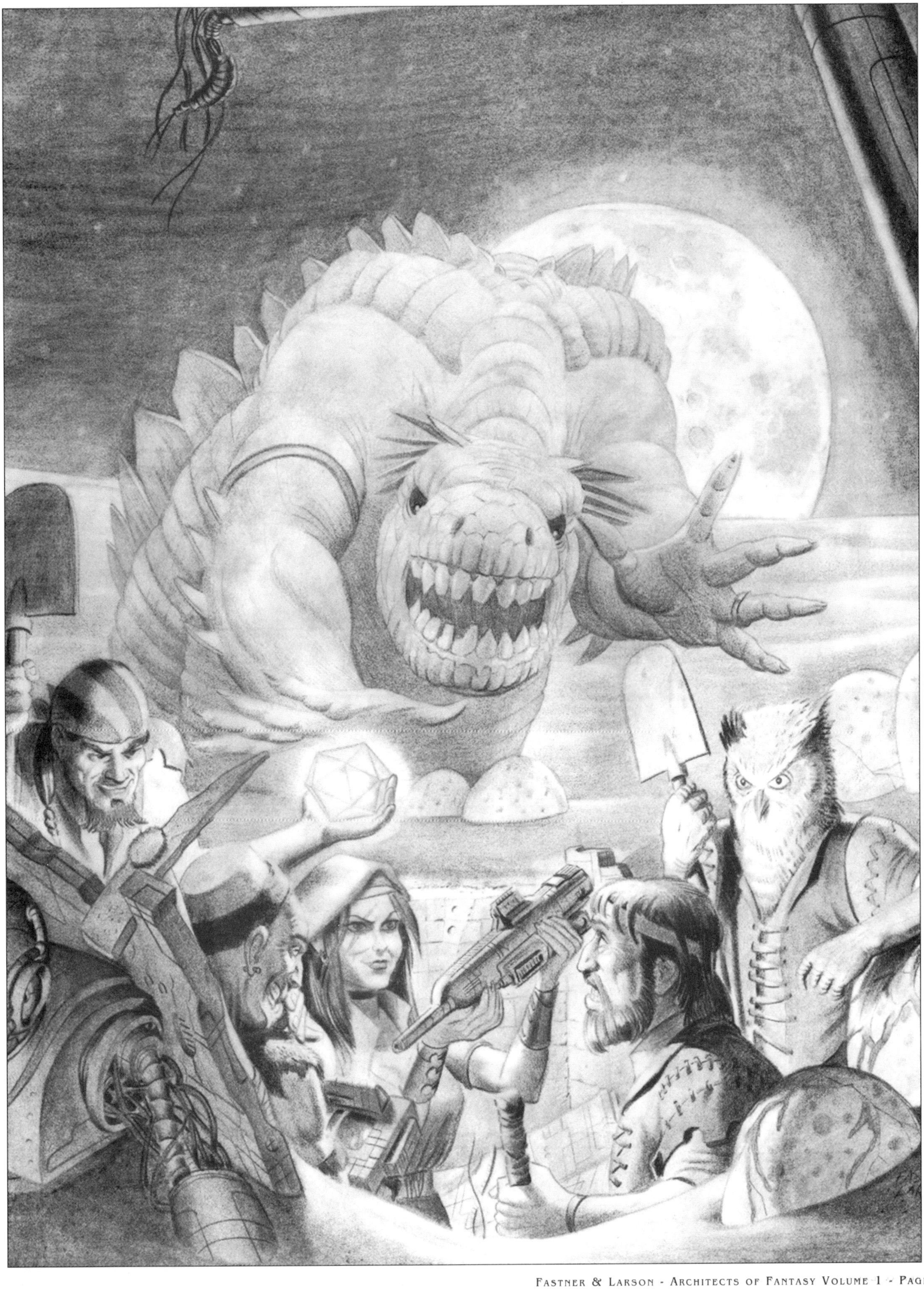

**STEVE:**

*"I've done several paperback covers, both alone and with artists like John Pierard supplying the pencils. 'My Teacher is an Alien' is a best-seller."*

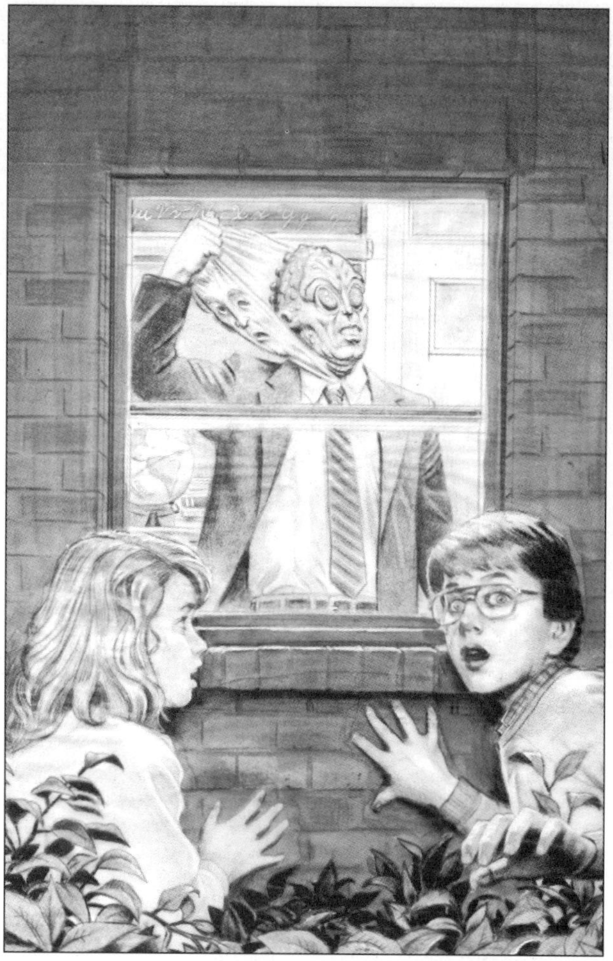

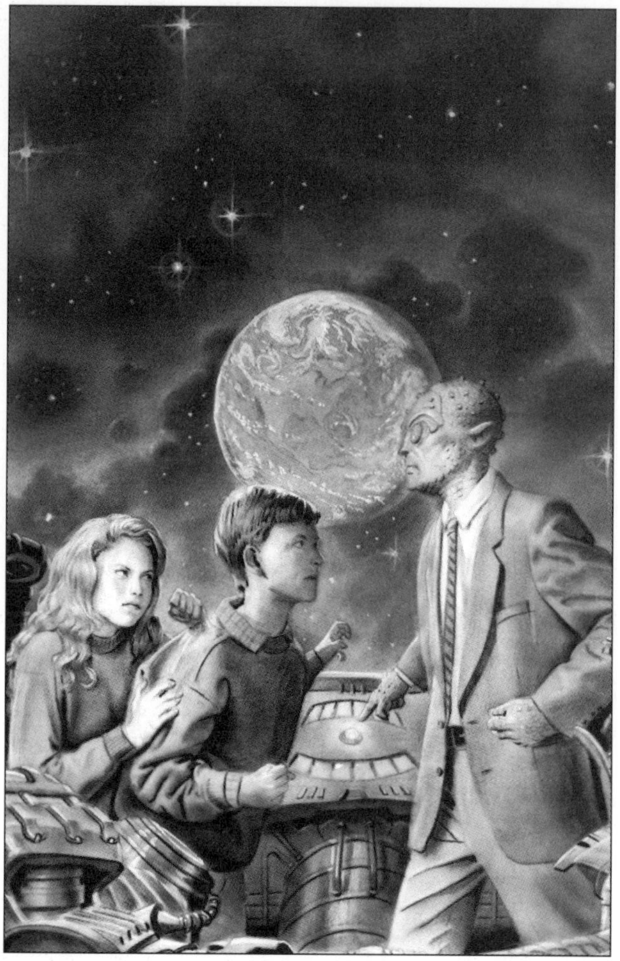

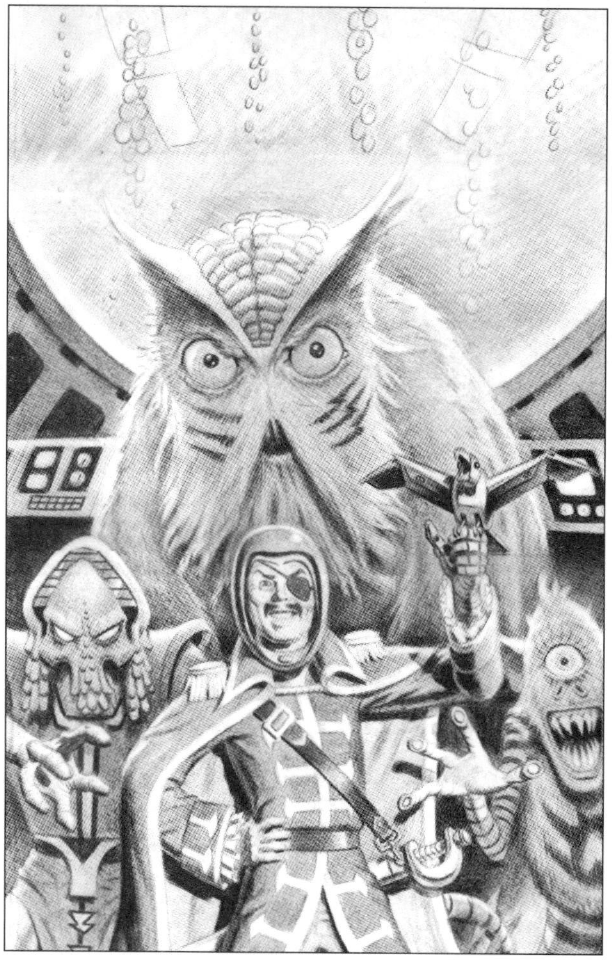

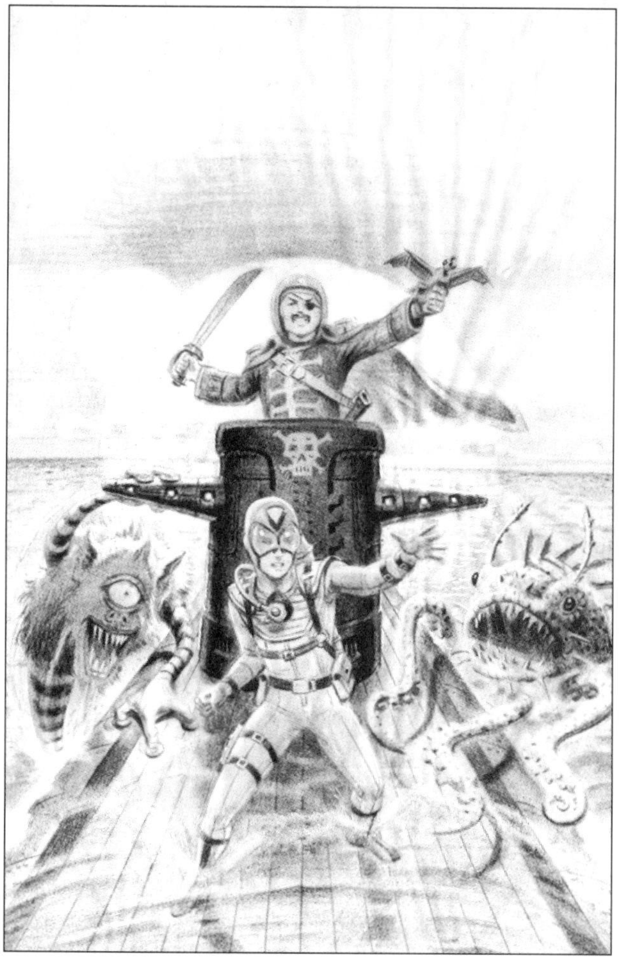

CLOCKWISE FROM TOP:

DESIGN FOR "MY TEACHER IS AN ALIEN"

DESIGN FOR "MY TEACHER FLUNKED THE PLANET" (LAYOUT BY JOHN PIERARD)

TWO SOLO STEVE "GALACTIC PIRATE" LAYOUTS

OPPOSITE PAGE: "BRUCE COVILLE'S MONSTERS" (LAYOUT BY JOHN PIERARD)

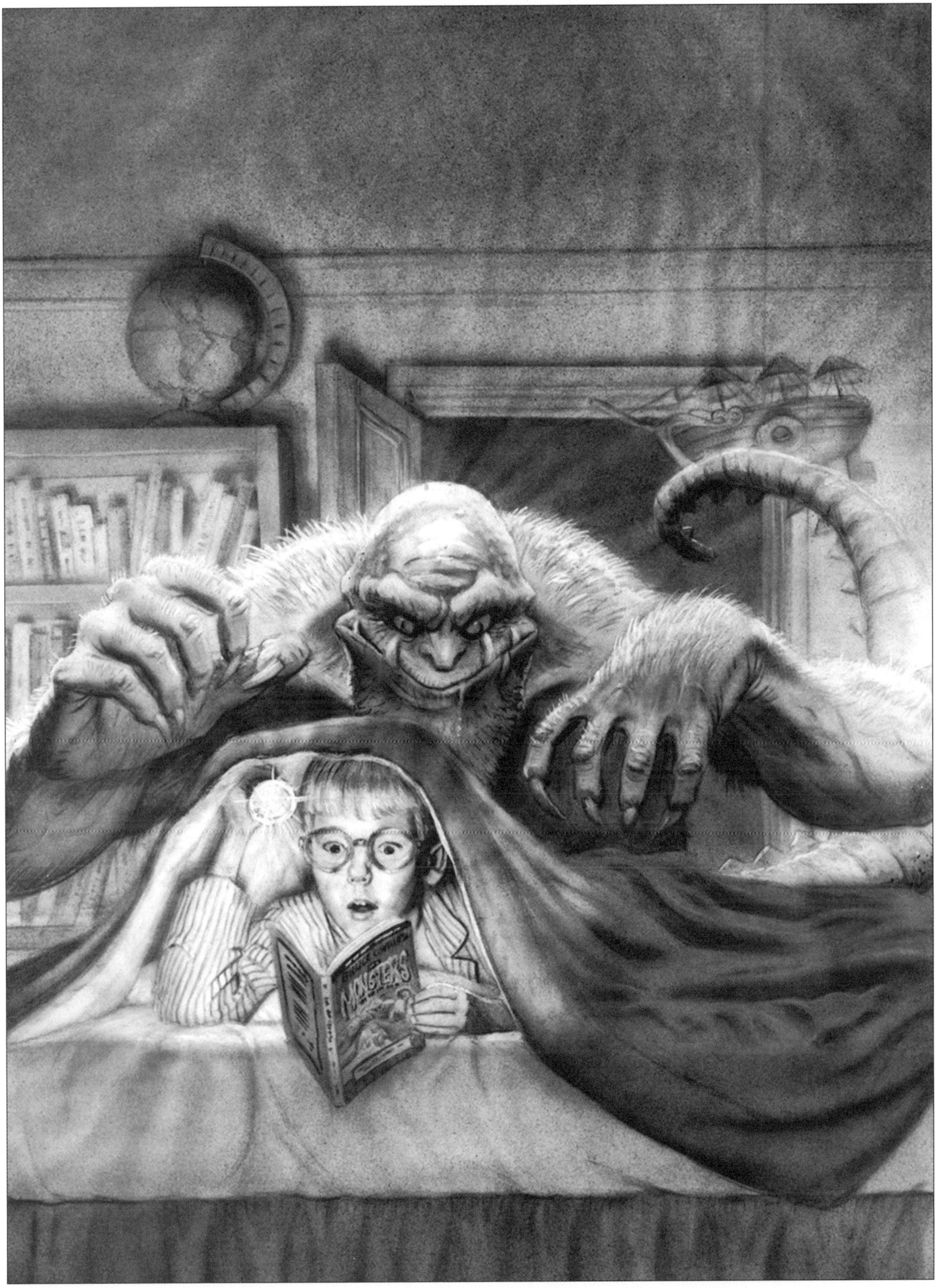
MONSTERS

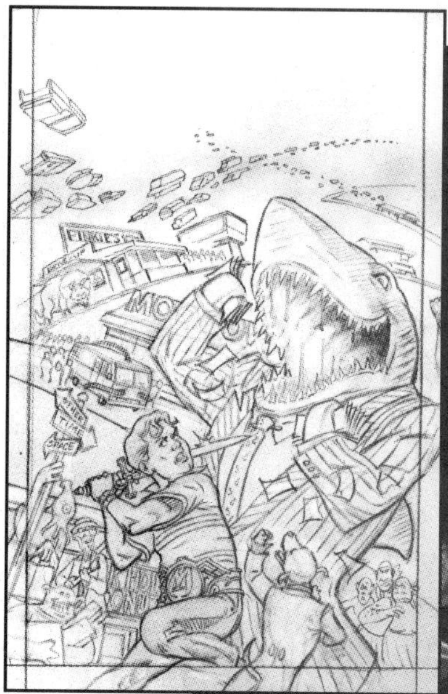

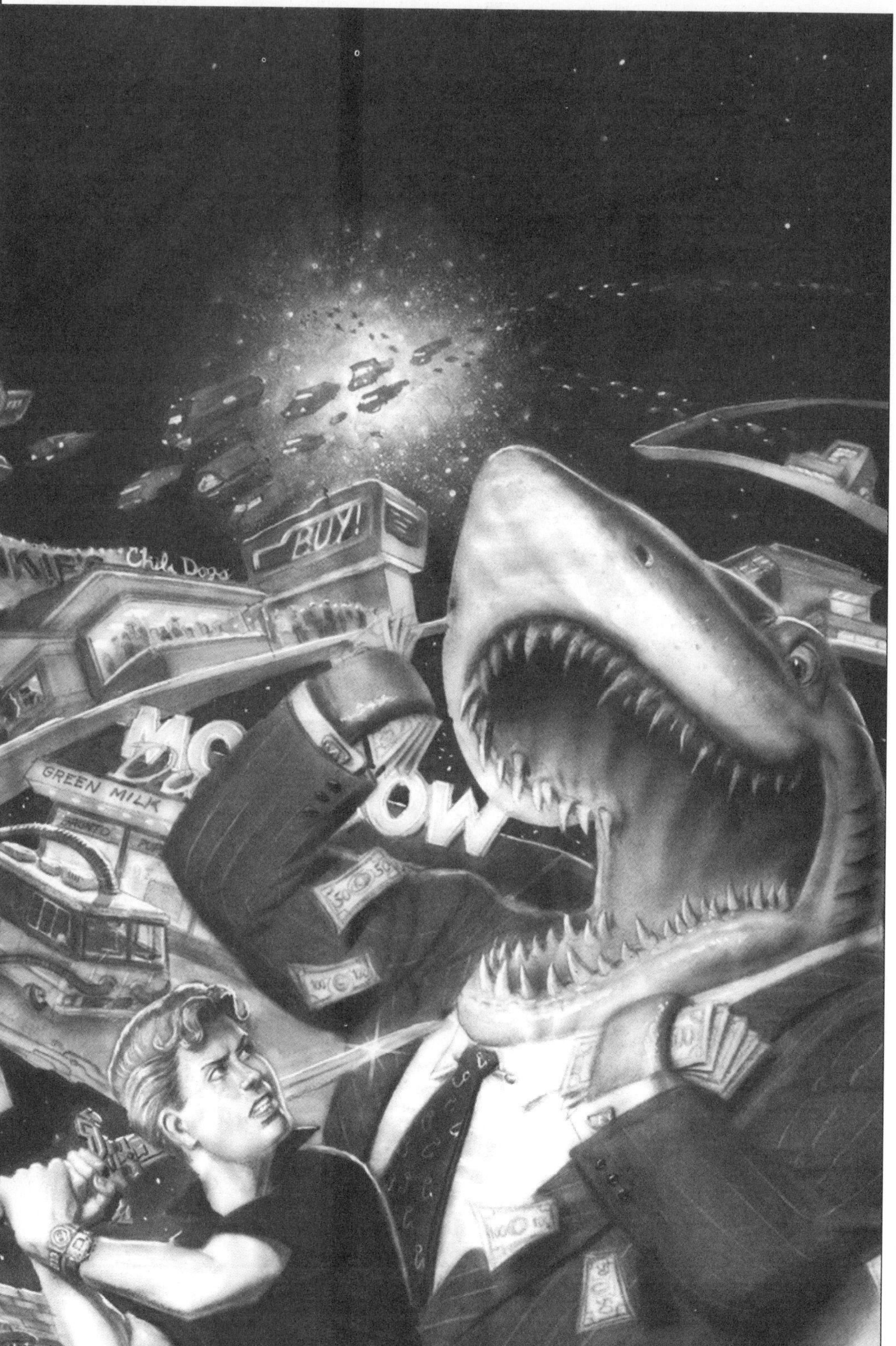


Tone study for the paperback of "Night Of The Living Shark"

Inset
Second pencil rough for cover

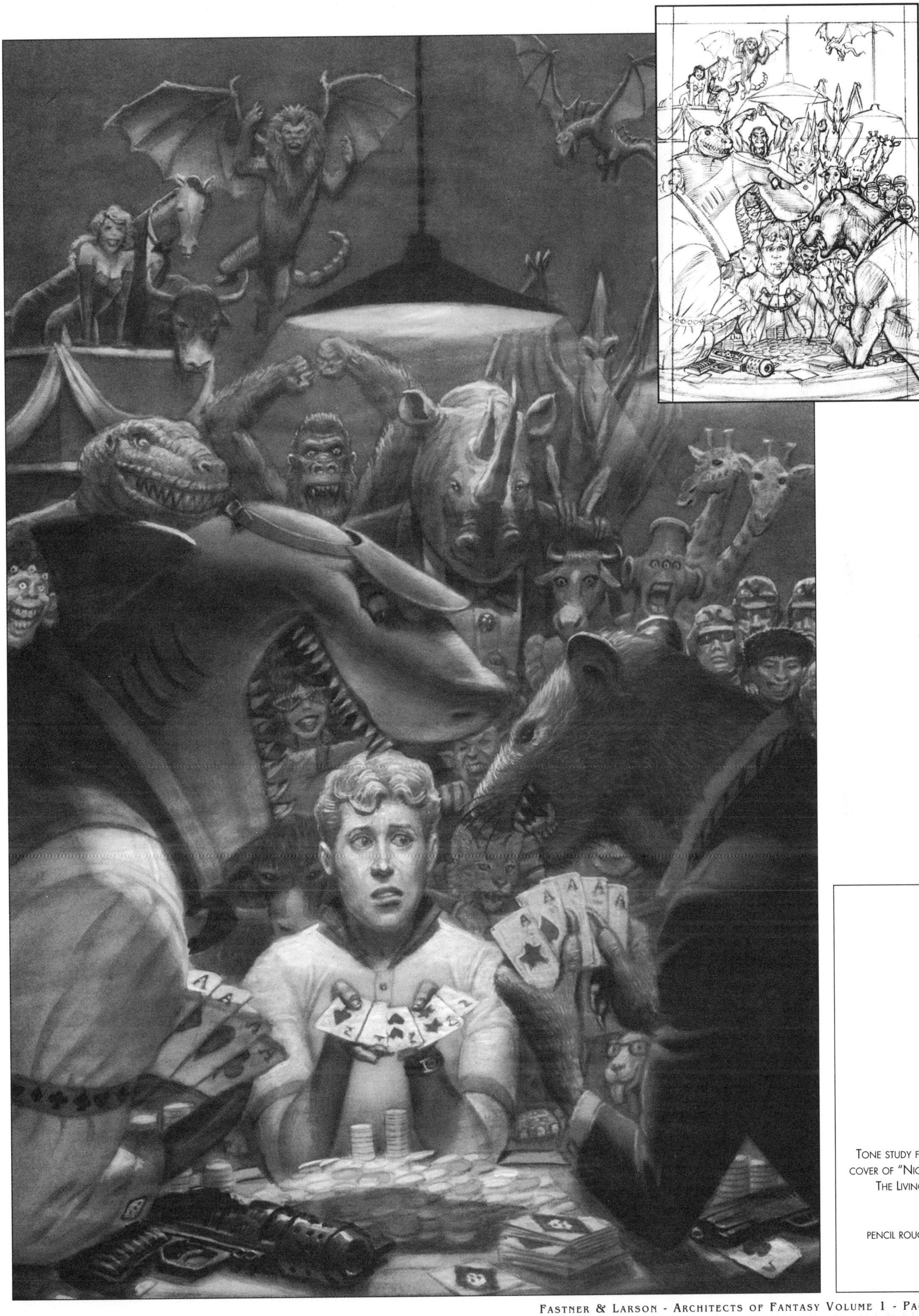

TONE STUDY FOR THE COVER OF "NIGHT OF THE LIVING RAT"

INSET PENCIL ROUGH FOR COVER

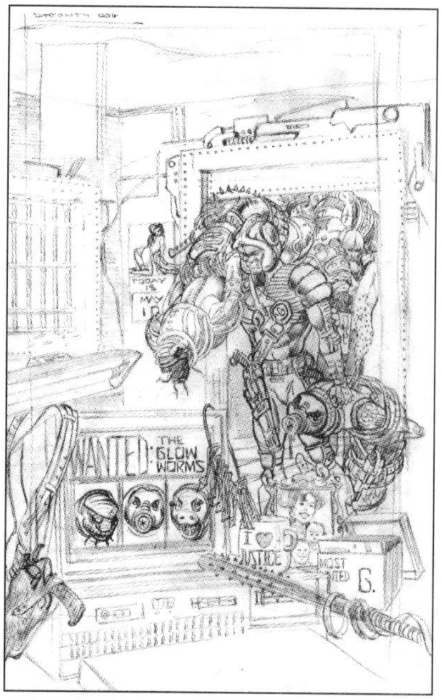


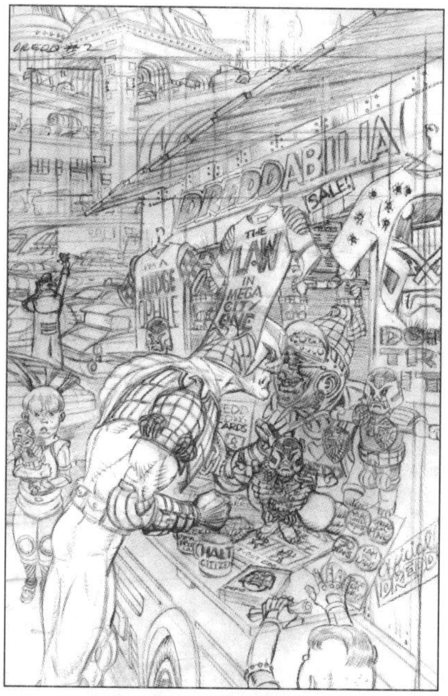


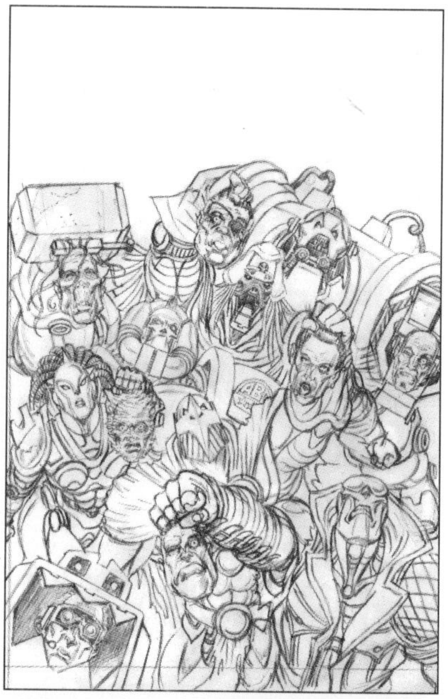

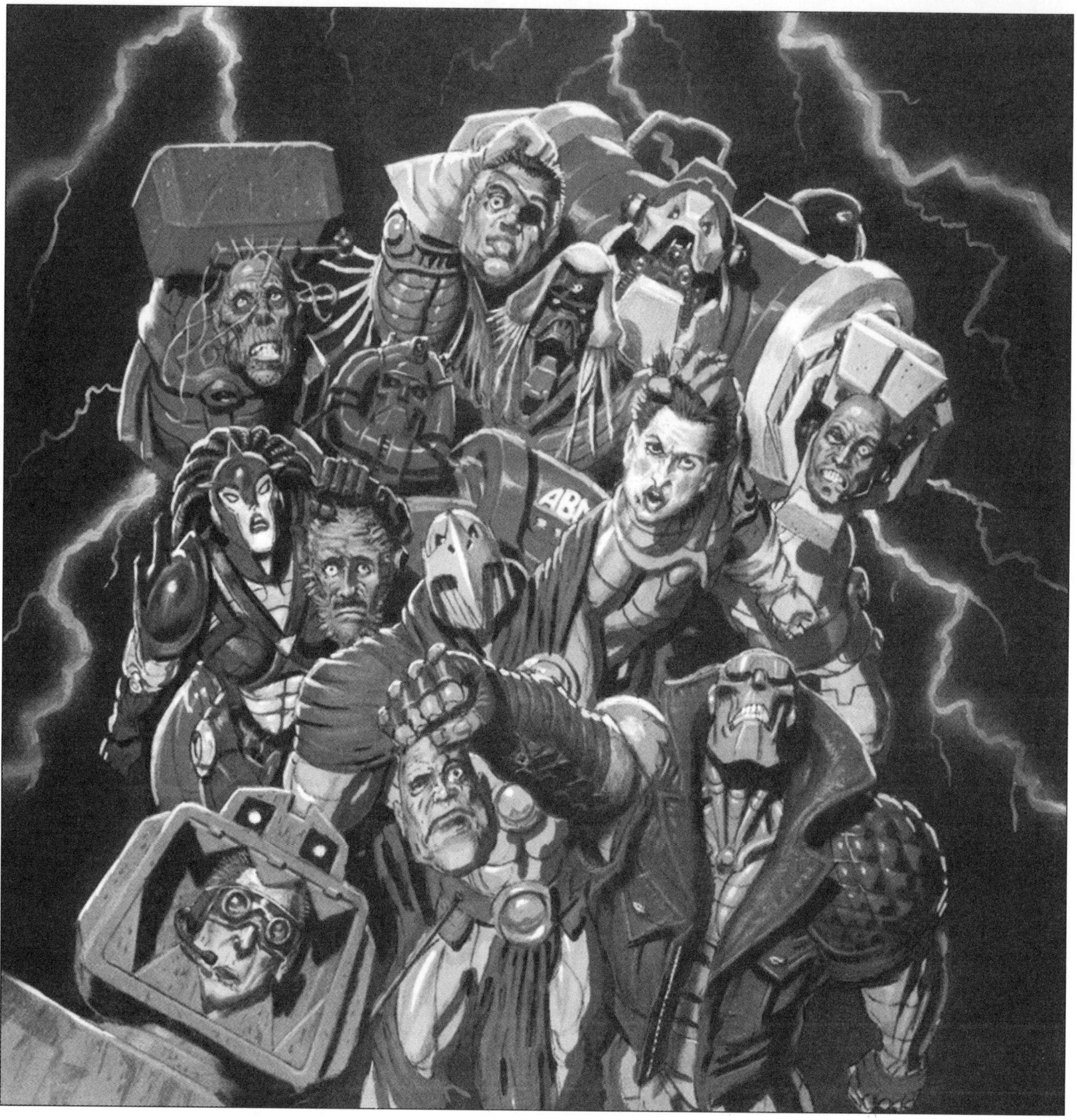

Clockwise from top left:

Pencils to a **Strontium Dog** cover

Pencils for a **Judge Dredd** cover

Pencils to **ABC Warriors** "Khronicles of Kaos"

Color study of **ABC Warriors**

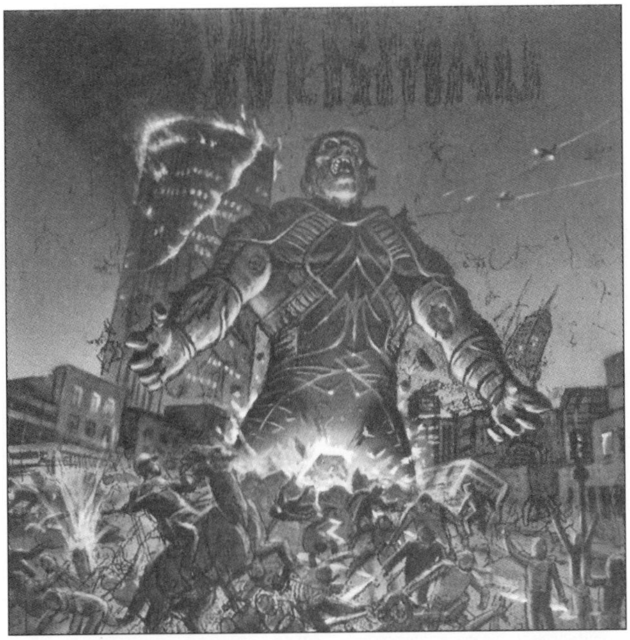

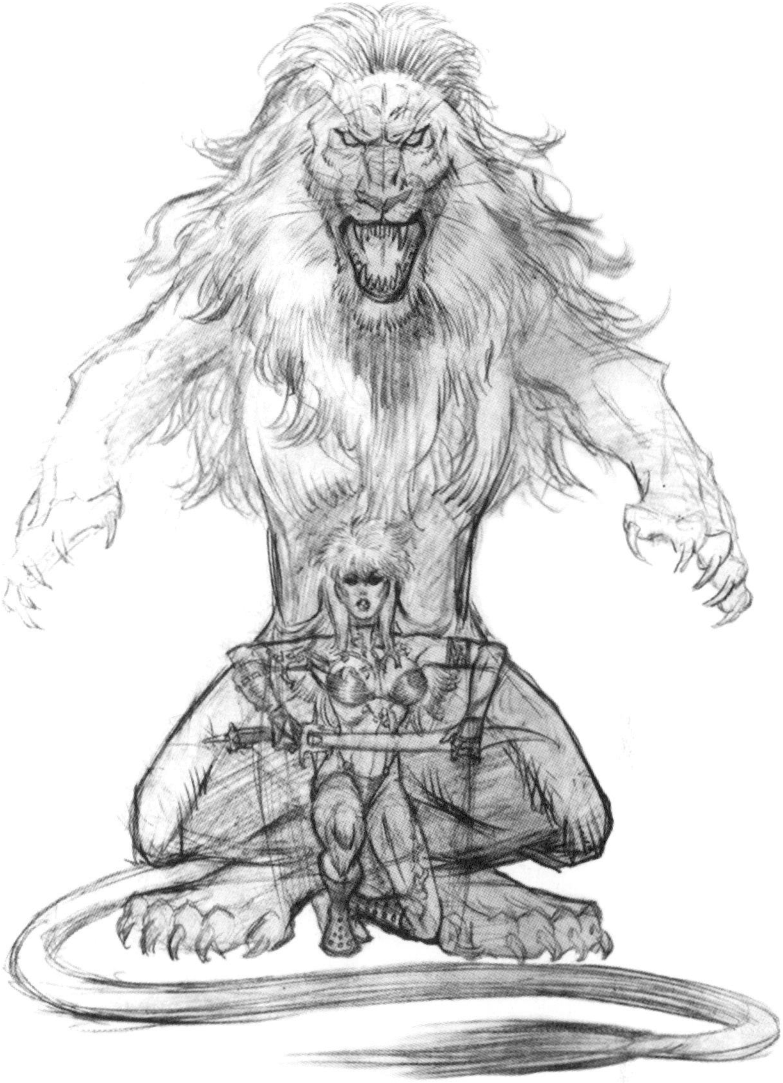

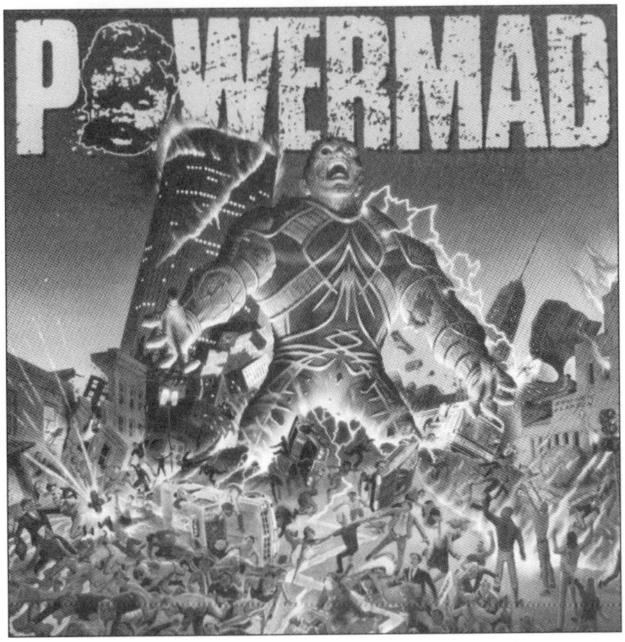


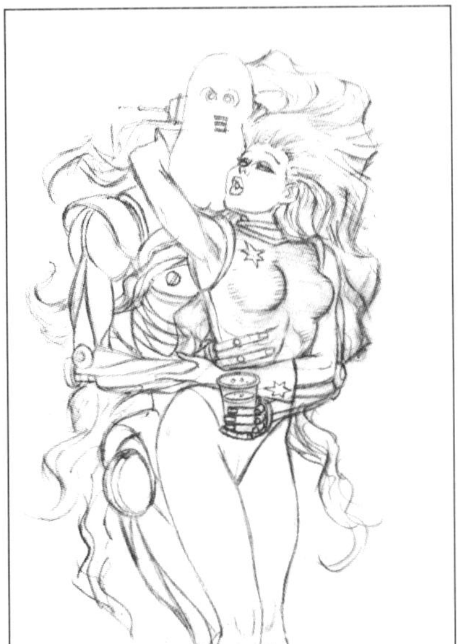

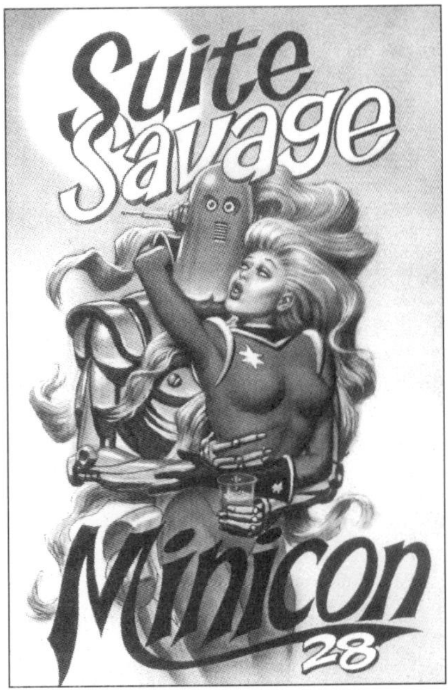


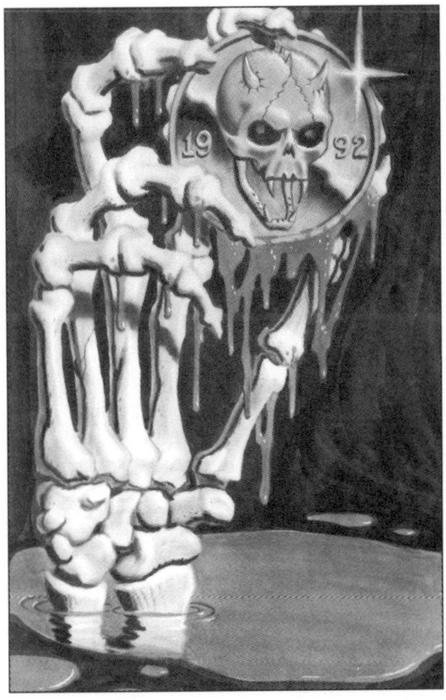


Clockwise from top left:

Color study for **Powermad** album cover

T-Shirt design for the band **White Lion**

T-Shirt design for **Overkill**

**Minicon** T-shirt design

Pencils for same

Finished artwork for **Powermad**

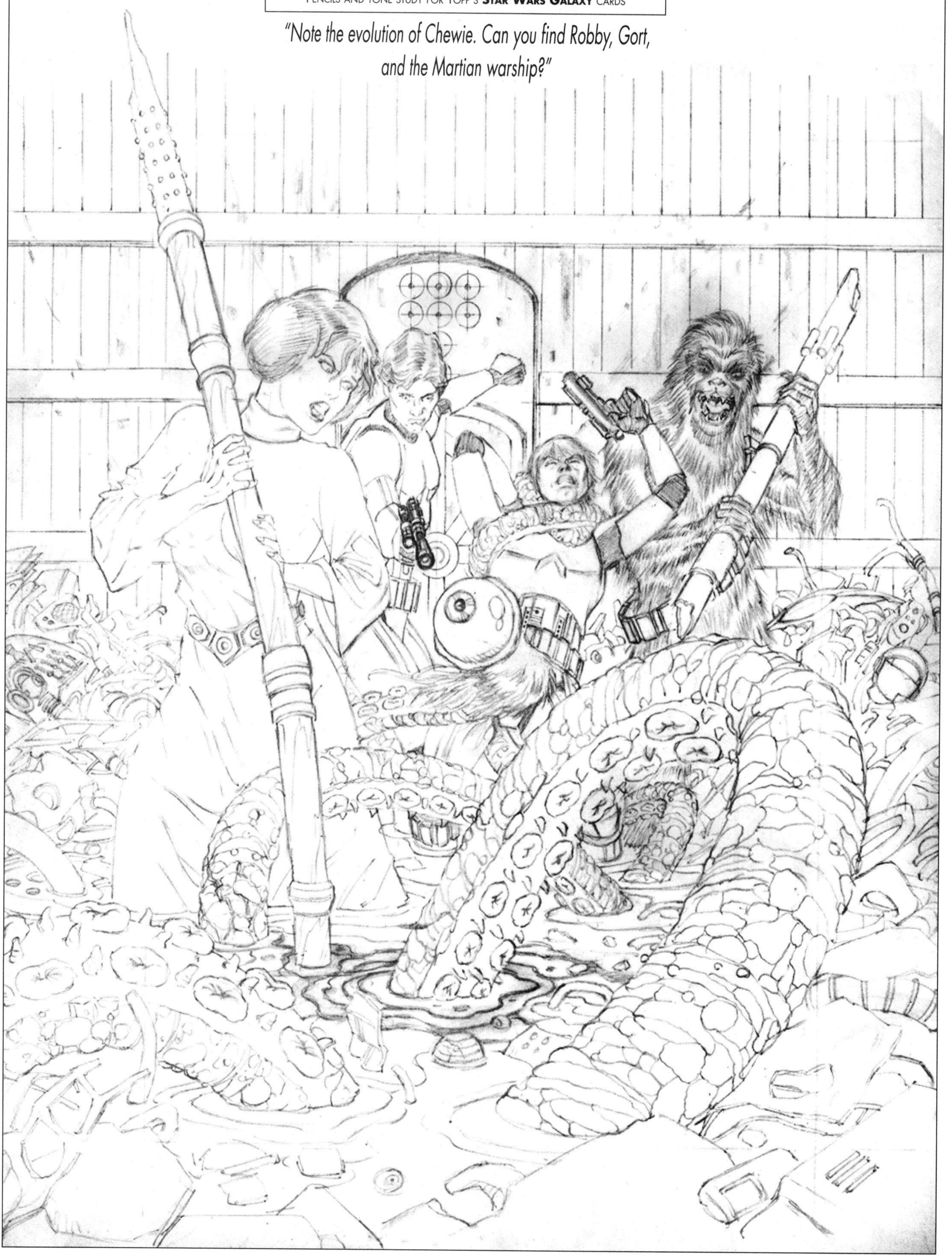

Pencils and tone study for Topp's **Star Wars Galaxy** cards

*"Note the evolution of Chewie. Can you find Robby, Gort, and the Martian warship?"*

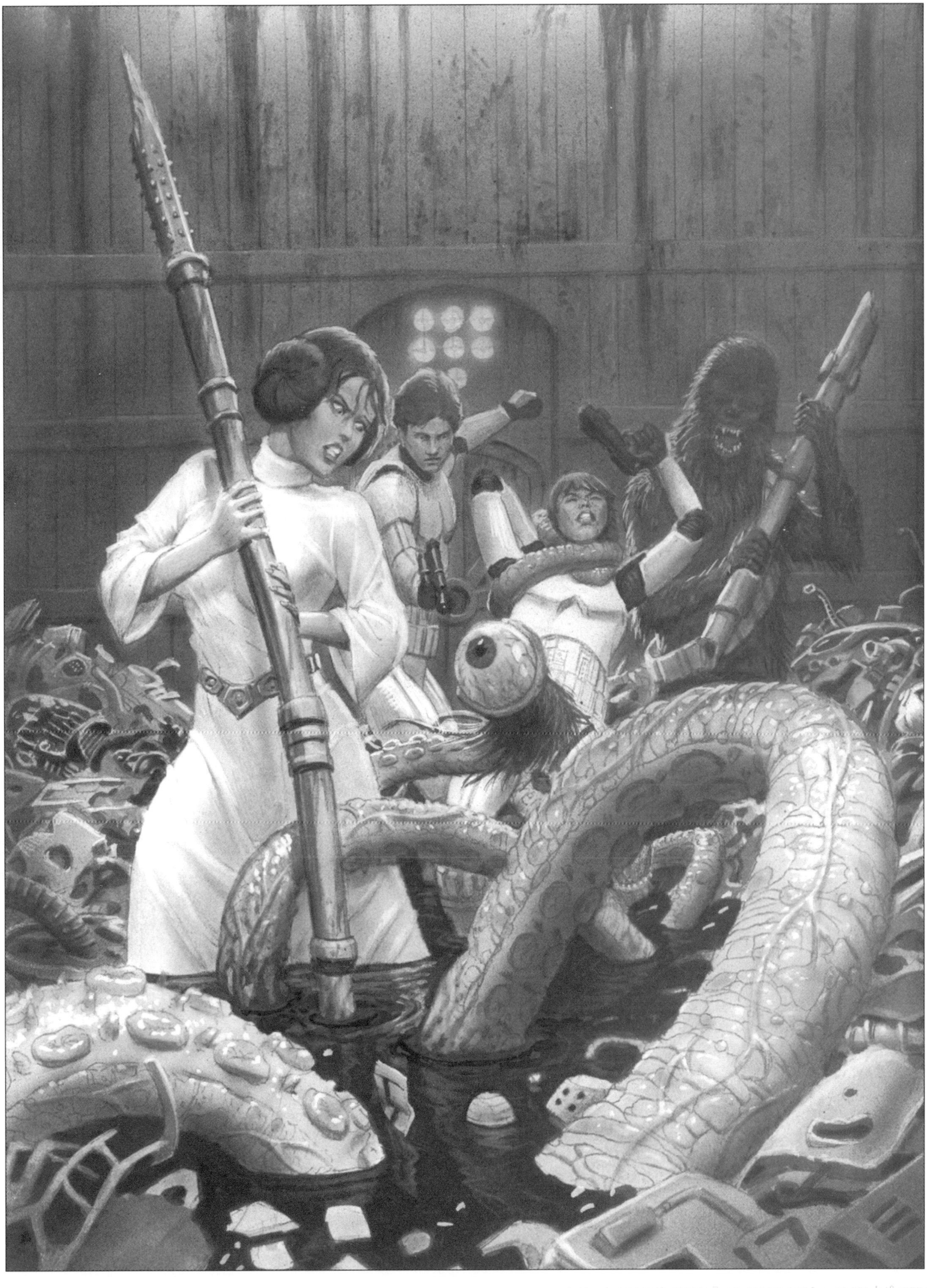

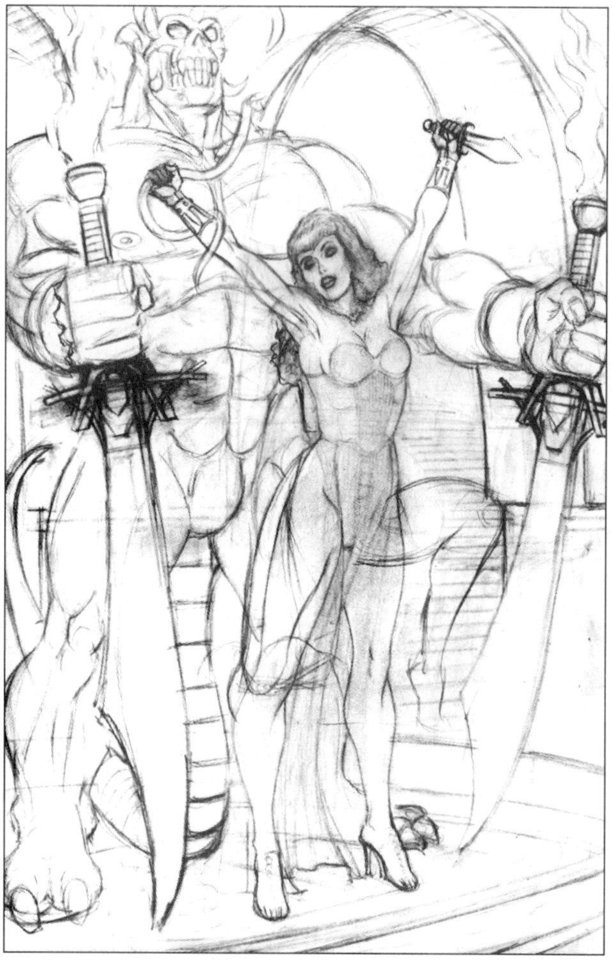

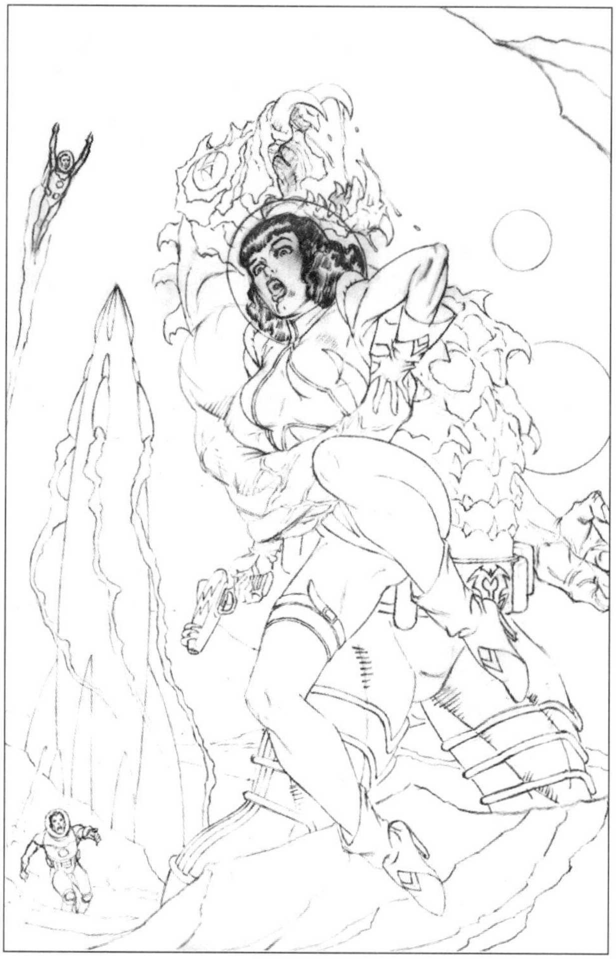

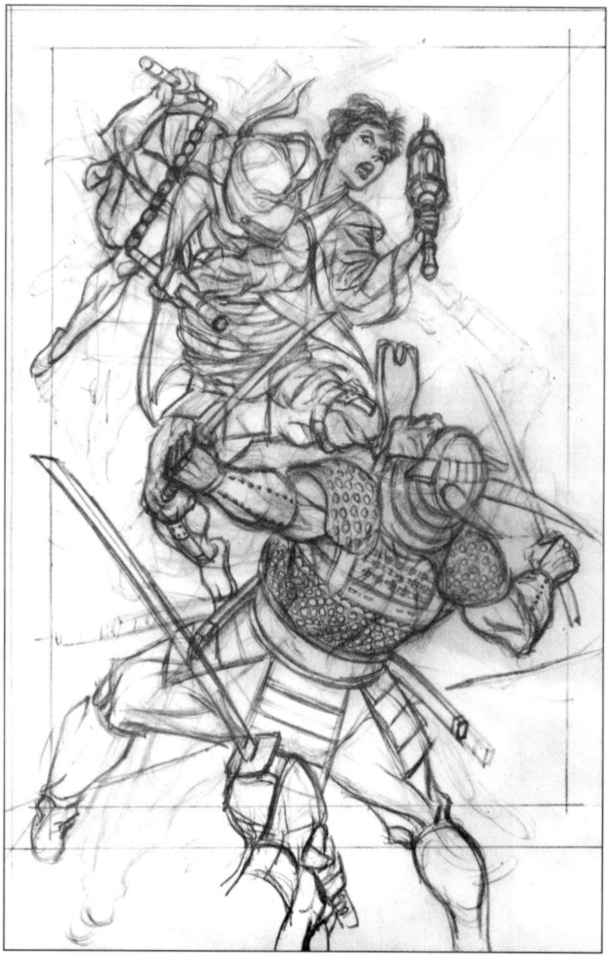

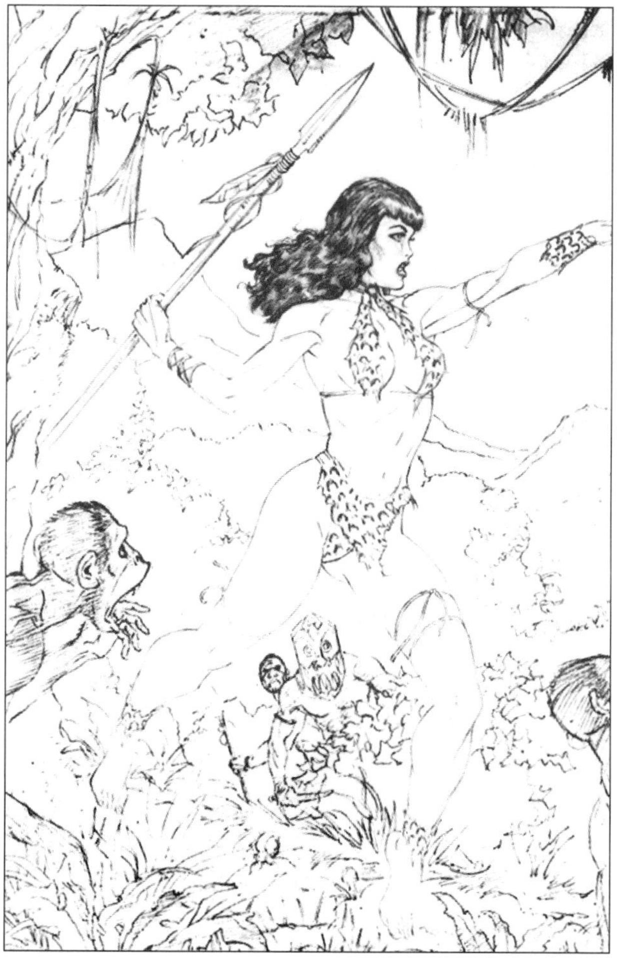

Clockwise from top left:

Three pencil sketches from a proposed **Betty Page** Portfolio

Pencil rough for **Teenage Mutant Ninja Turtles** cards

Following page: Tone study from the **Spider-Man** Portfolio

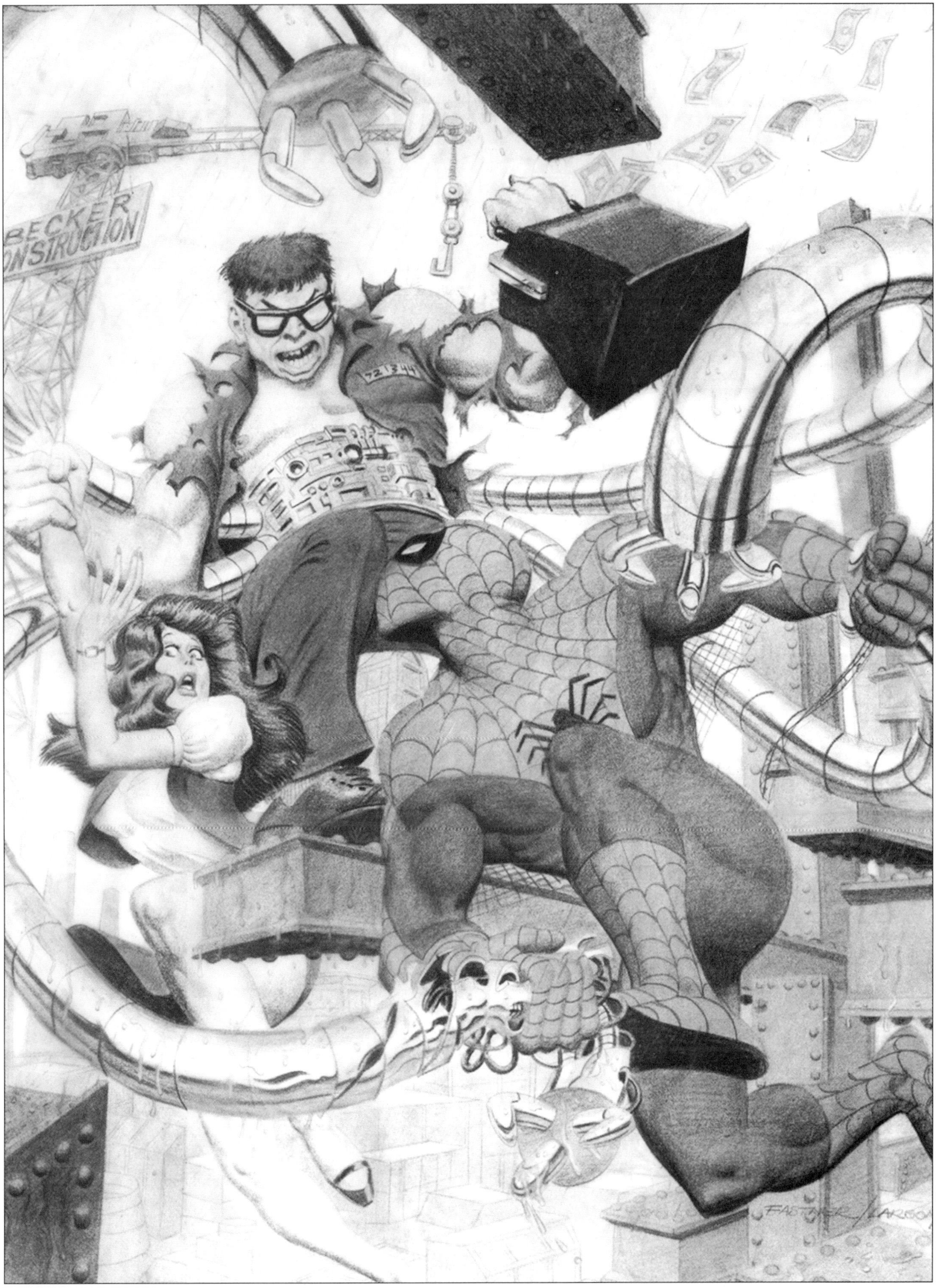
BECKER
ONSTRUCTION

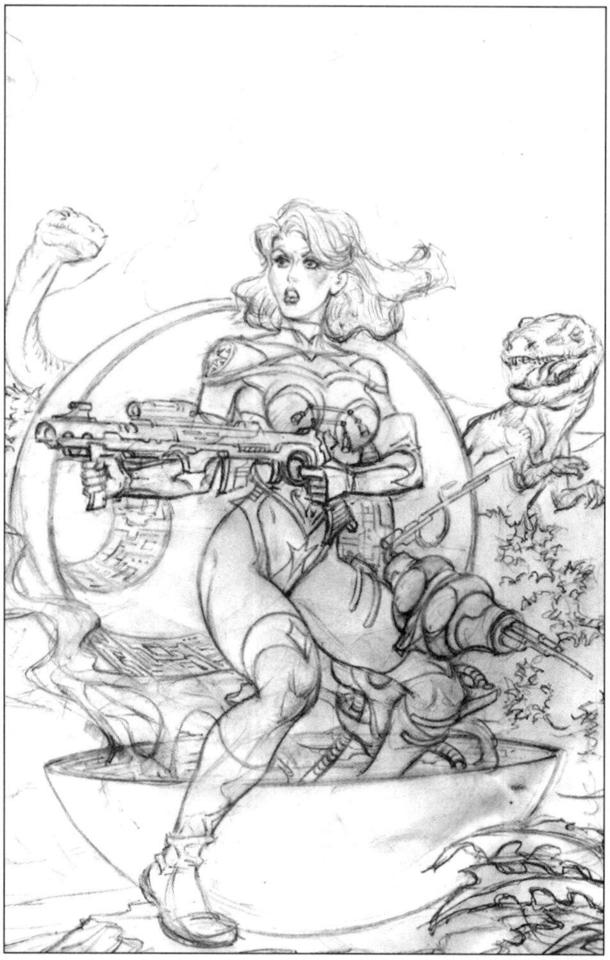

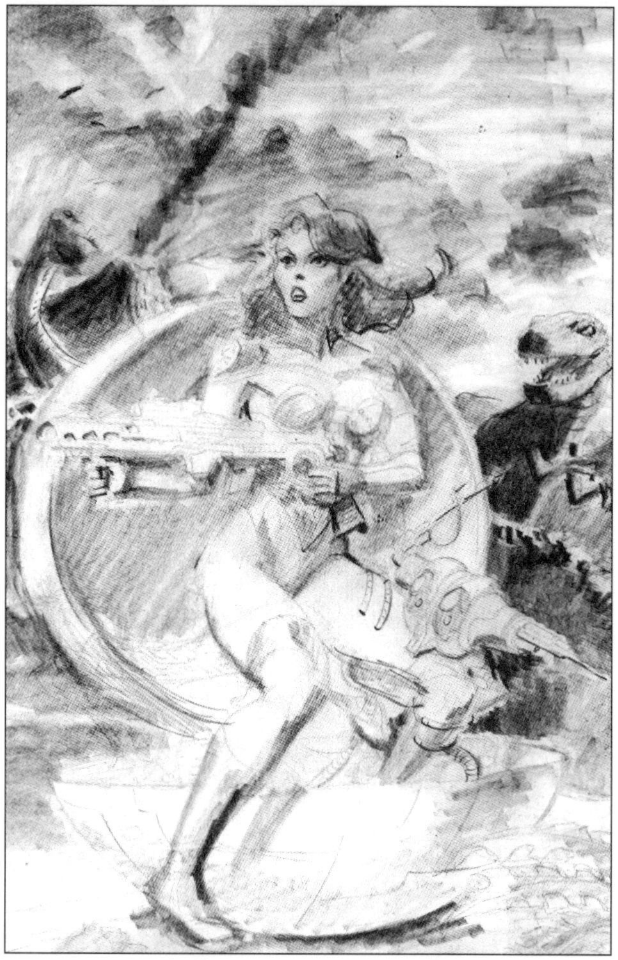

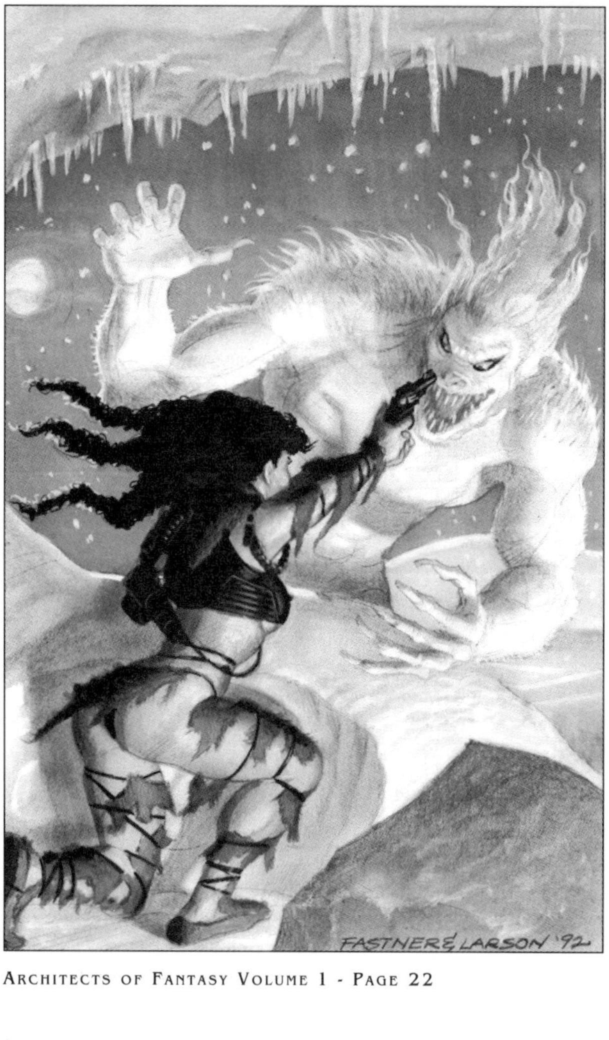


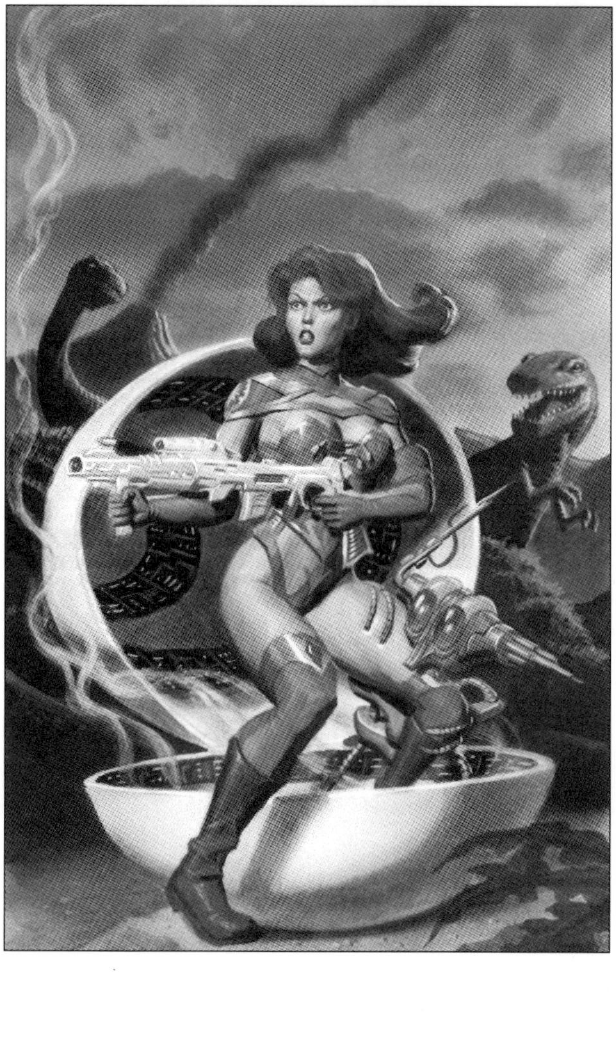

Clockwise from top left:

A plate from the **Space Runners** Portfolio, from sketch, to lighting study, to color rough

Tone study from **DarkeWorld** Portfolio

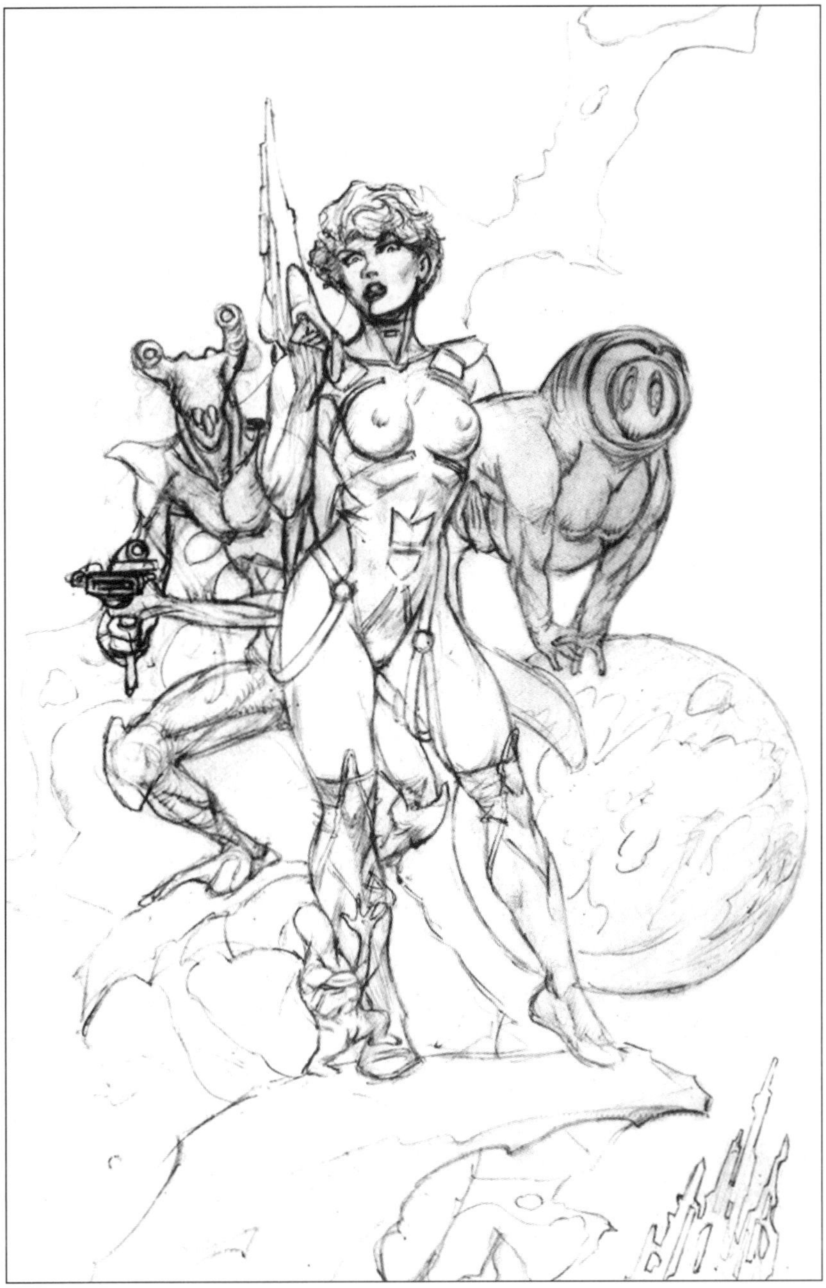

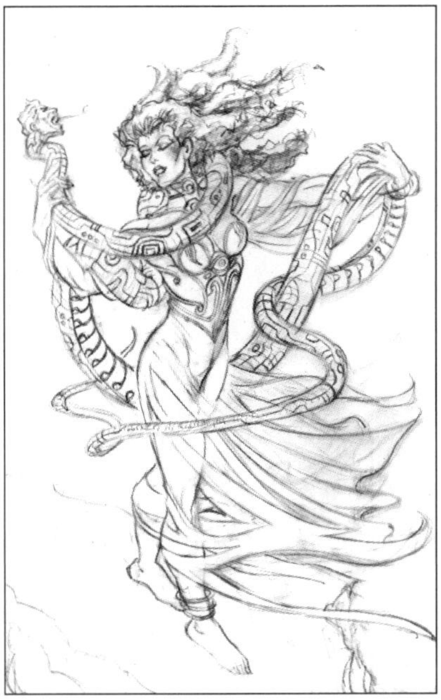

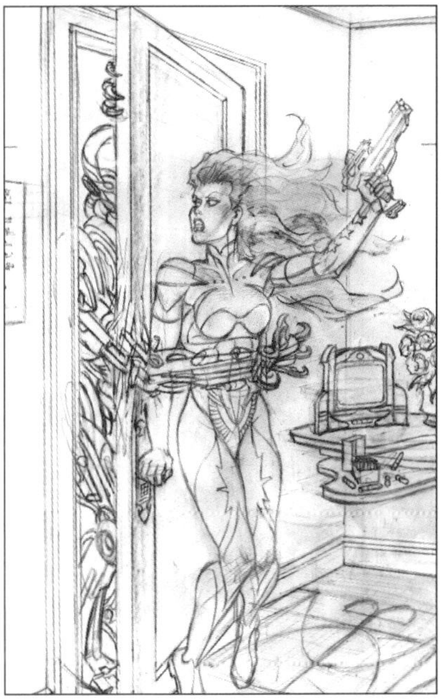

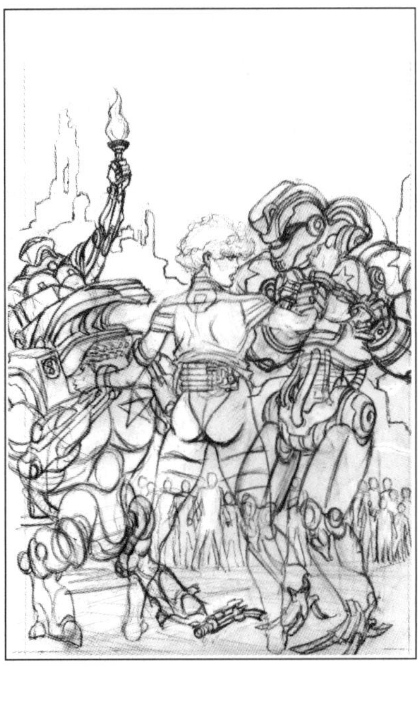

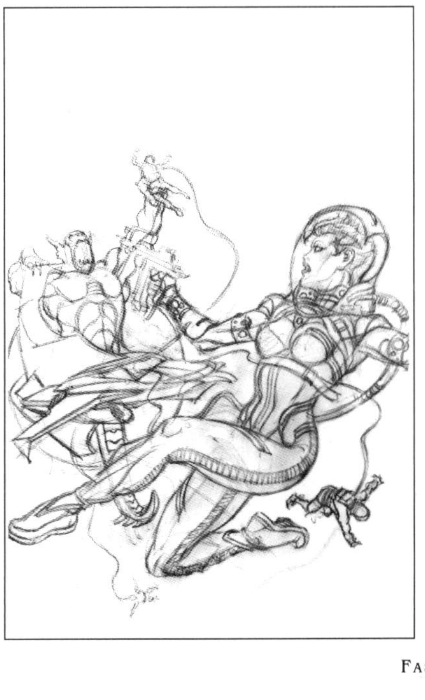

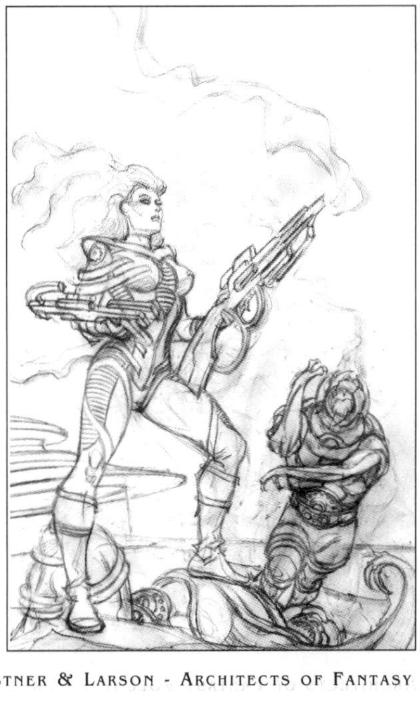

Clockwise from top left:

Pencils for "Guns of Klarn".

Various cover designs for **666: Mark of the Beast** and **Time Killers** comics

Following page: "It's Only a Game" SF convention program illo

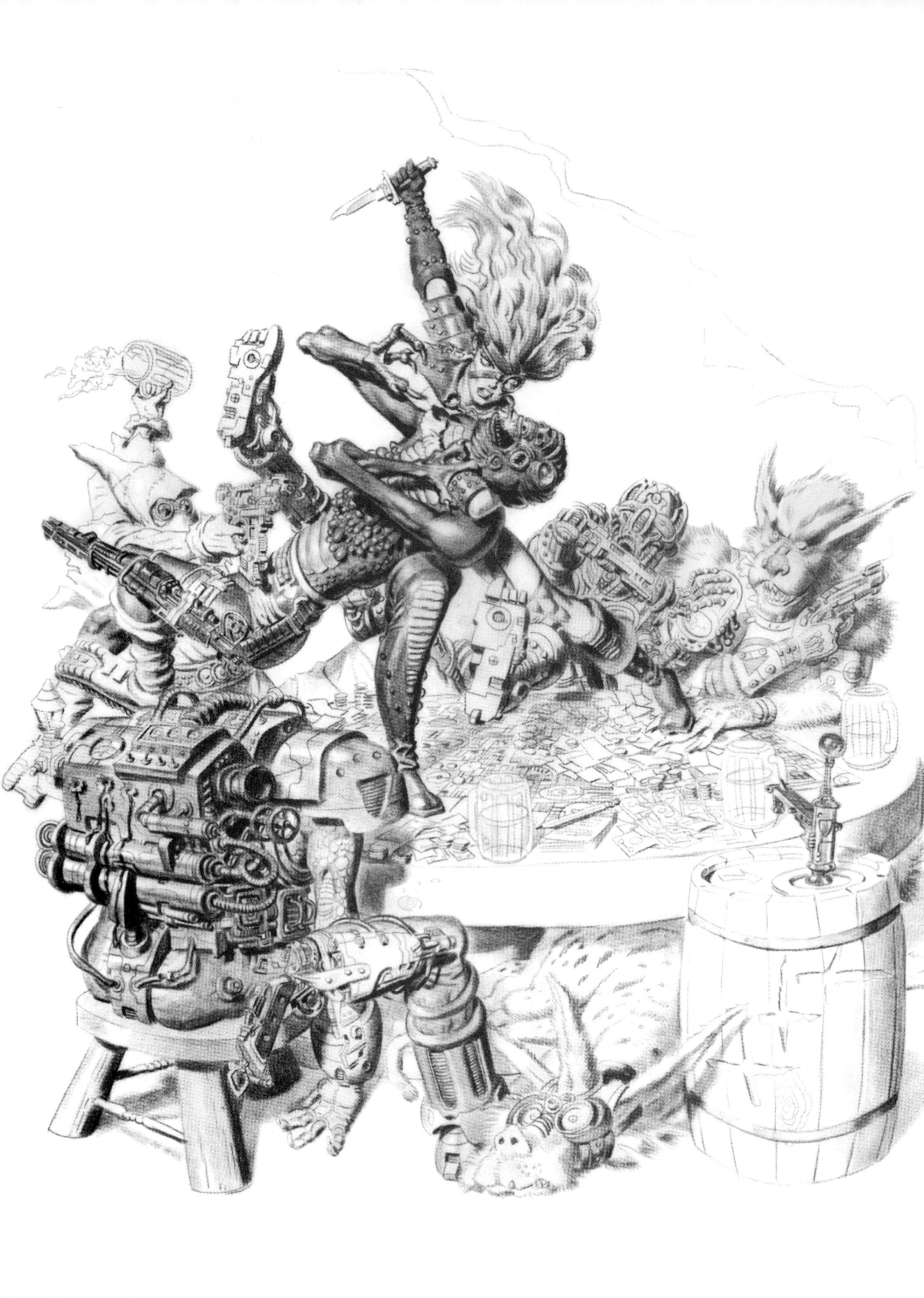

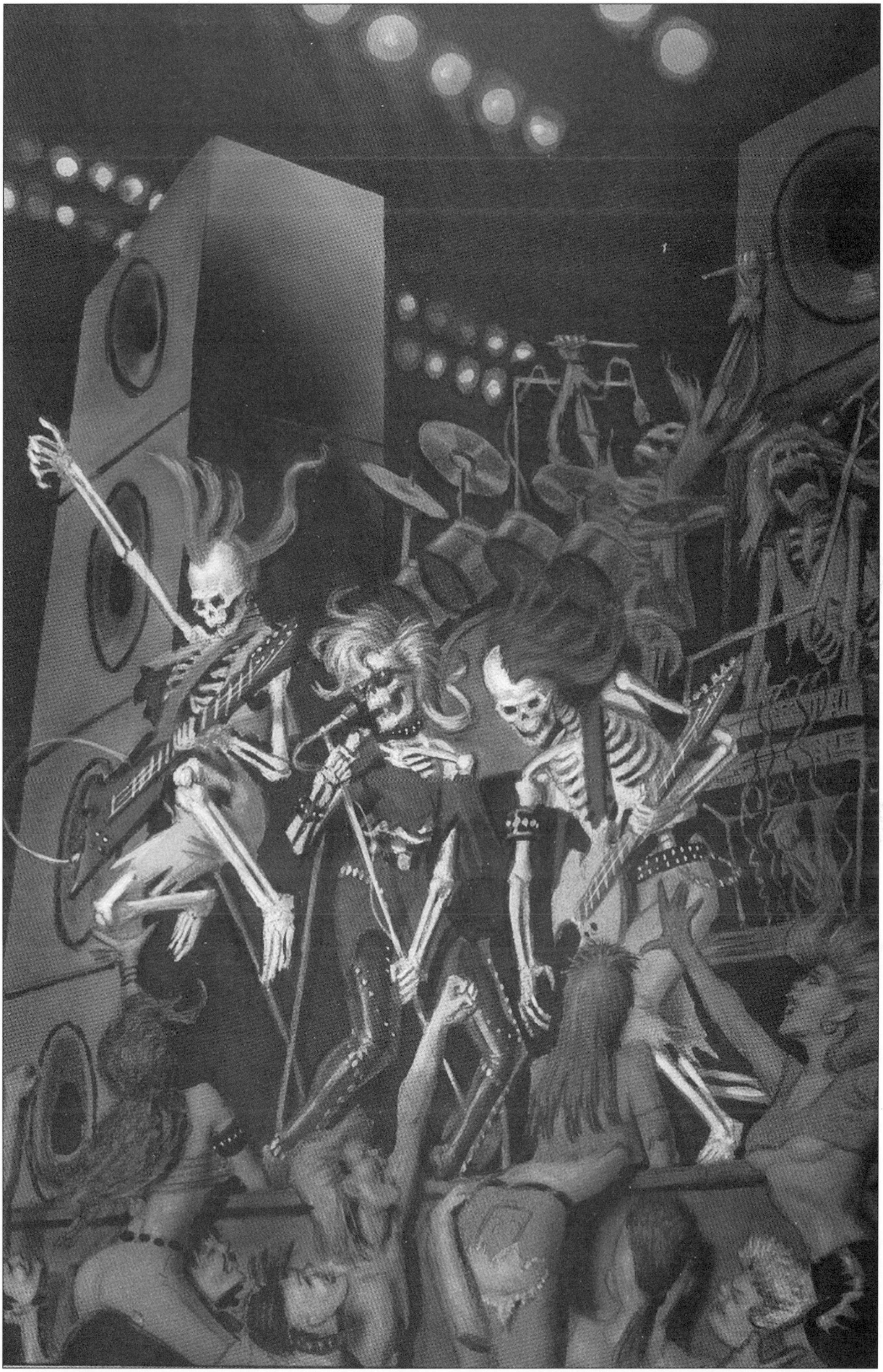

Concept sketch for toy and model sculptor Steve Kiwus

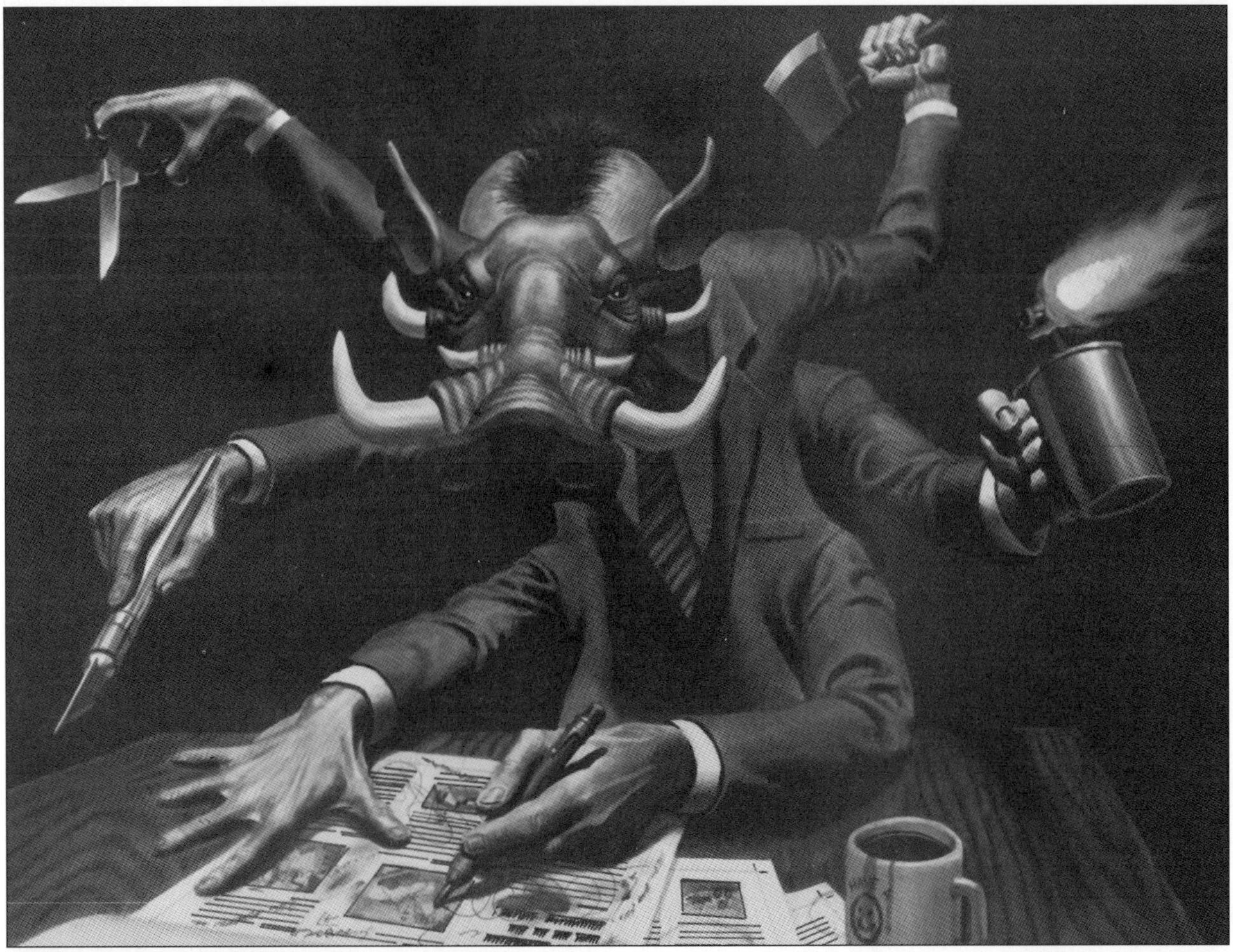

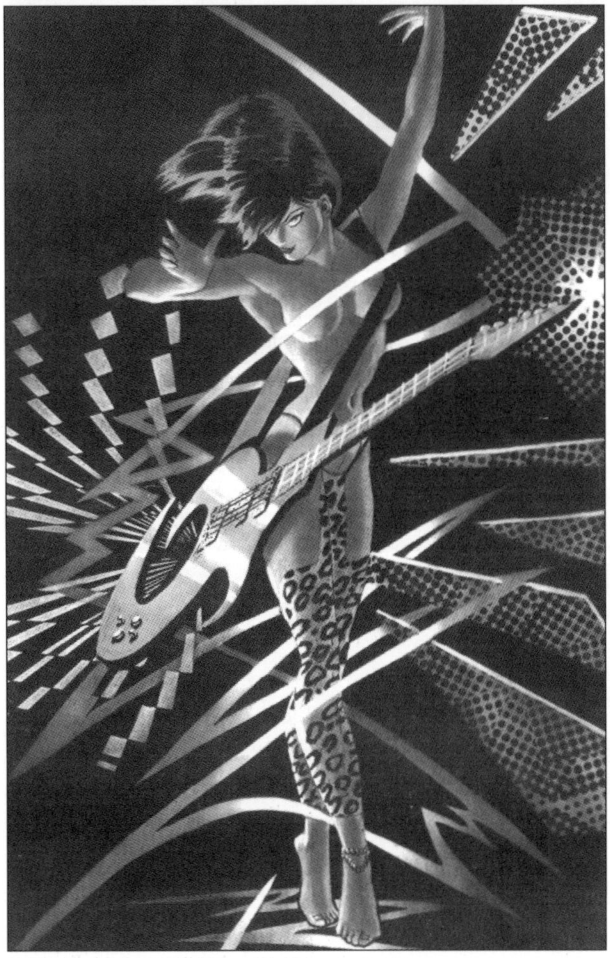

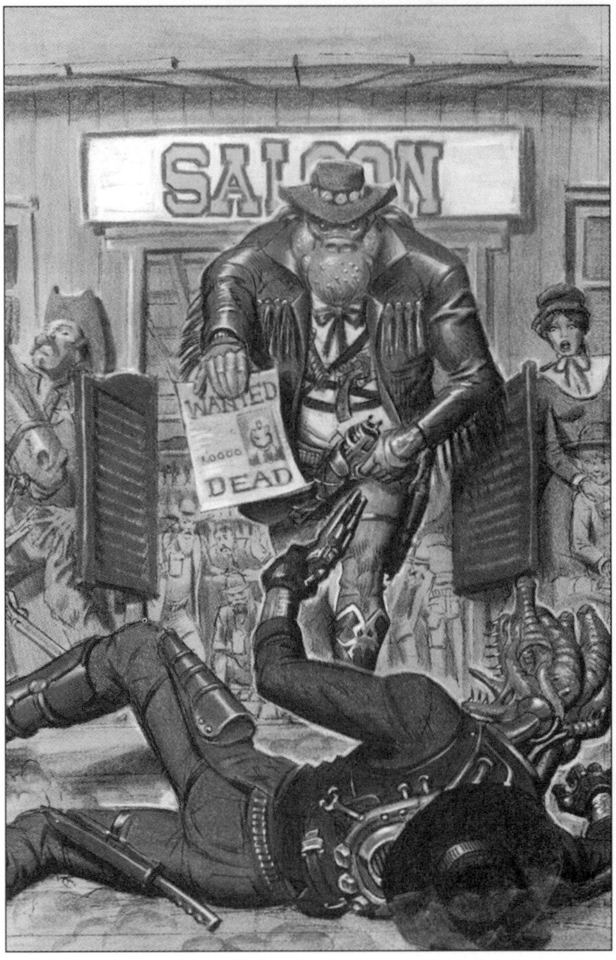


CLOCKWISE FROM TOP:

ADVERTISING WORK ENTITLED "THE CARELESS CLIENT"

COLOR STUDY FOR A COVER OF **TIME TWISTERS**

A COLOR STUDY FOR A T-SHIRT

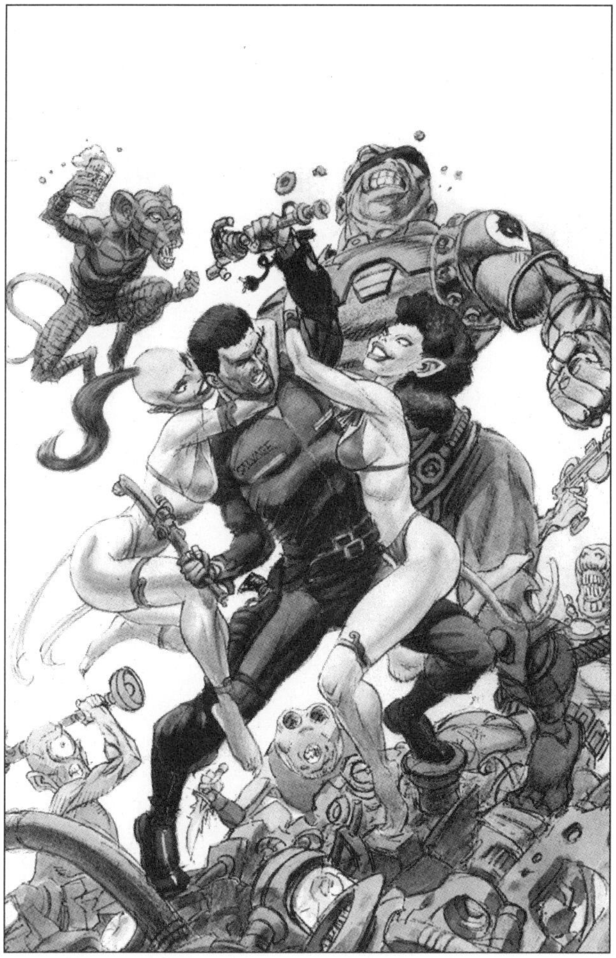

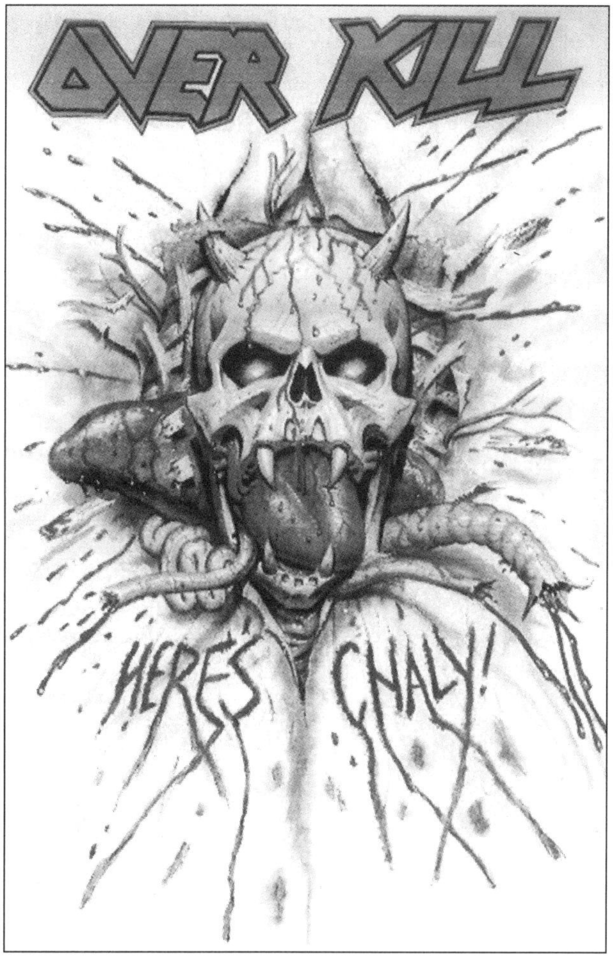


**RICH:**

*"This t-shirt was worn by one of the punks who beat up Nicholas Cage at the end of 'Wild At Heart'"*

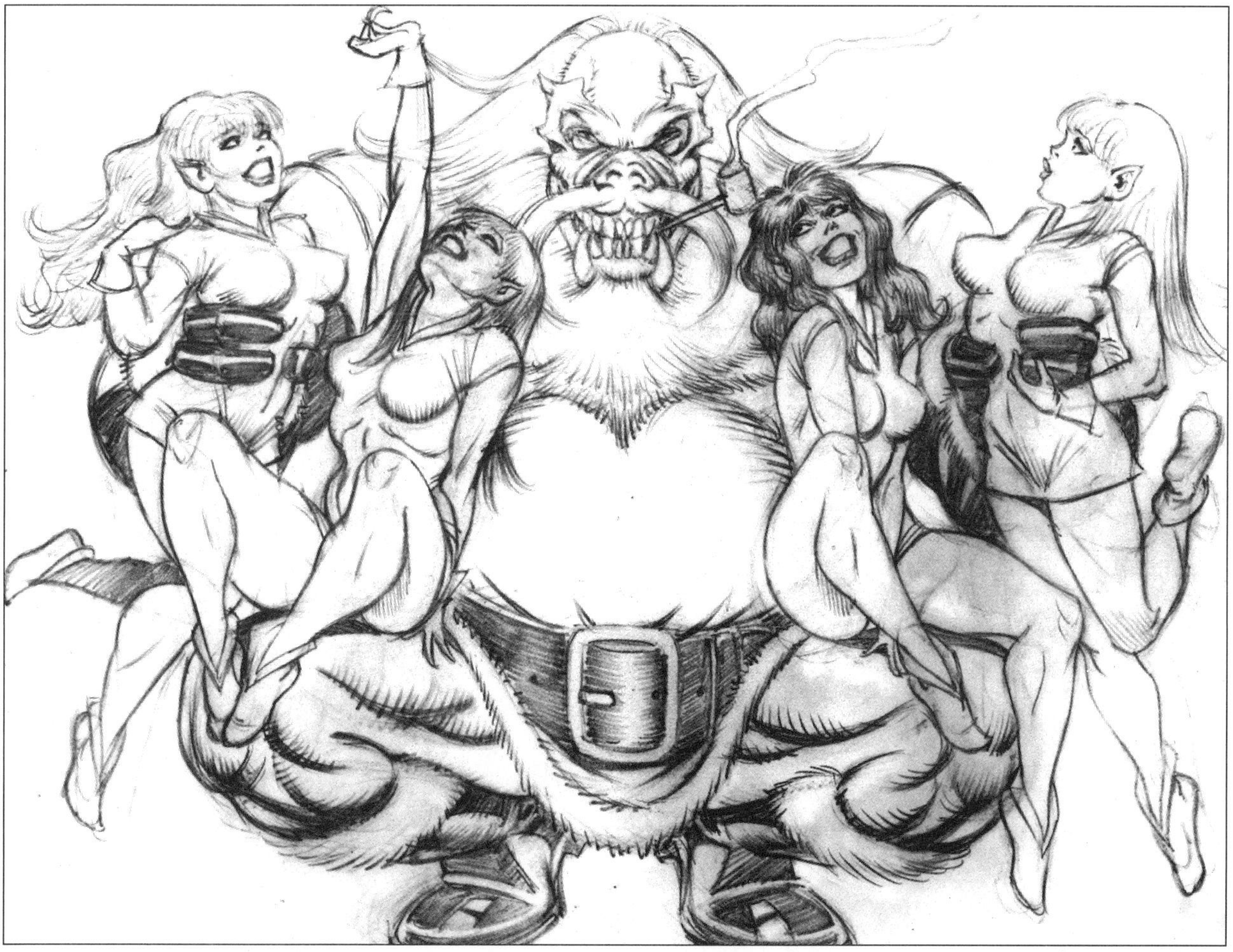

CLOCKWISE FROM TOP LEFT:

COLOR STUDY FOR COVER OF **JUNKER** 1

T-SHIRT DESIGN FOR SOCIALLY CONCERNED FOLK ROCKERS **OVERKILL** - "HERE'S CHALY"

PENCIL SKETCH OF A CHRISTMAS CARD DESIGN DONE FOR **SQP**

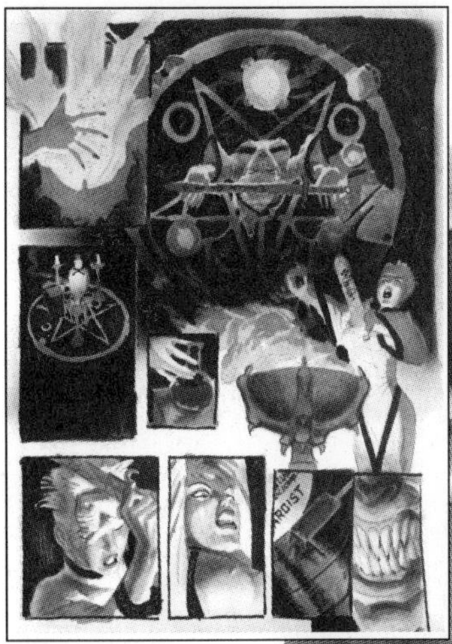

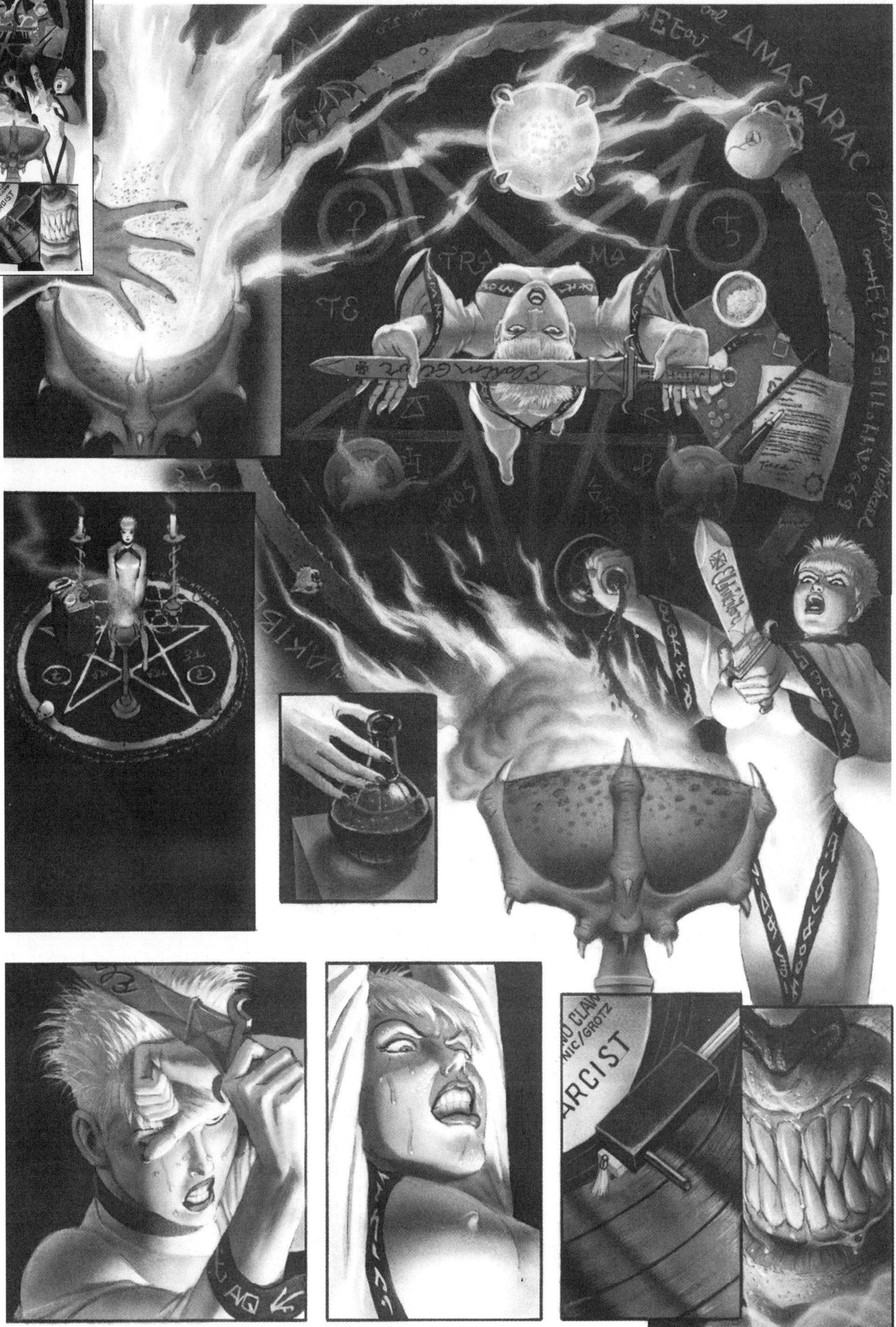


Inset:
Tone study of page two from "Demon Baby", a proposed comic project by Fastner and Larson

Final art from page two of Demon Baby

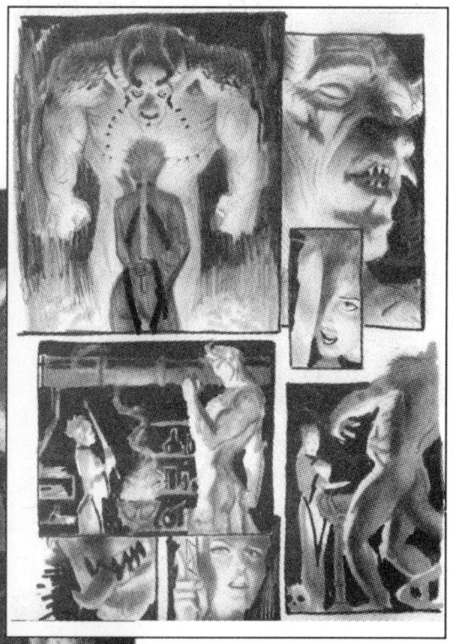

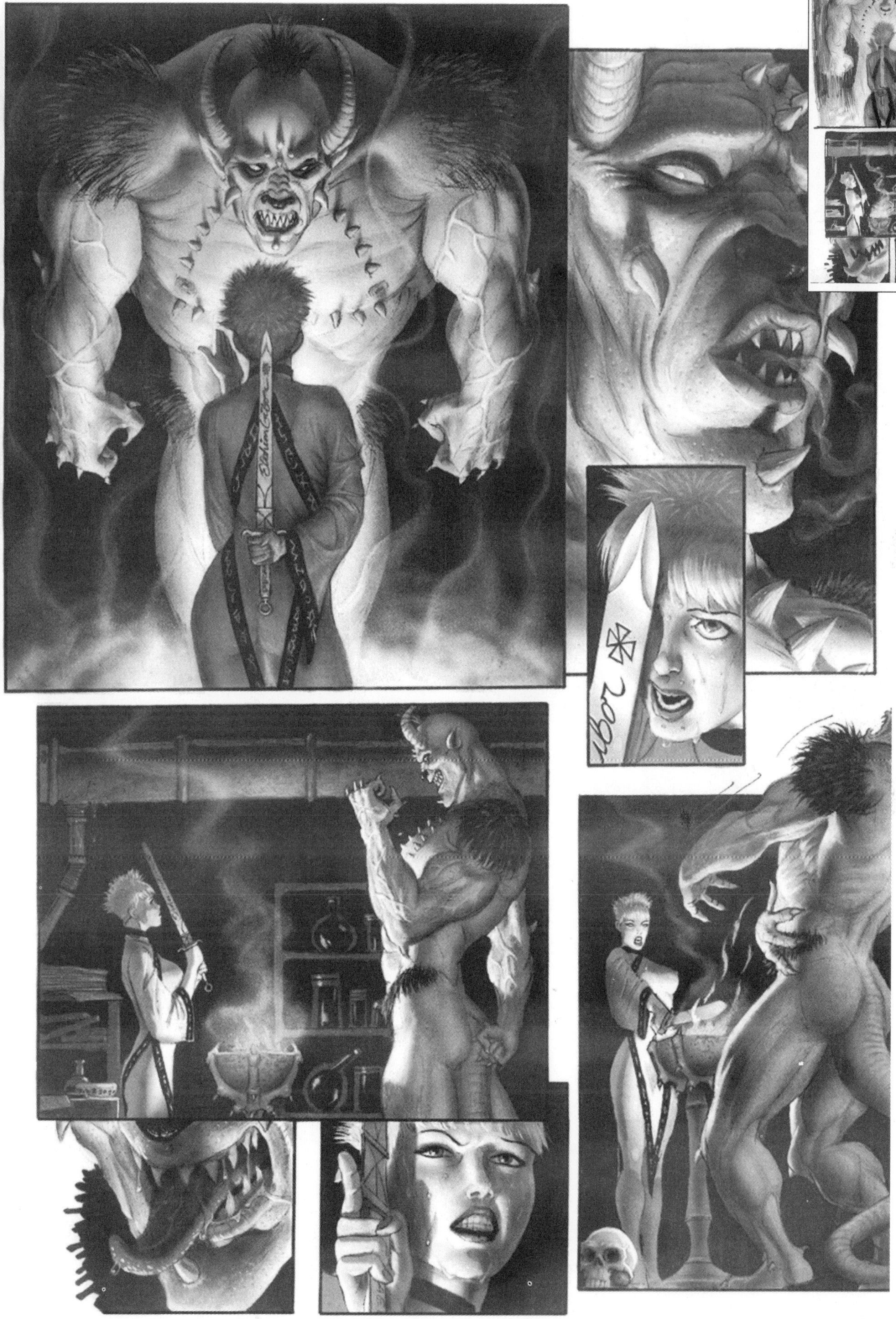

INSET:
TONE STUDY OF PAGE THREE FROM THE STORY "DEMON BABY"

FINISHED ART OF PAGE THREE

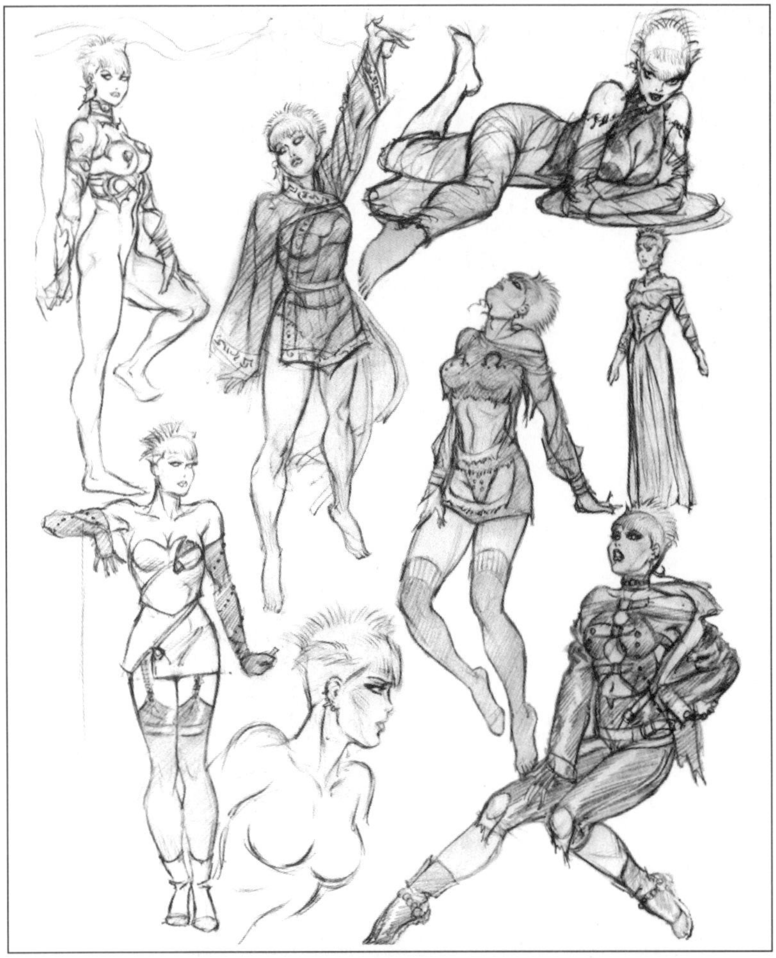

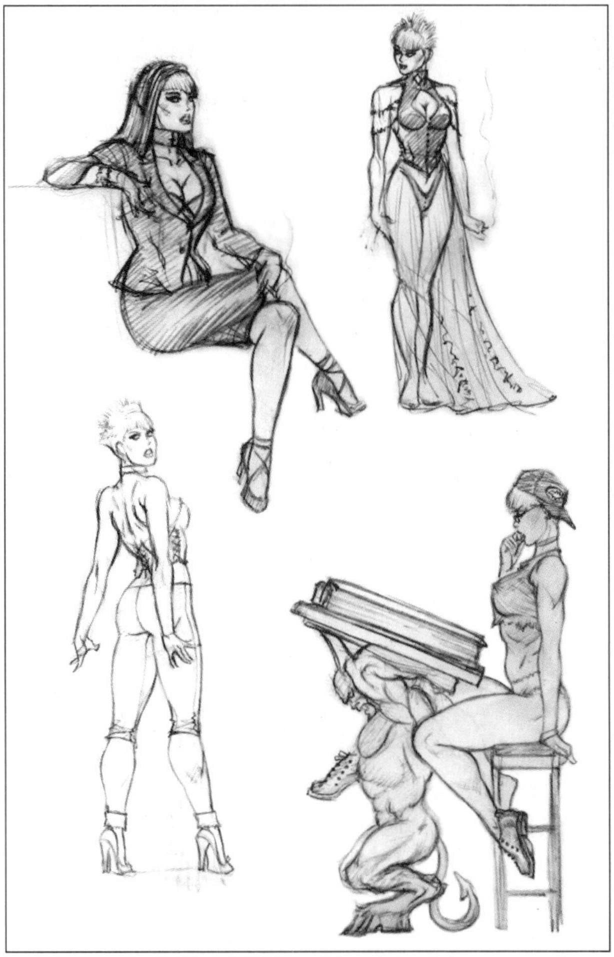

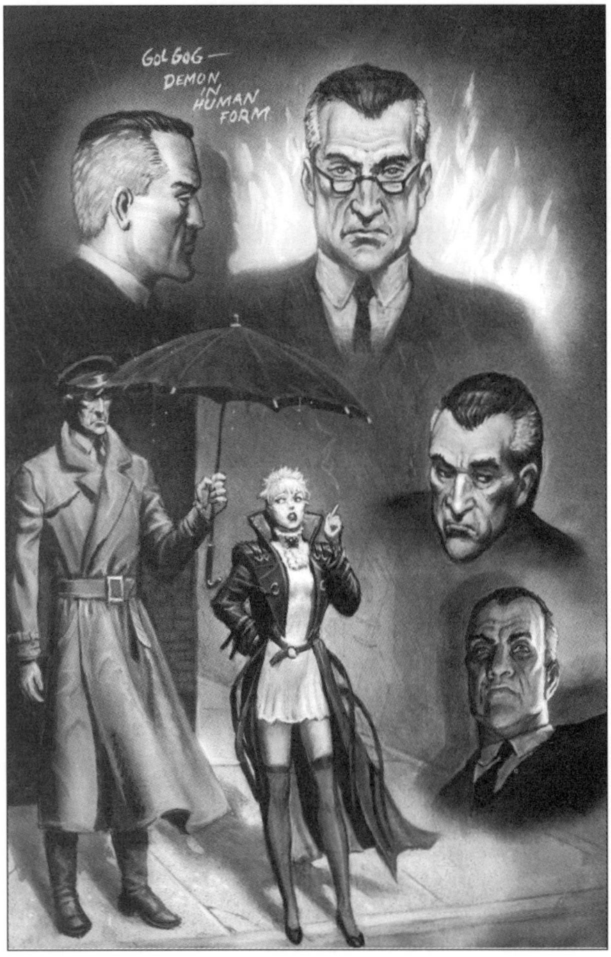



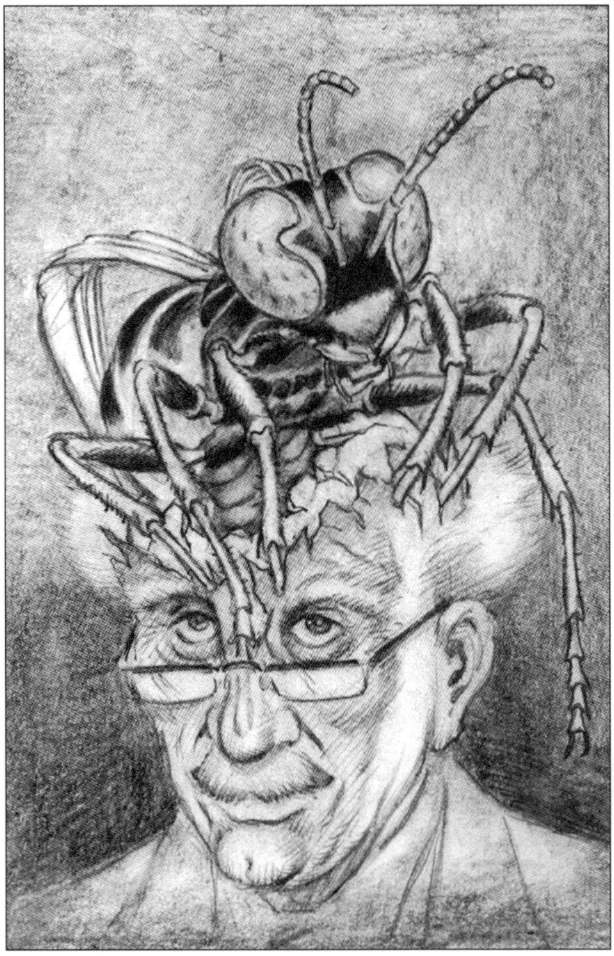

CLOCKWISE FROM TOP LEFT:

VARIOUS CHARACTER AND COSTUME DESIGNS FOR "DEMON BABY"

SELF PORTRAIT, RICH

CHARACTER AND TONE STUDIES FOR THE DEMON GOLGOG, OF "DEMON BABY"

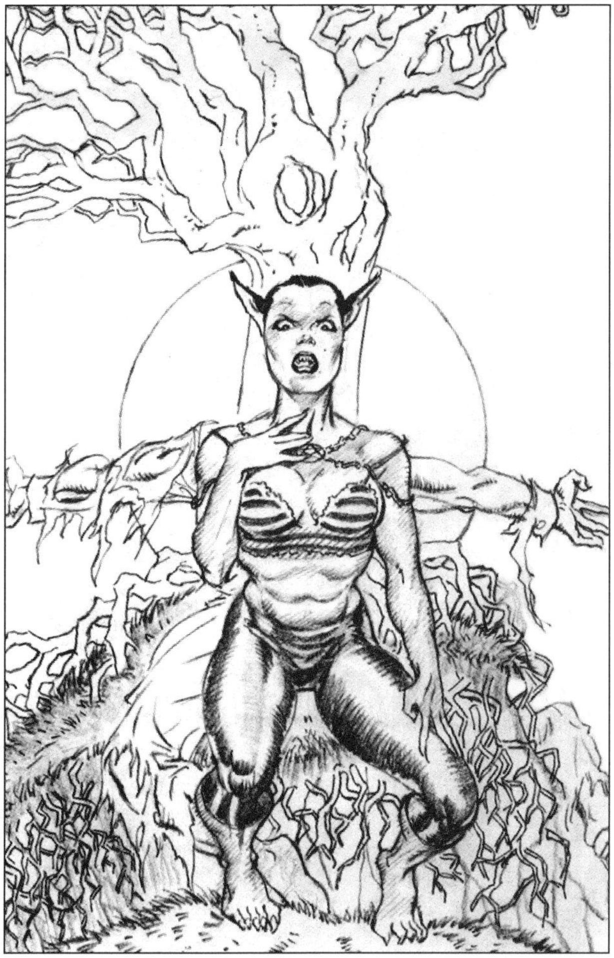

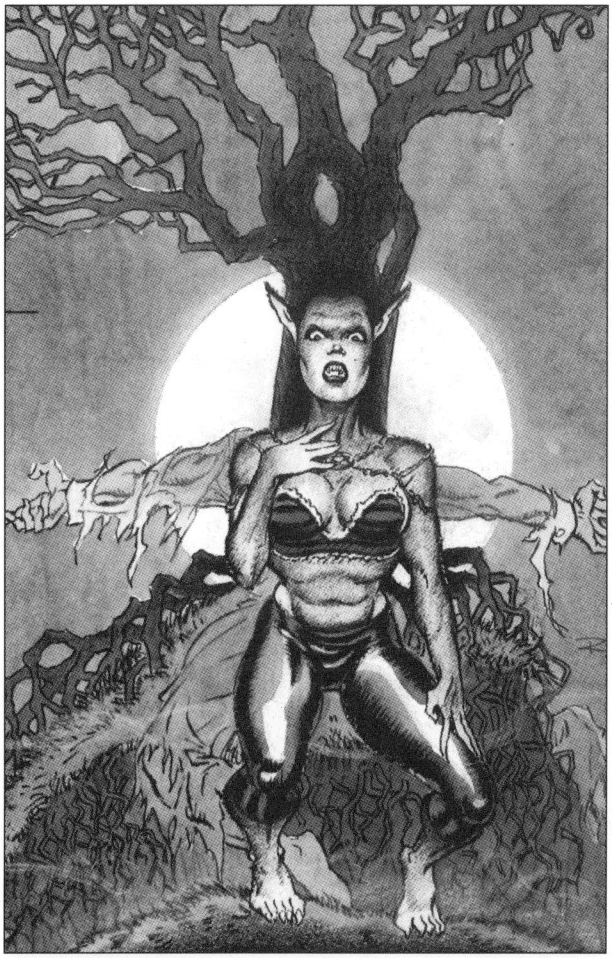

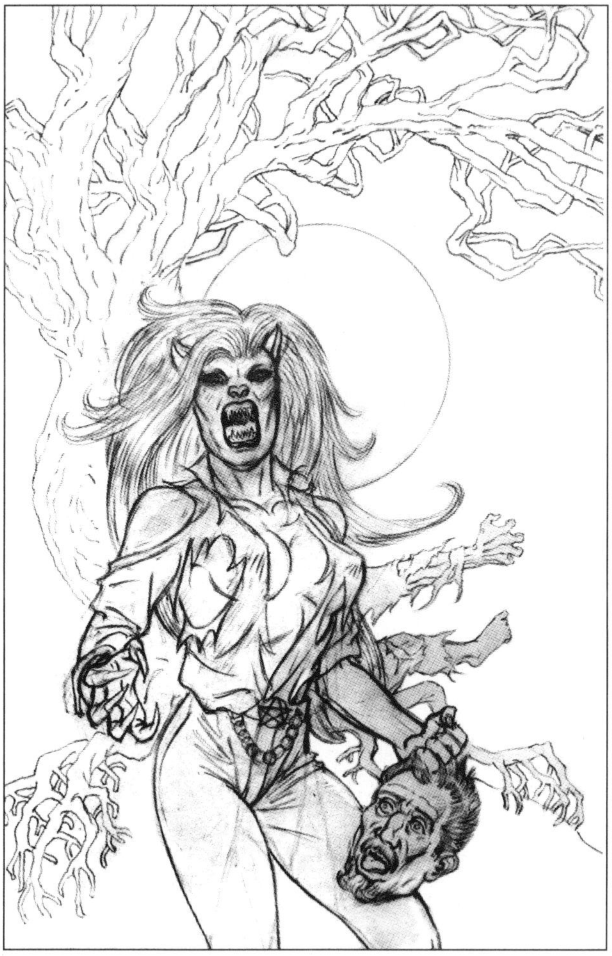

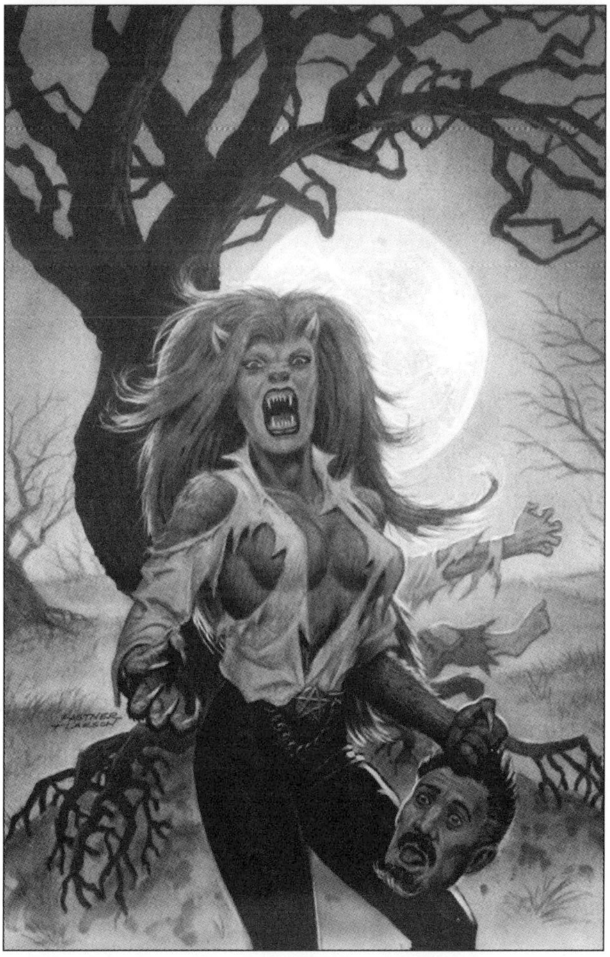

Werebabe roulette

Clockwise from top left:

Initial pencil sketch for the cover of **666** #3, featuring a female she-wolf on the run from a murder spree

Tone study of same

Revised version with longer hair and someone to hold

Pencils of the finished design

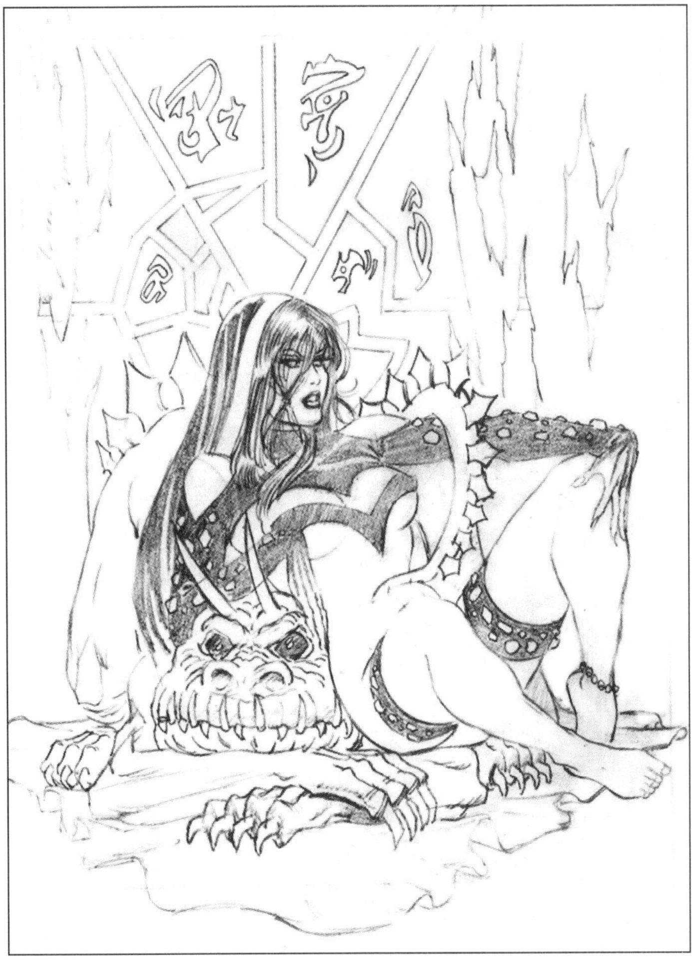

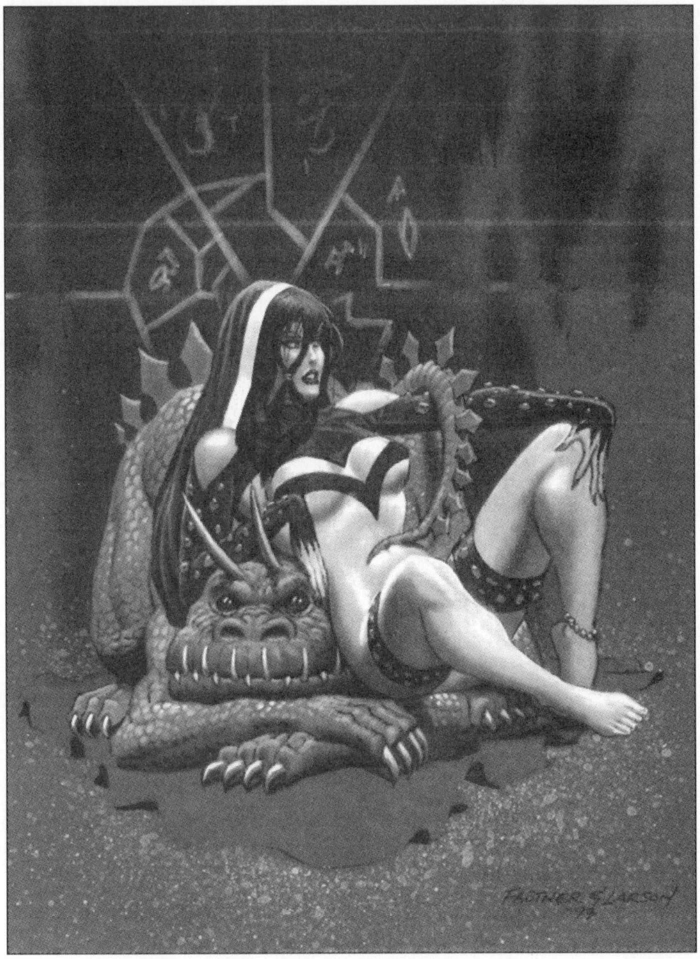


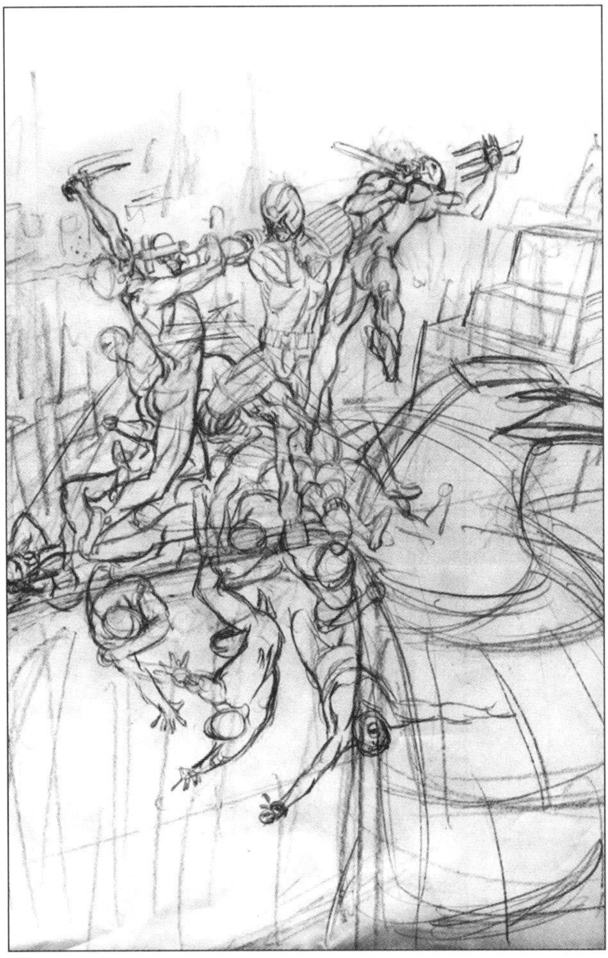

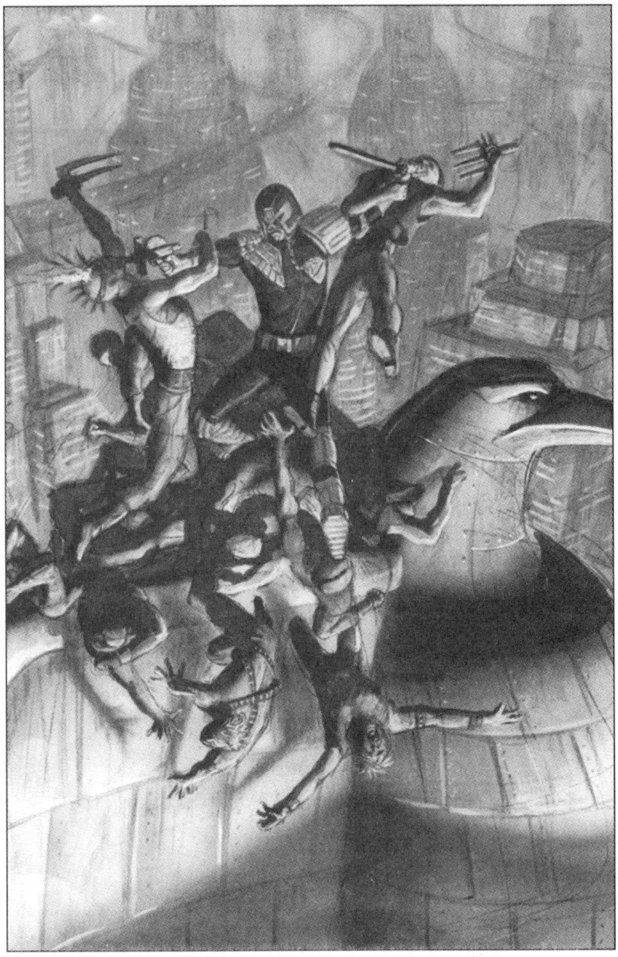

Clockwise from top left:

Proposed pencil sketch for a cover of **666**

Color study of same

Final design for **Judge Dredd** "Hall of Justice" cover

Pencil rough of same

Following page:

Full size (20"x30") tone study of "Hall of Justice" before giant finished painting is created

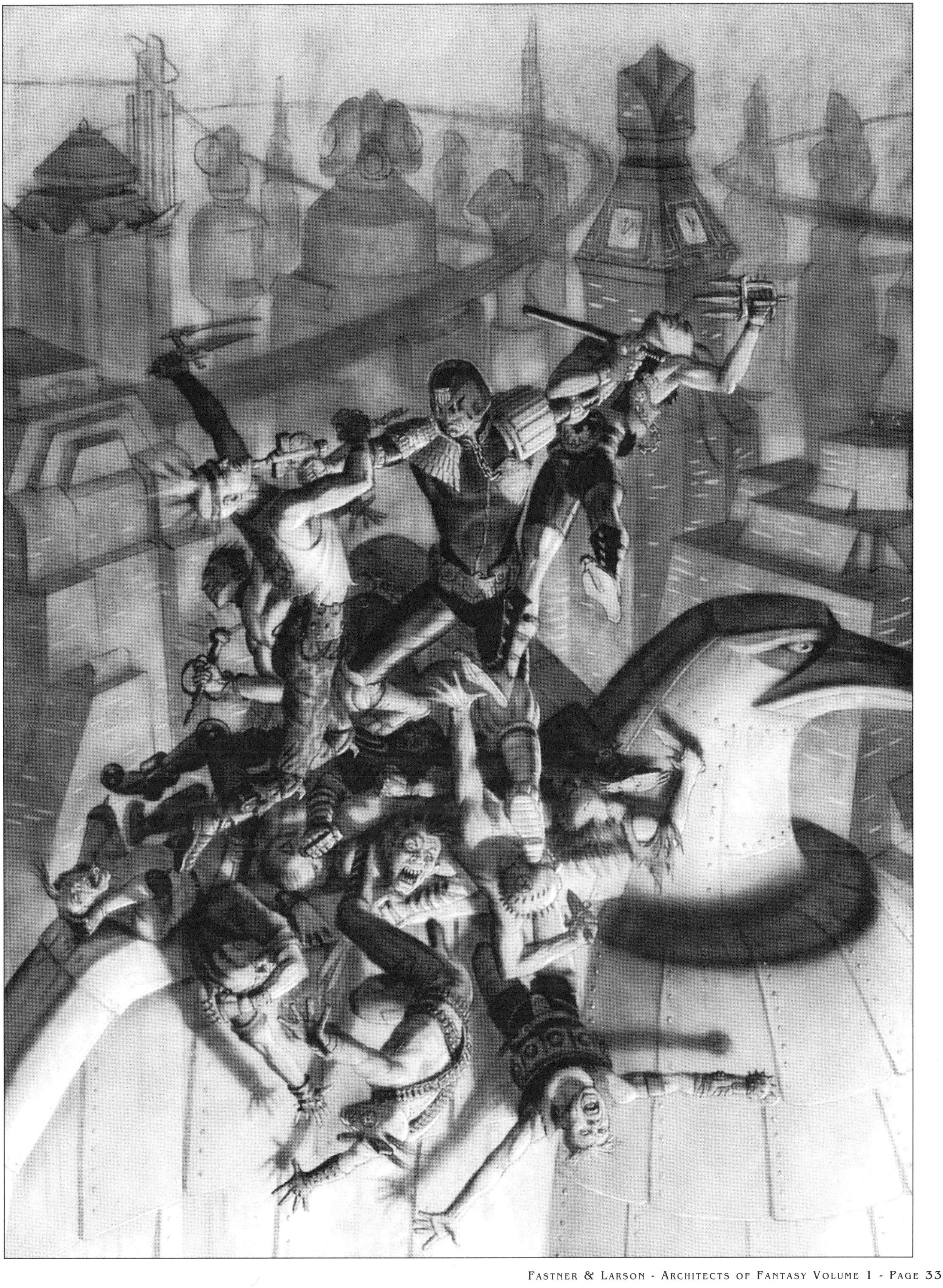

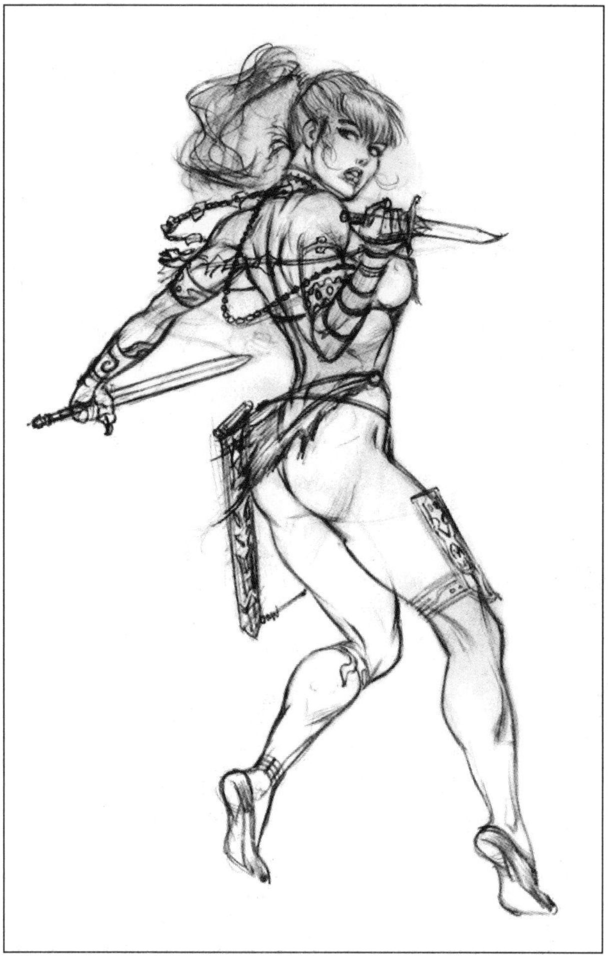

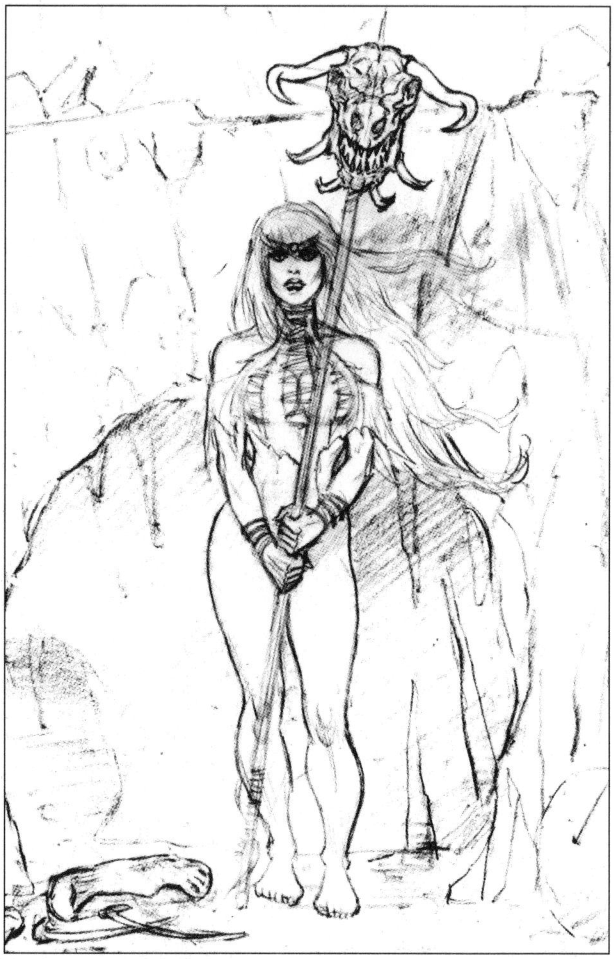

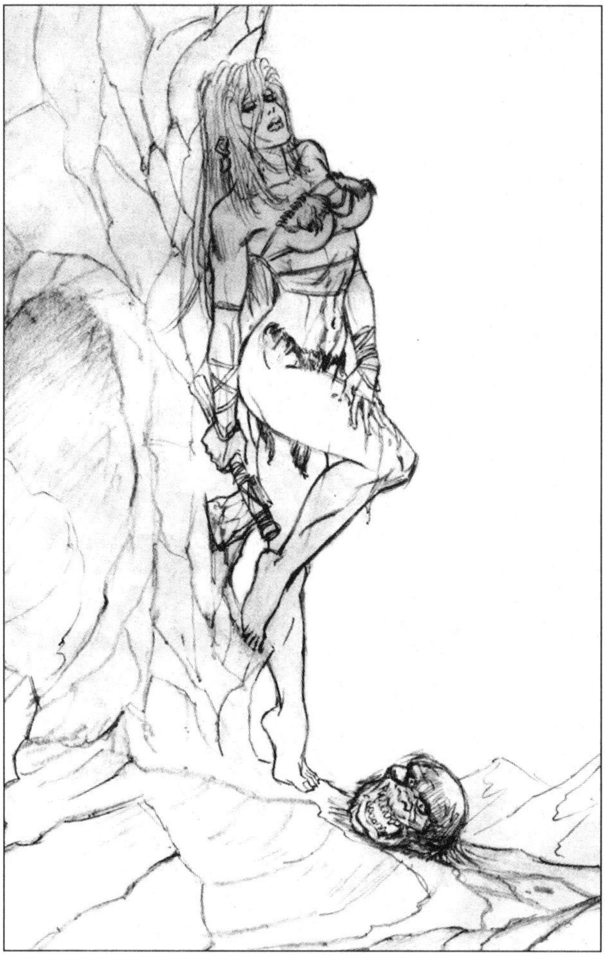

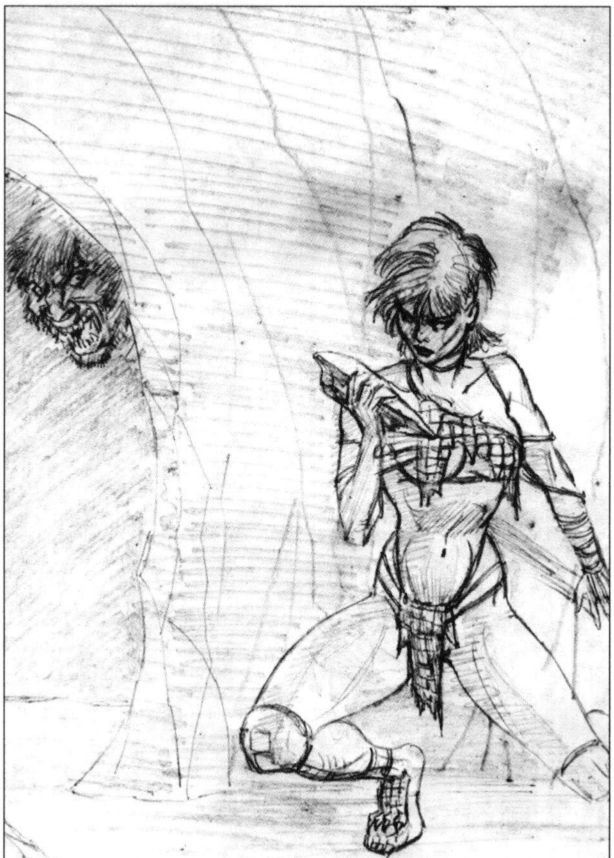

Clockwise from top left:

Pencil rough for the portfolio **Angels of Death**

Three pencils for **Clan of the Claw** Portfolio Set 1

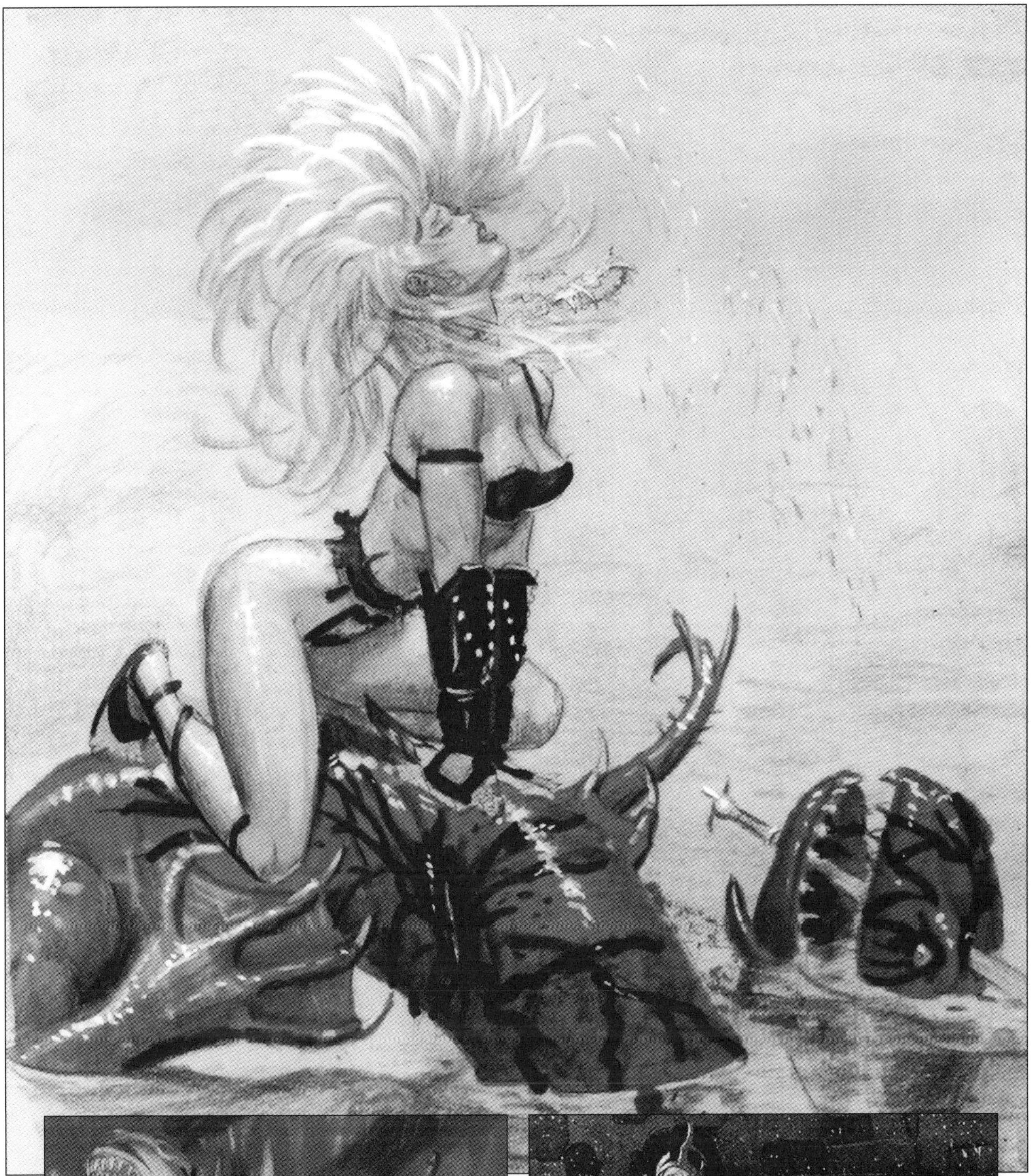

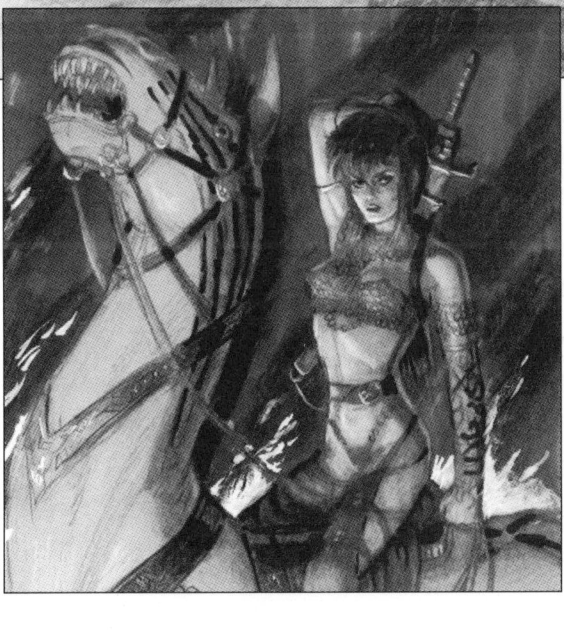

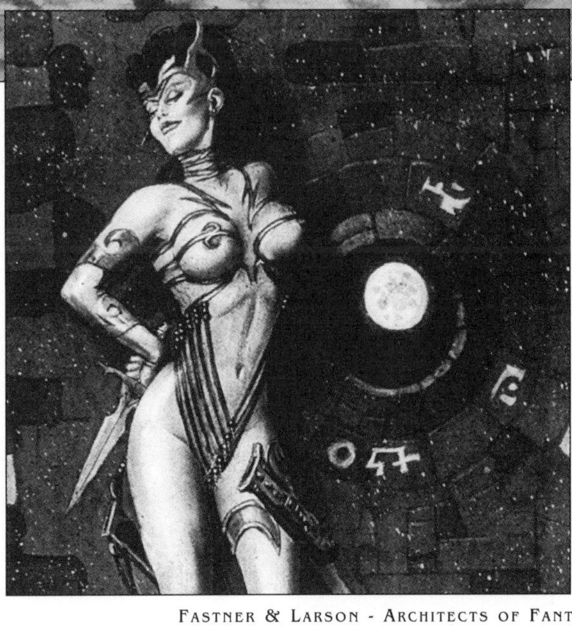

Clockwise from top :

Tone study for a plate in the **Petz** Portfolio

Tone study for a plate in **Flesh & Blood** Portfolio Set 2

Another **Petz** tone Study

Following page: Pencil layout for **Tyranny Rex** graphic novel cover art

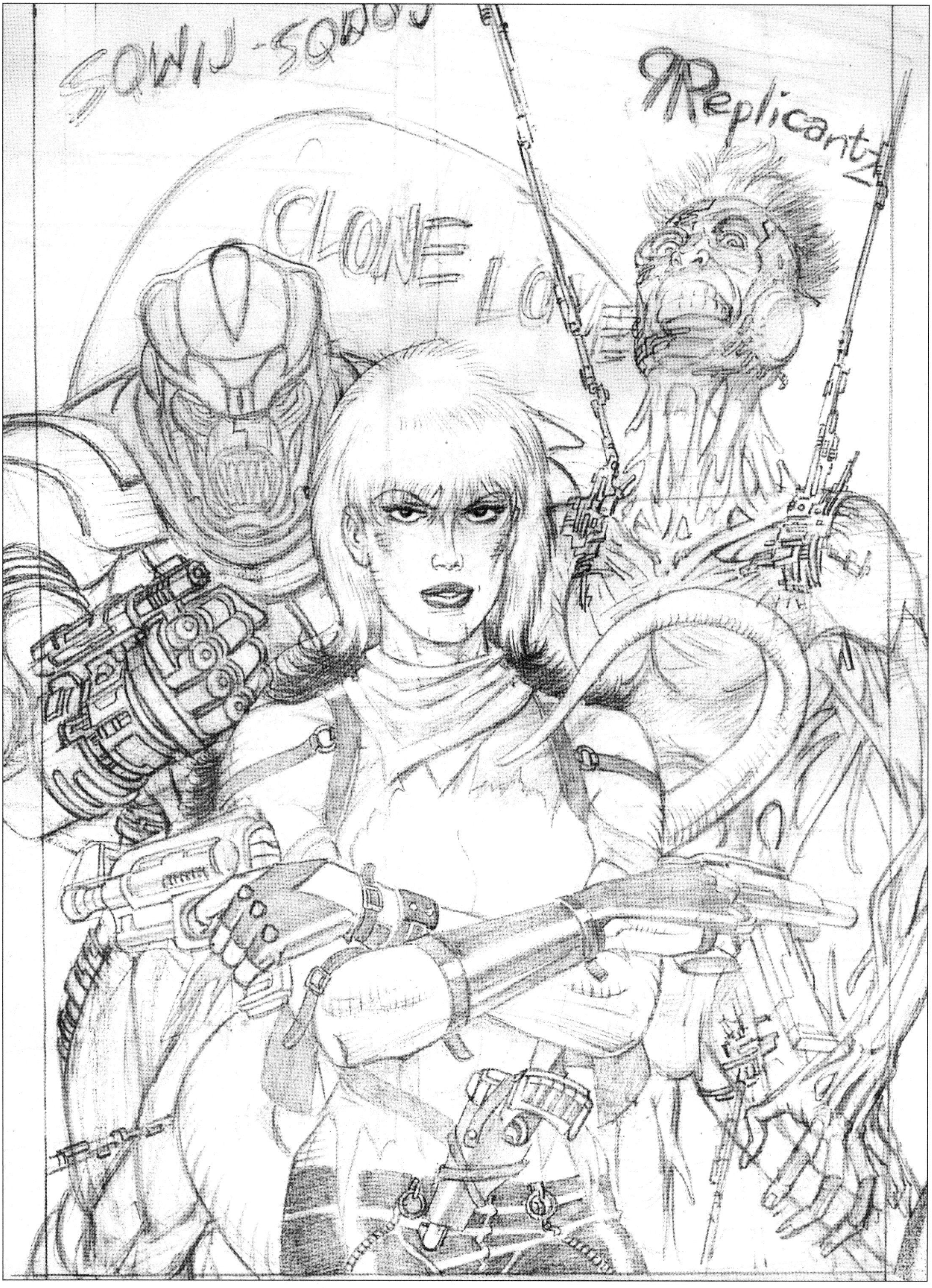
SQWIJ-SQDOJ
Replicantz
CLONE LOVE

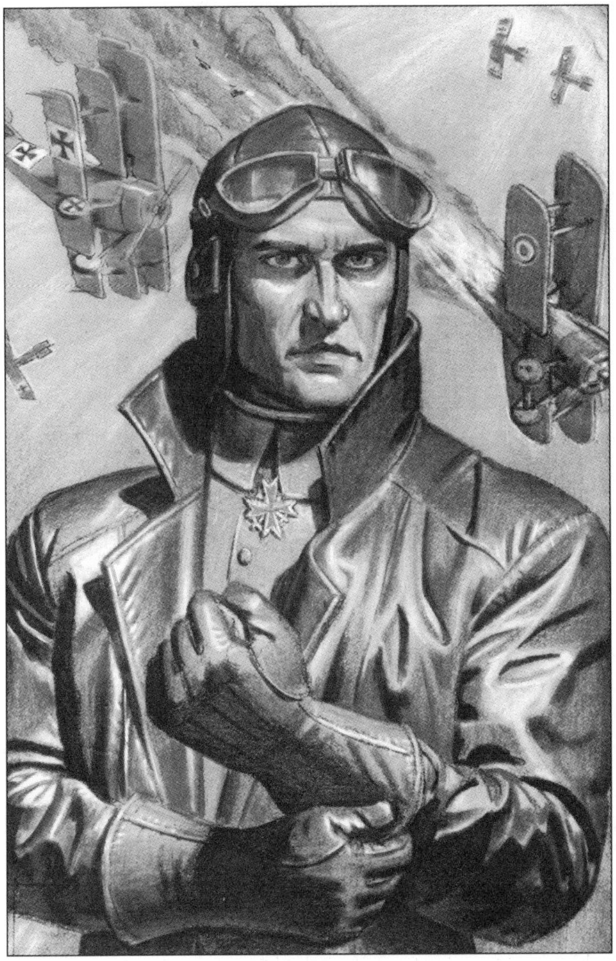

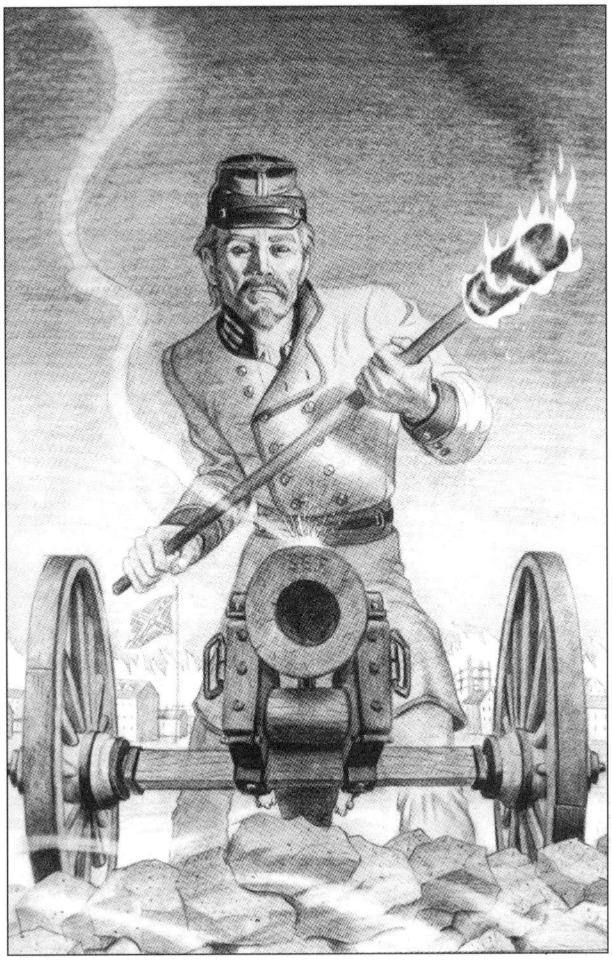

**STEVE:**

*"I've been lucky to work with comics legends like Harvey Kurtzman, Mike Kaluta, and Jim Steranko"*

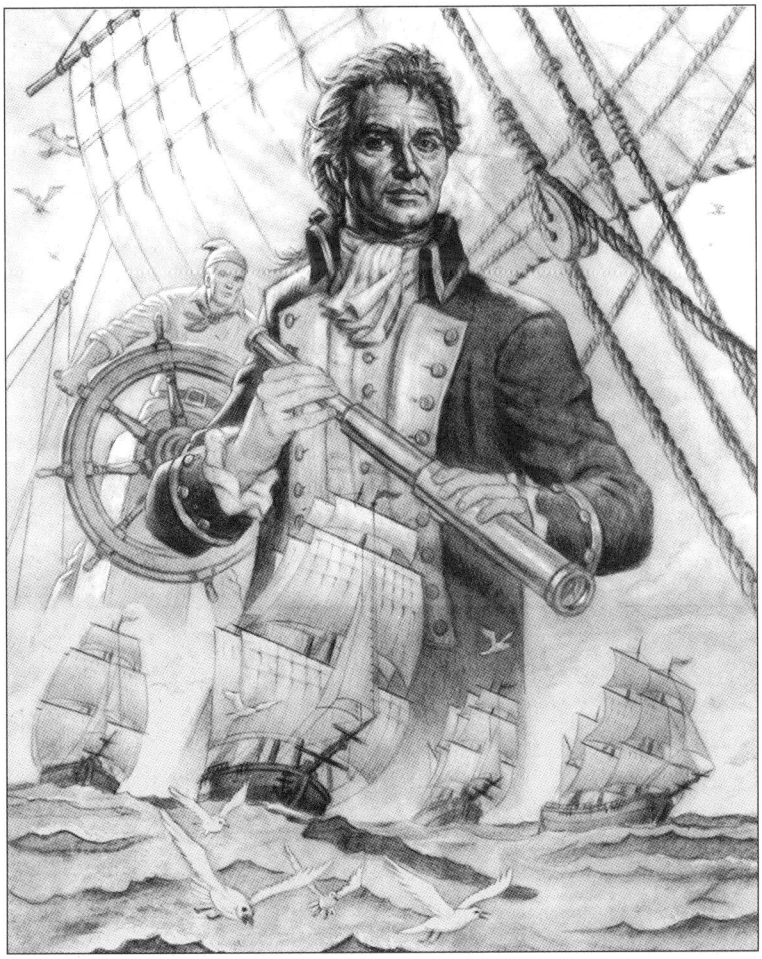

Clockwise from top left:

Red Baron (Kaluta layout)

Civil War Agent (Steve solo)

Captain Cook (Steranko layout)

Steve plays it straight with 3 tone and color studies for **The Time Machine** paperback series

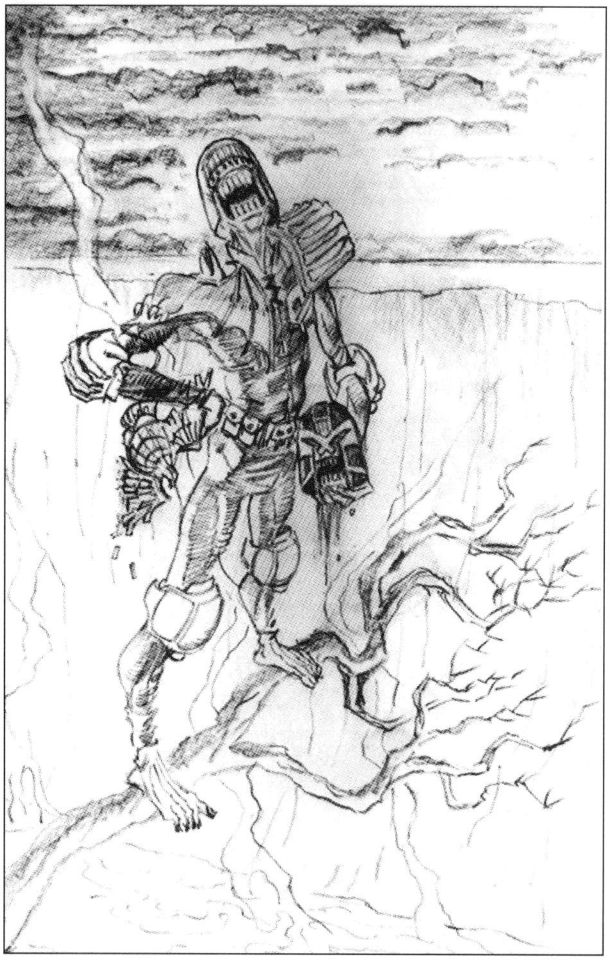

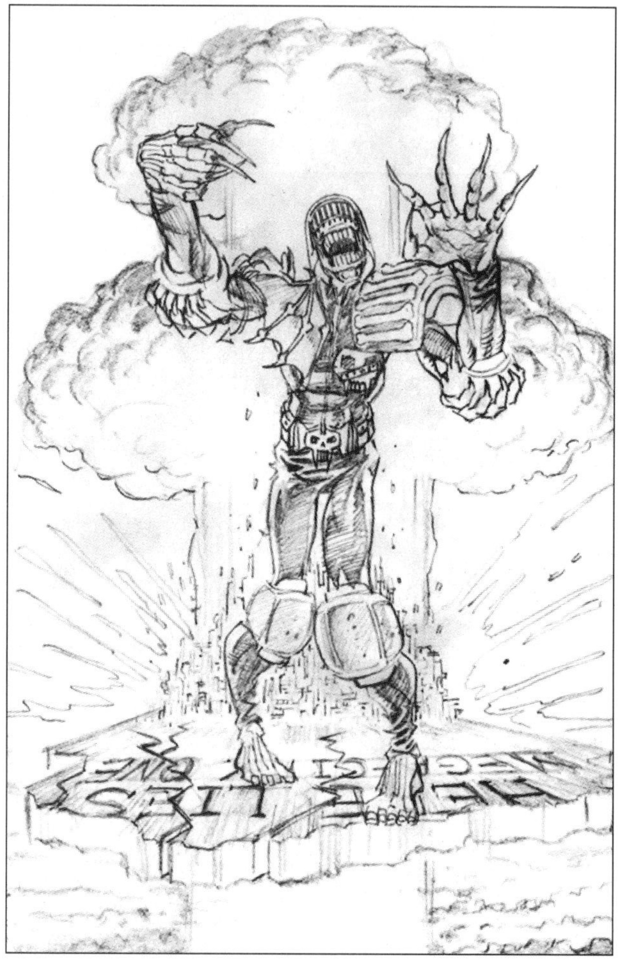

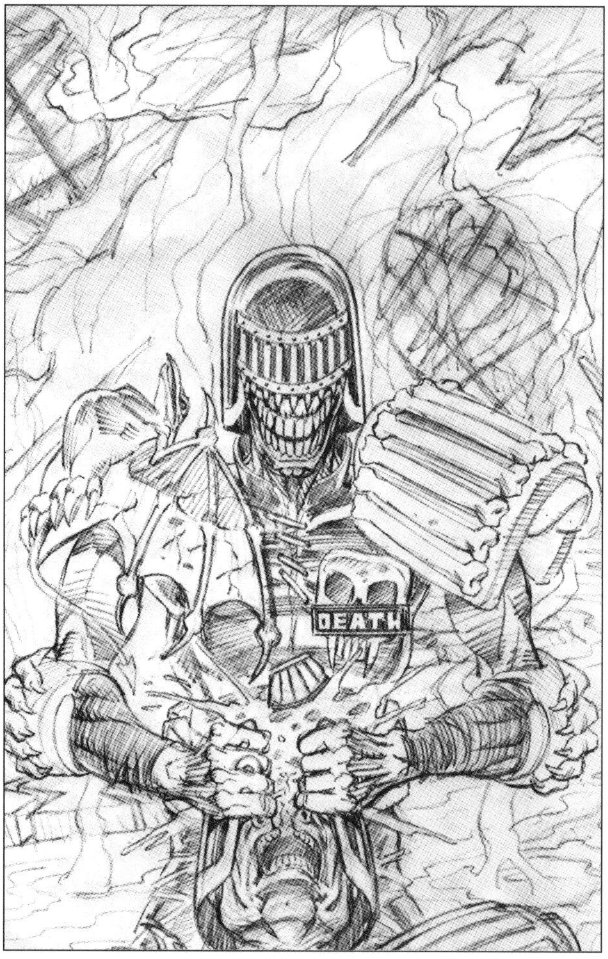


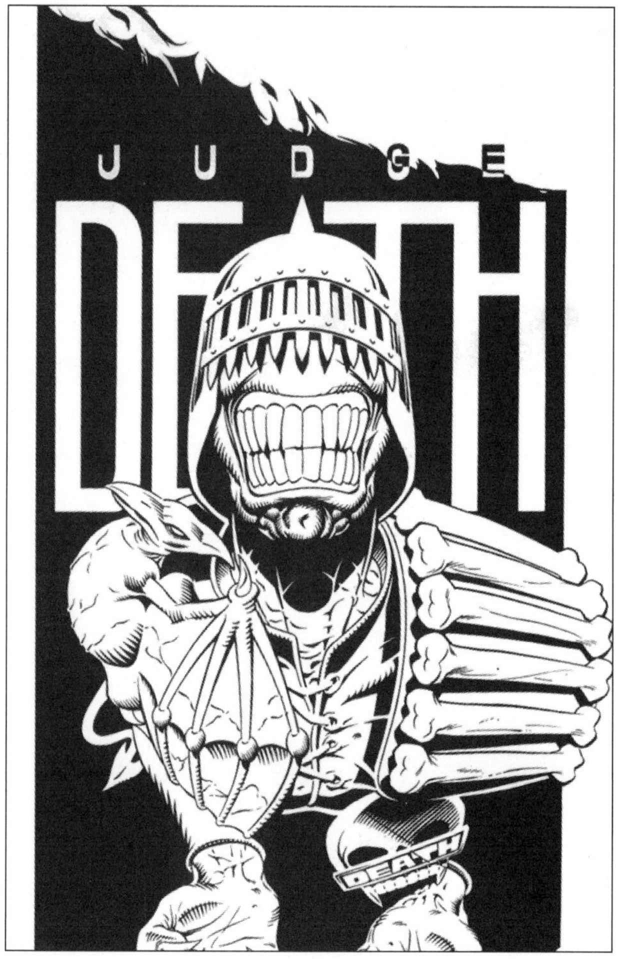


Death in extreme detail!

Clockwise from top left:

Proposed cover idea for a **Judge Death** collection

Second cover concept

Ink t-shirt design

Approved pencils

Following page: Tone study for final art

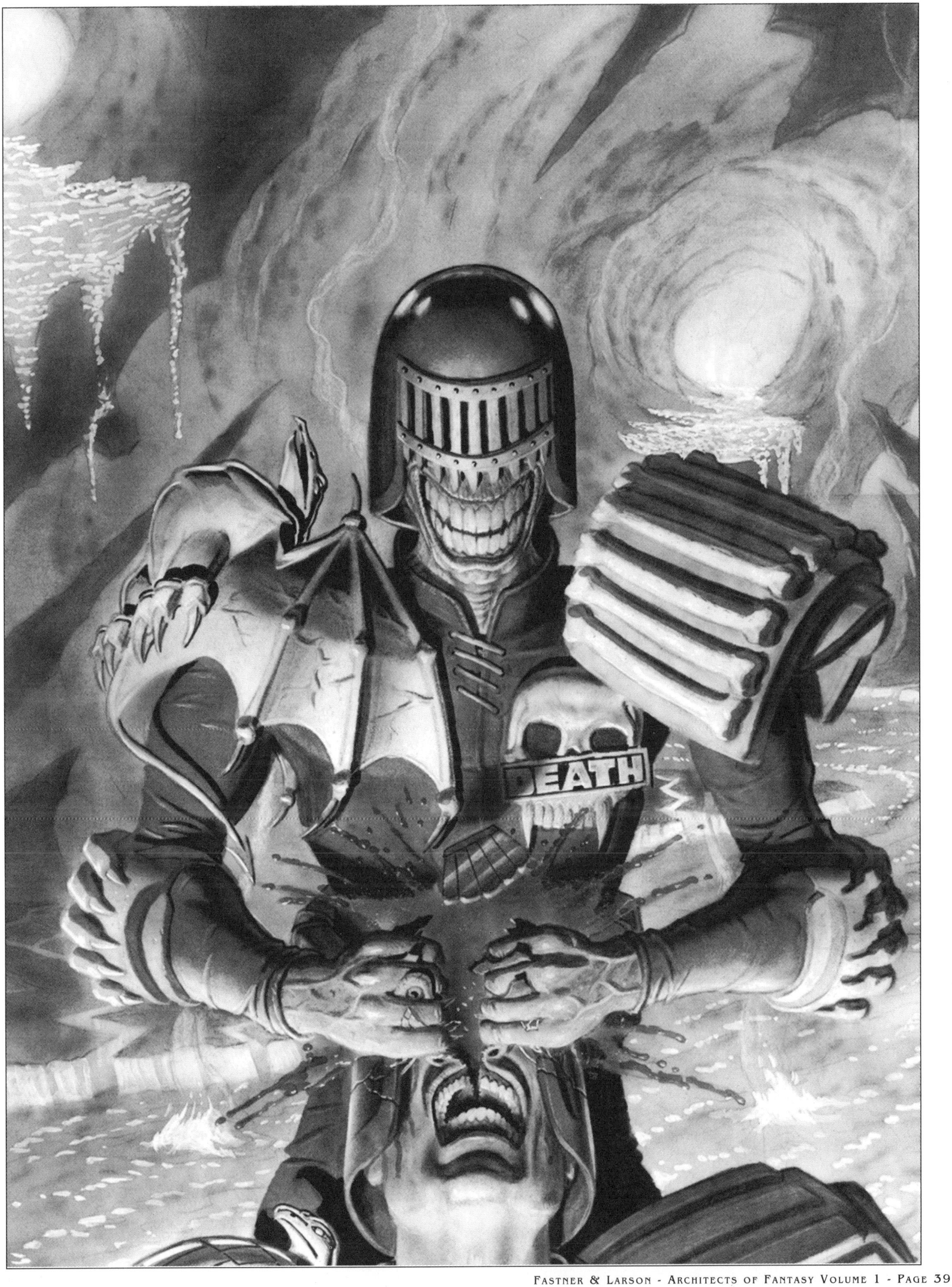
DEATH

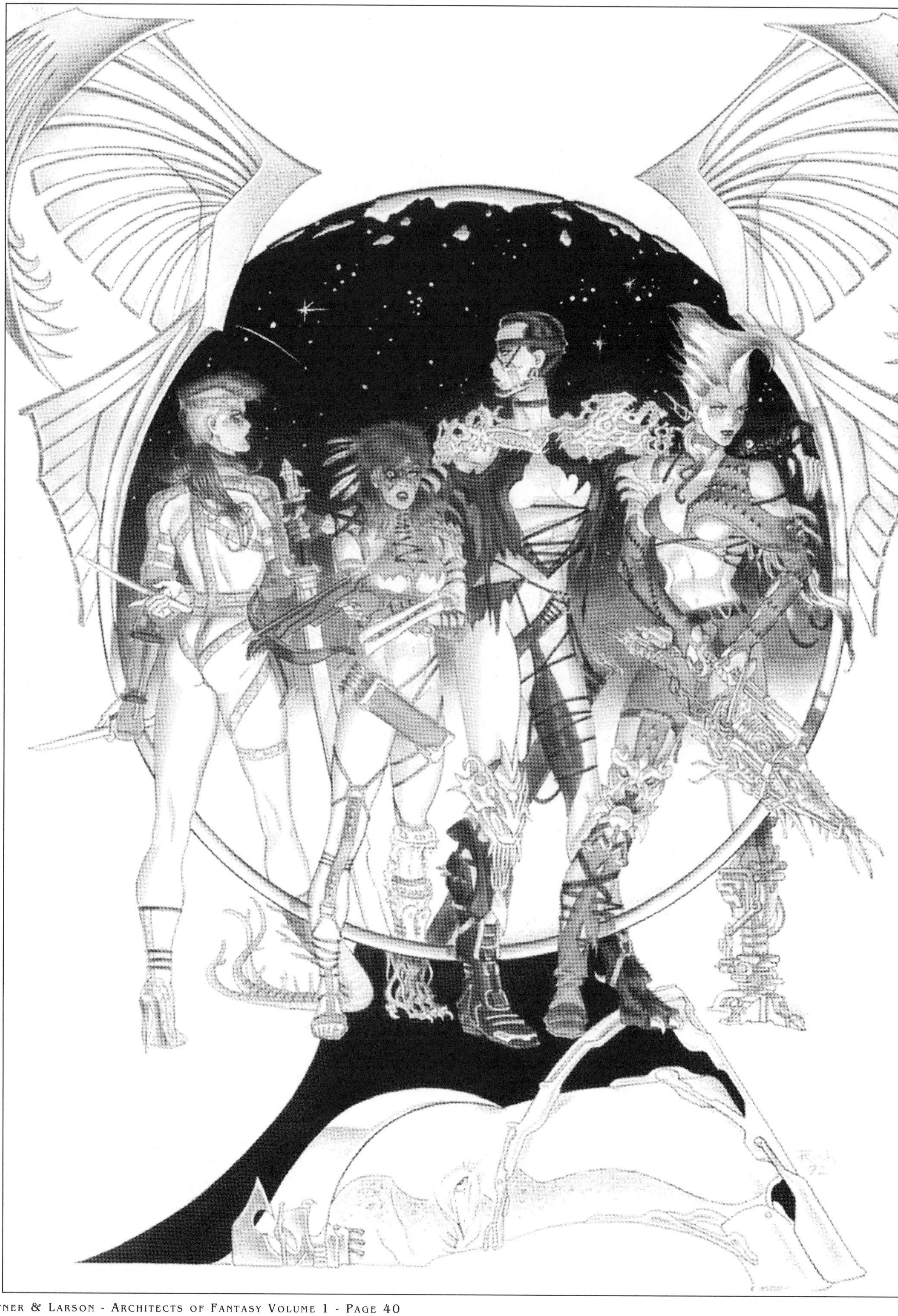

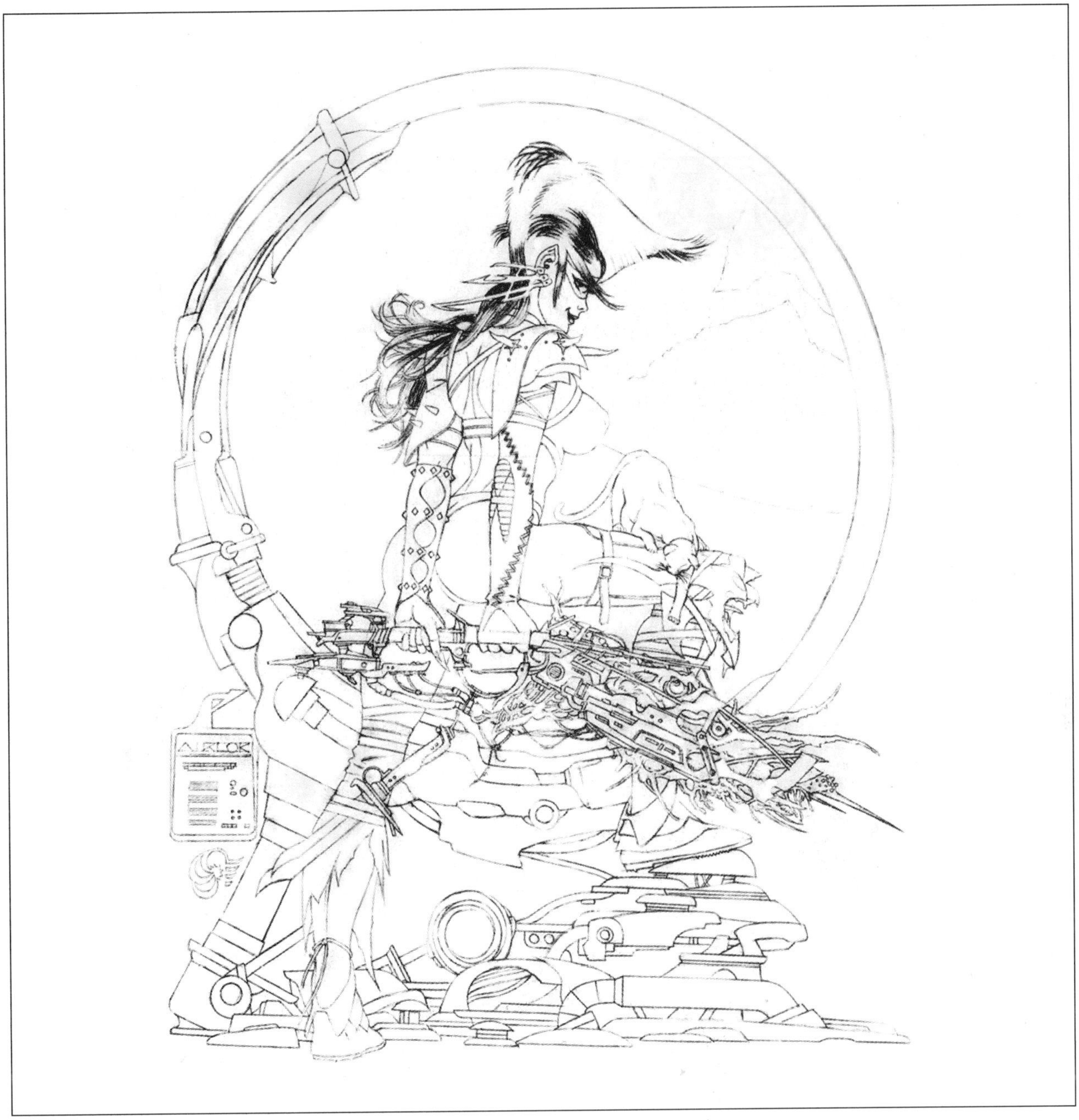

**RICH:**

*"'Daughters of the Disk' was inspired by 'The Road Warrior' - probably the best comic book on film."*

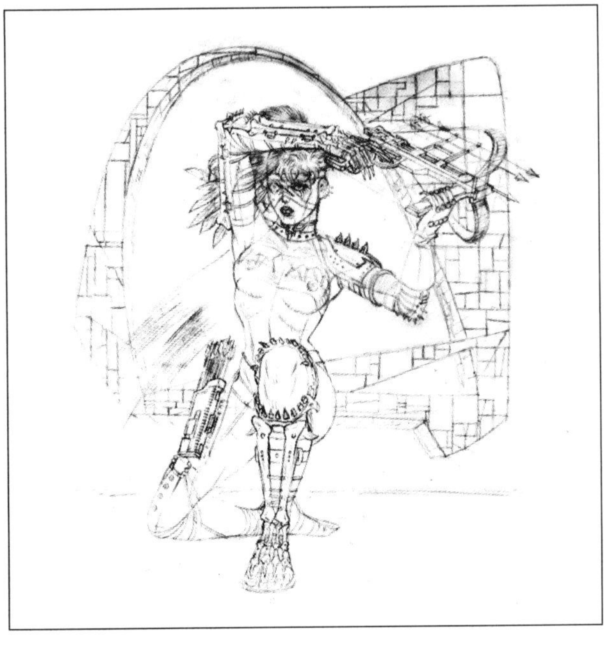

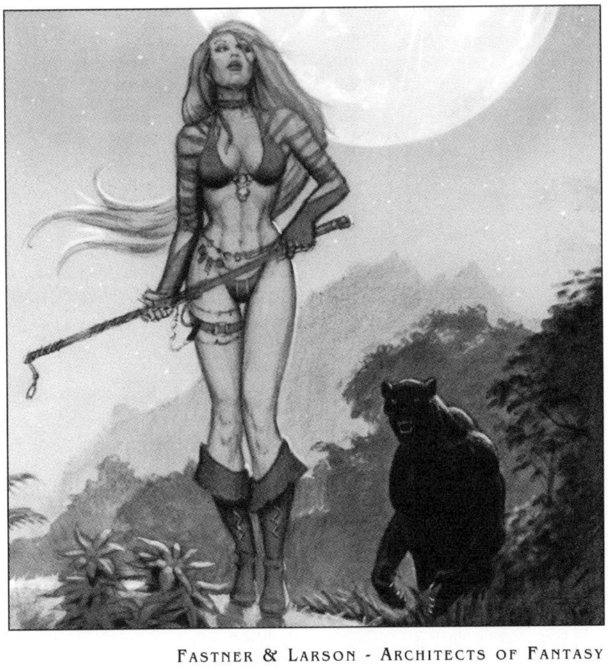

PRECEDING PAGE:
COLOR STUDY FOR **DAUGHTERS OF THE DISK** PORTFOLIO

THIS PAGE CLOCKWISE FROM TOP:

PENCIL STUDY OF JENNIS FROM **DAUGHTERS OF THE DISK**

TONE STUDY FOR A PLATE FROM **SEVEN OF SWORDS** PORTFOLIO

PENCILS FROM **DAUGHTERS OF THE DISK**

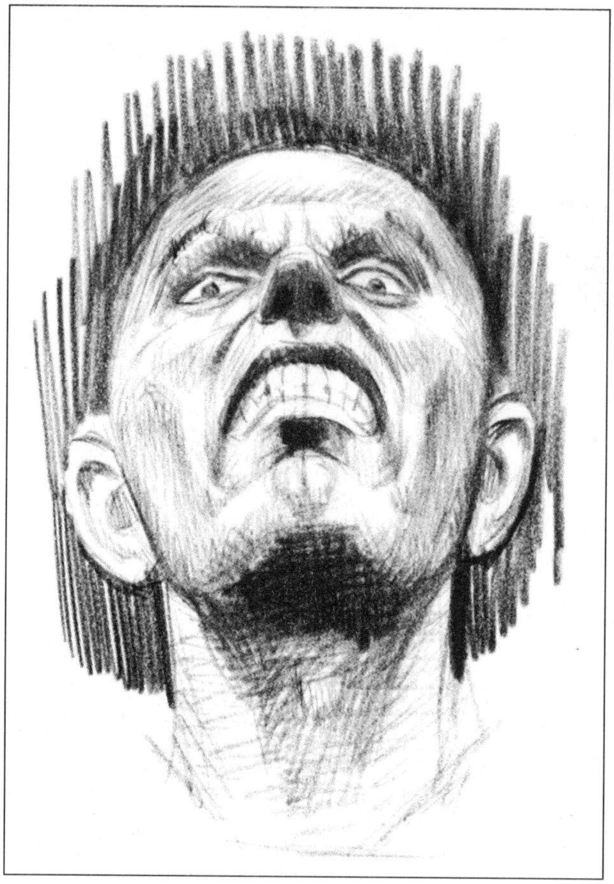

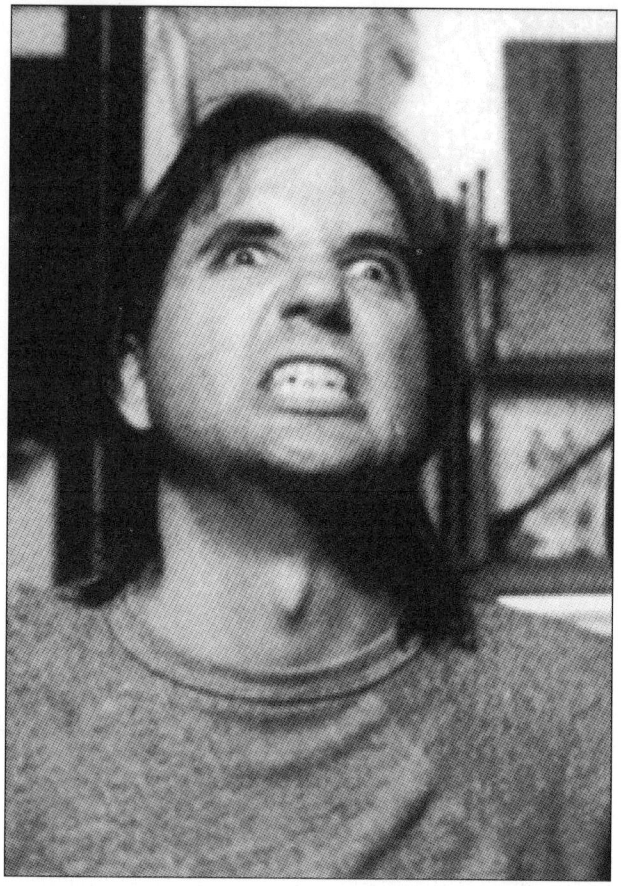

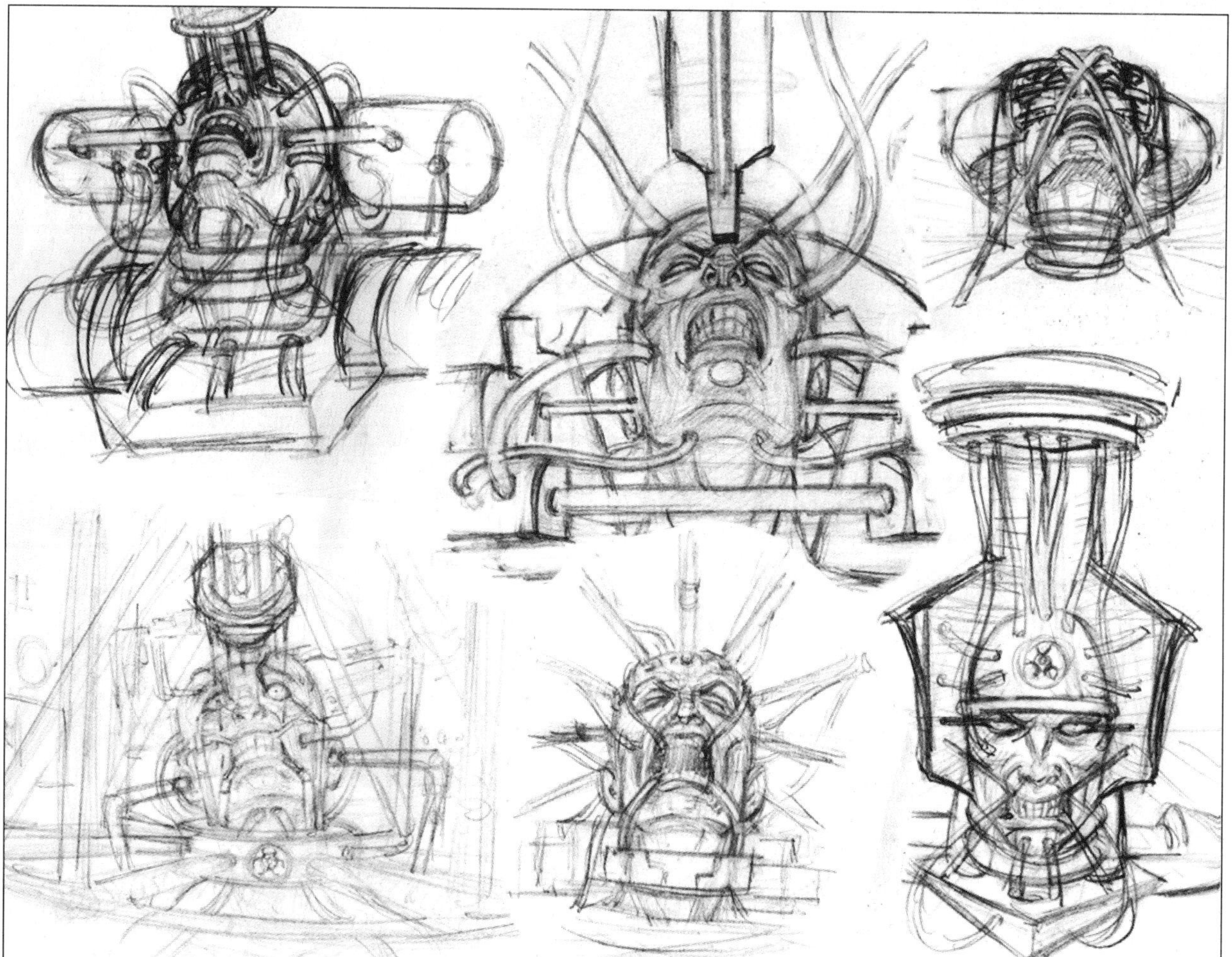

CLOCKWISE FROM TOP LEFT:

"ESCAPE FROM PAIN" FACIAL STUDY

STEVE FASTNER, STUDYING HIS OWN FACIAL FOR THE PIECE!

VARIOUS TORTURE DEVICES FOR "ESCAPE"

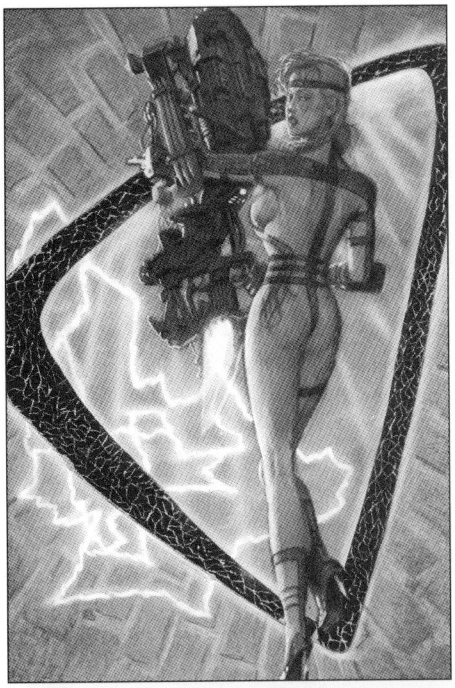

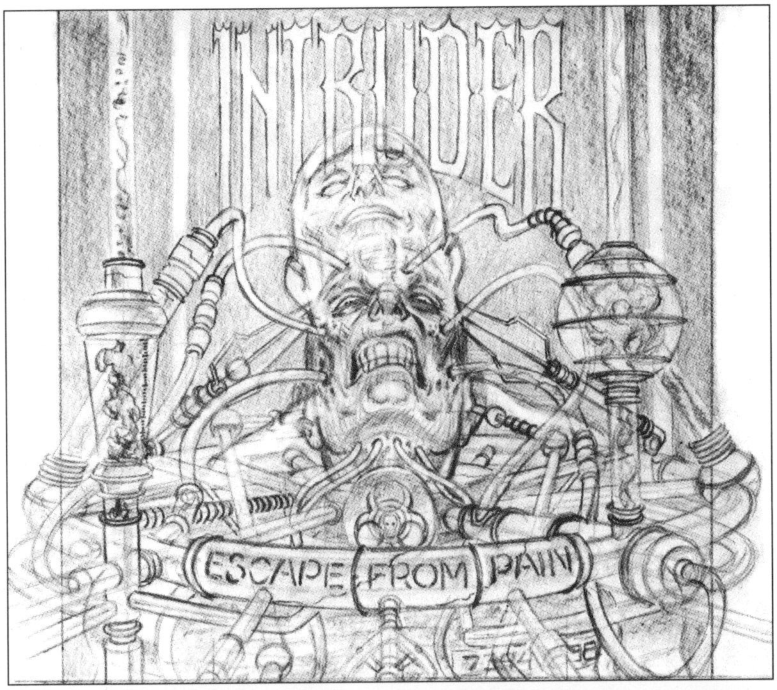


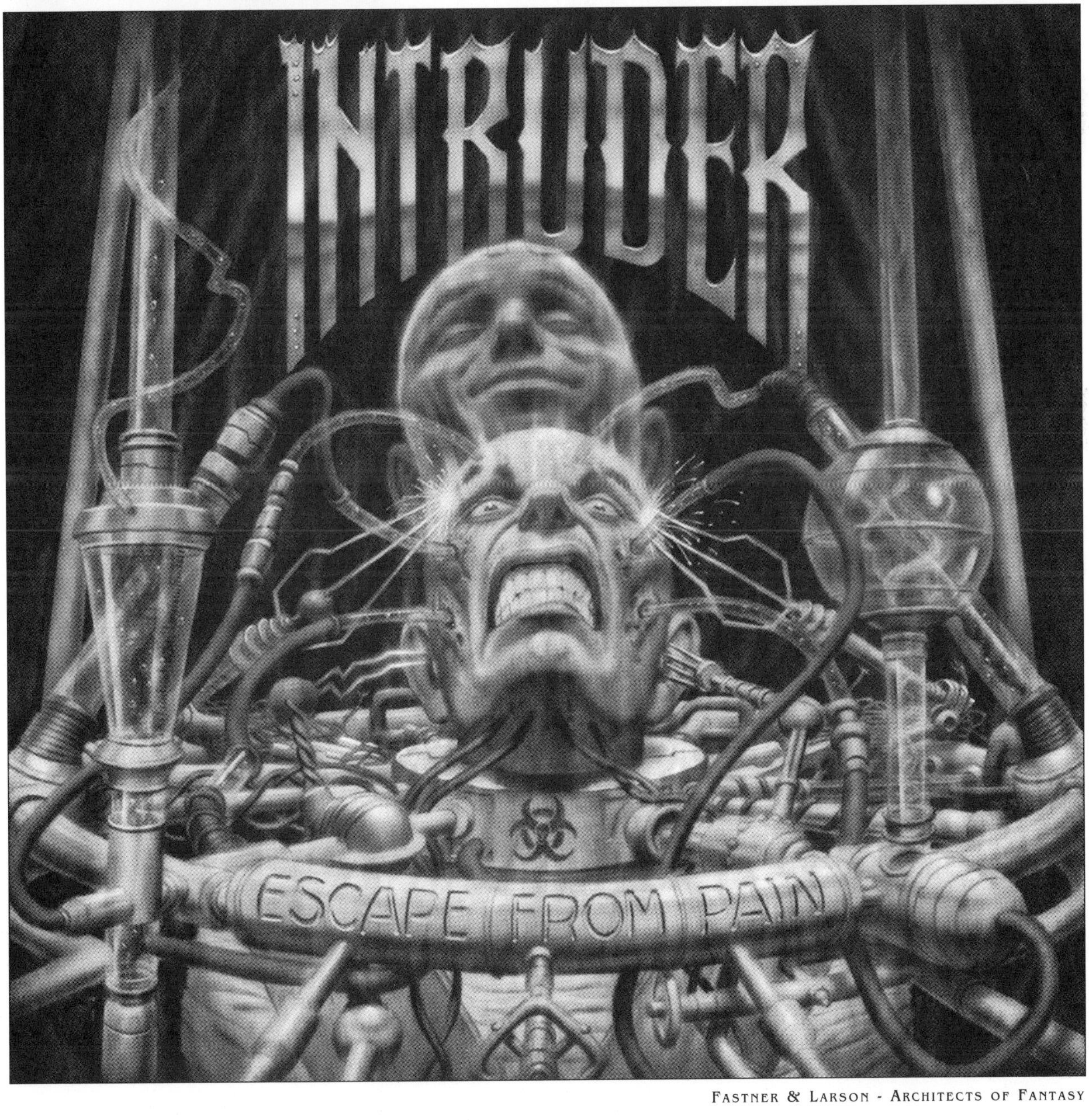


Clockwise from top left:

Tone Study from **Daughters of the Disk** Portfolio

Pencil rough for "Escape From Pain" album cover

Tone study from same.

Following page: Tone study for "Laser Punks"

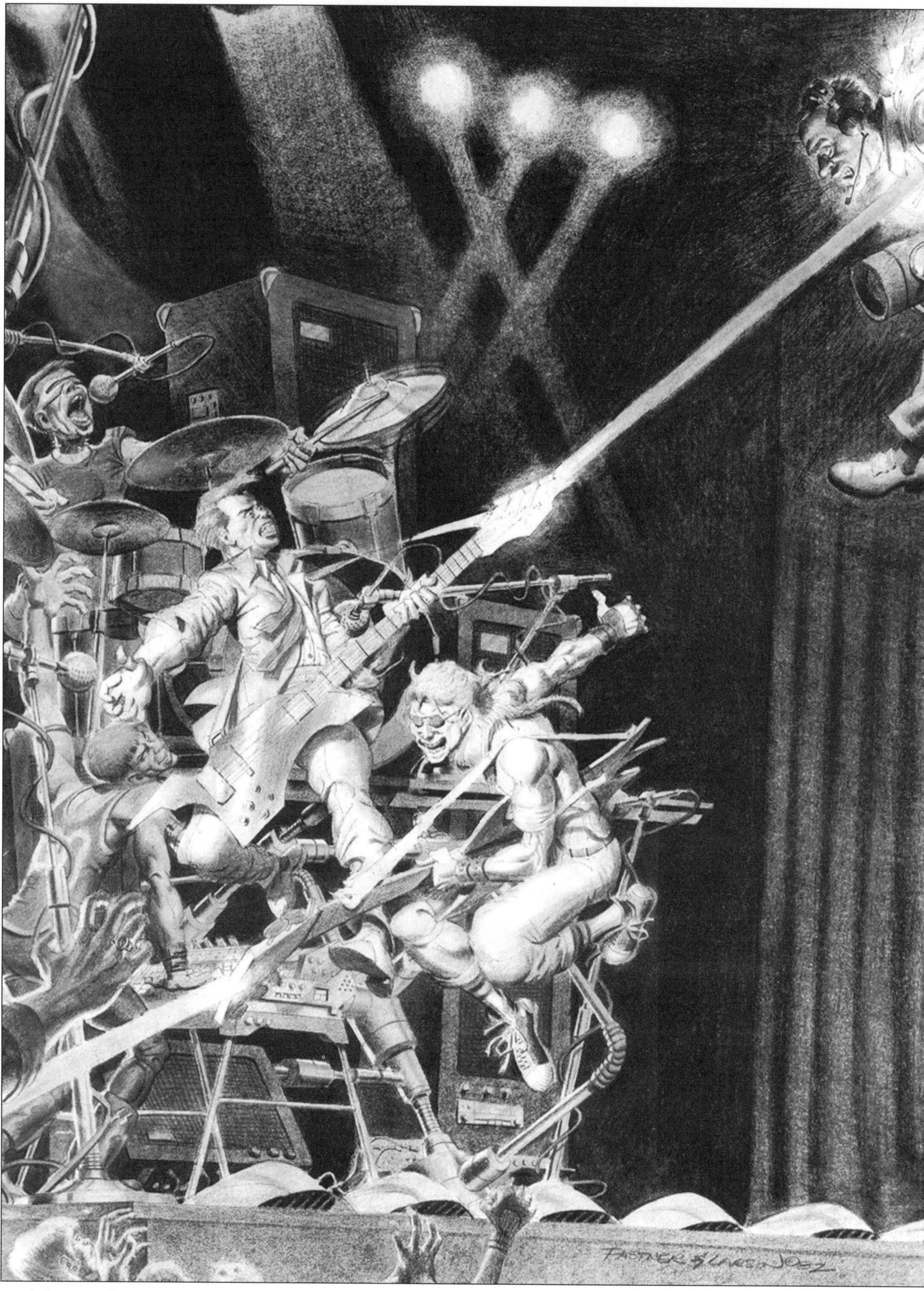

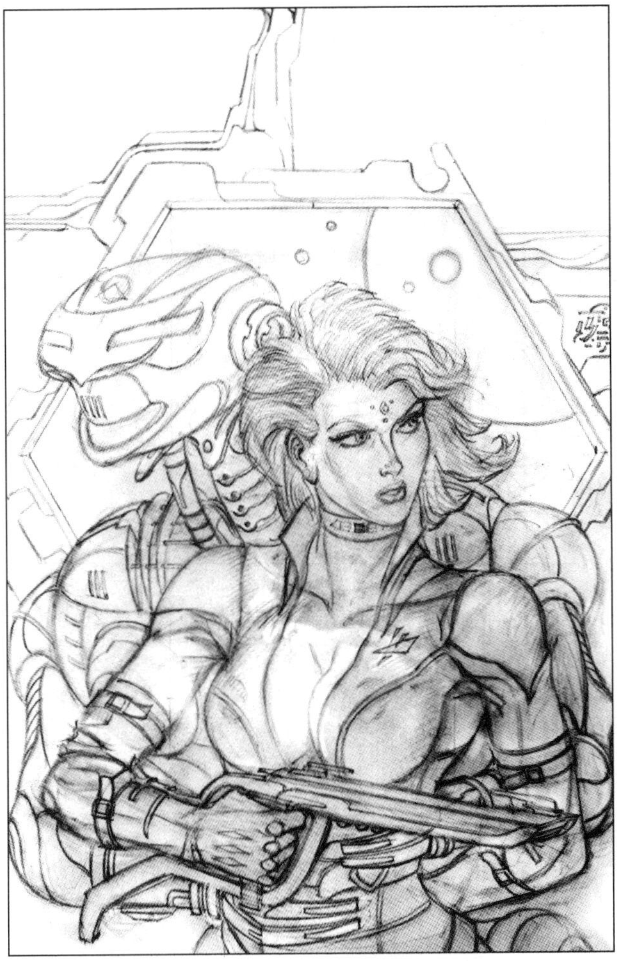

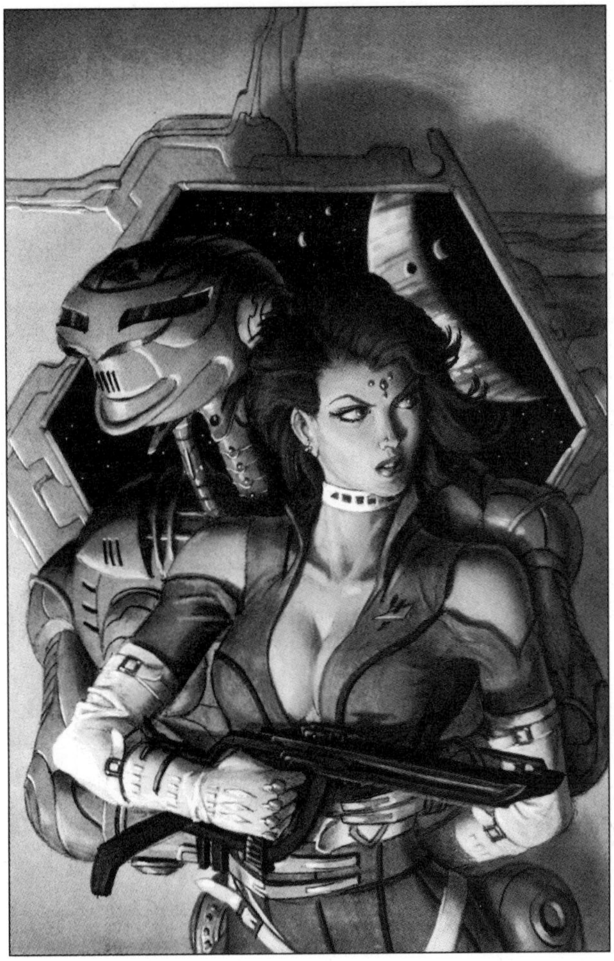

**RICH:**

*"Our favorite (and luckiest) robot"*

**STEVE:**

*"This was inspired by Michael Whelan's 'Friday' painting."*

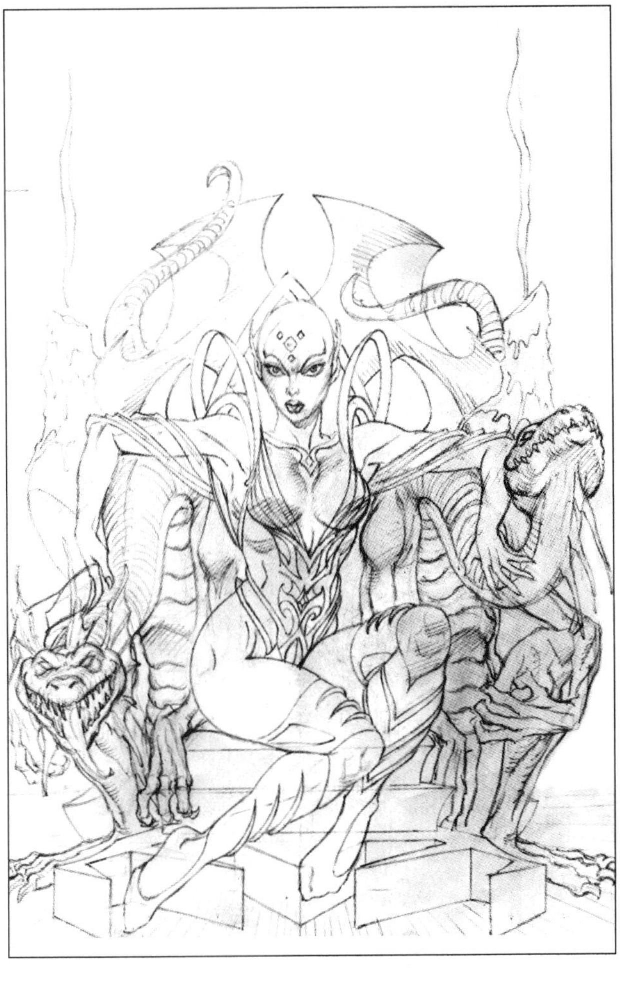

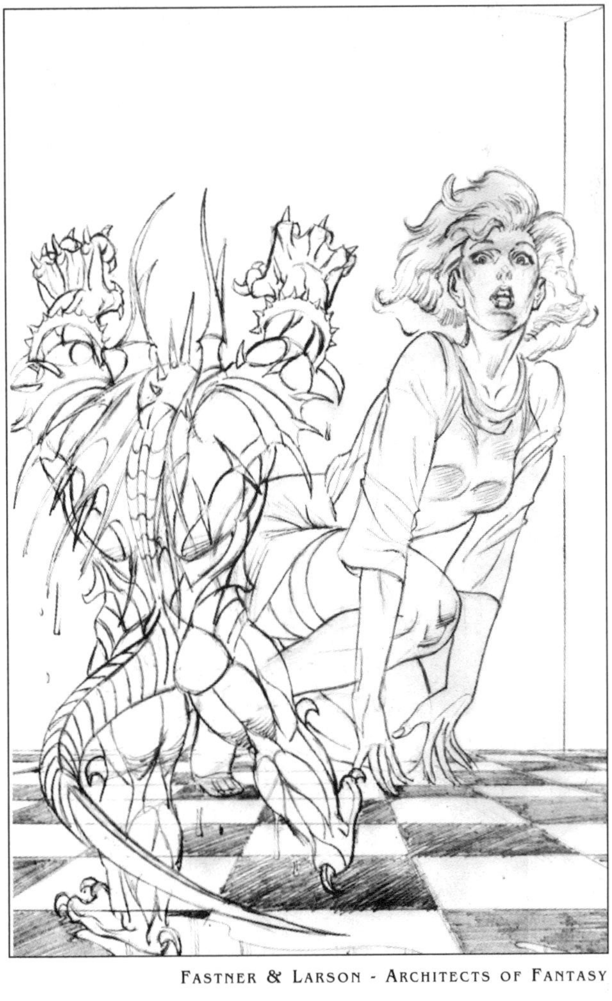

Clockwise from top left:

Pencil sketch for the cover of **Time Killers #4**

Color study for same

Proposed cover concepts for **Time Killers**

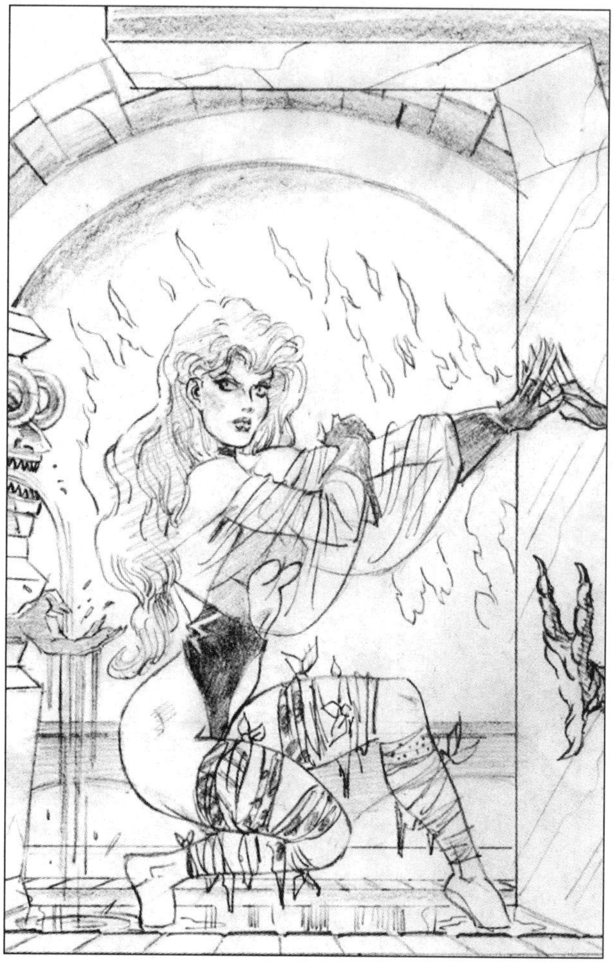

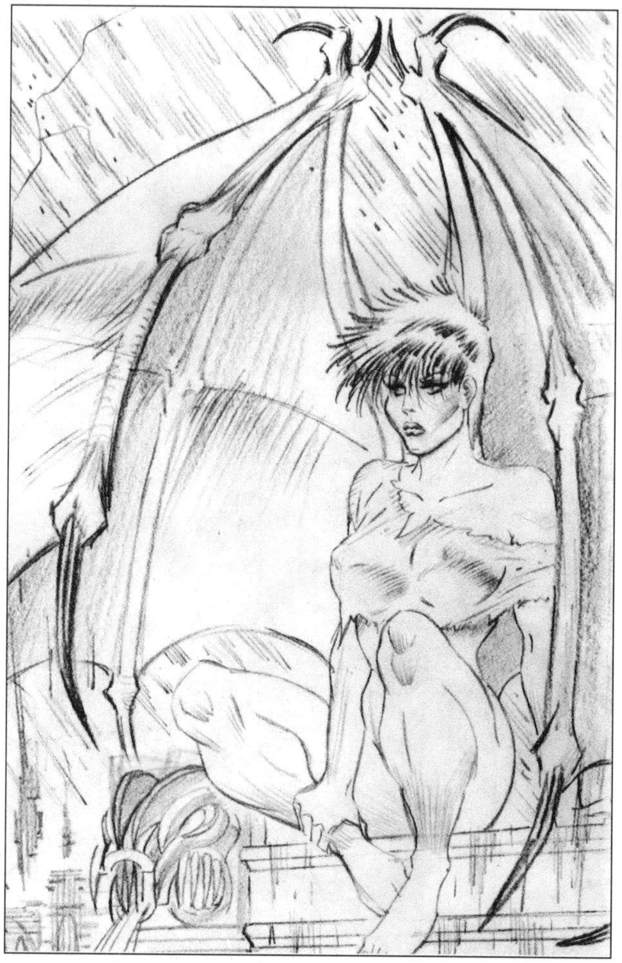

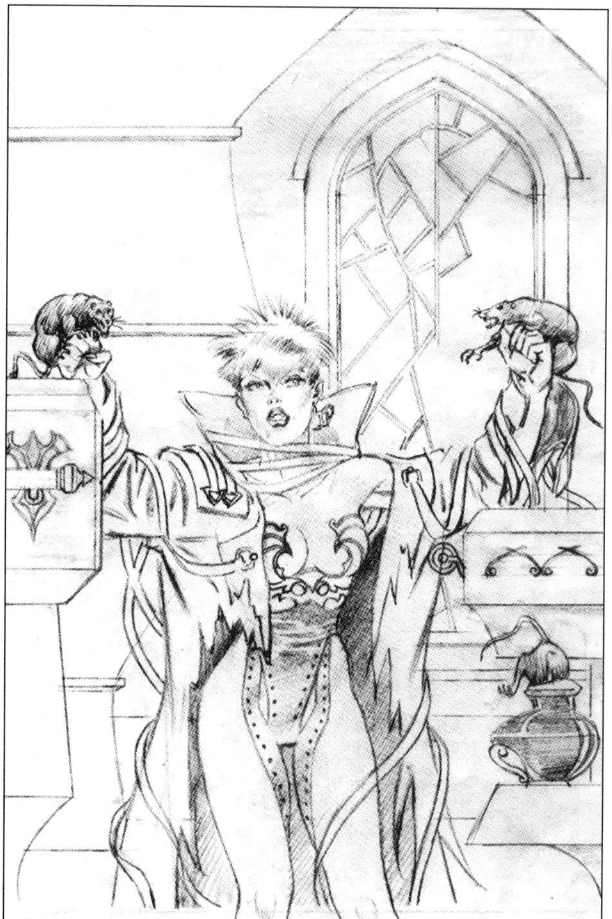

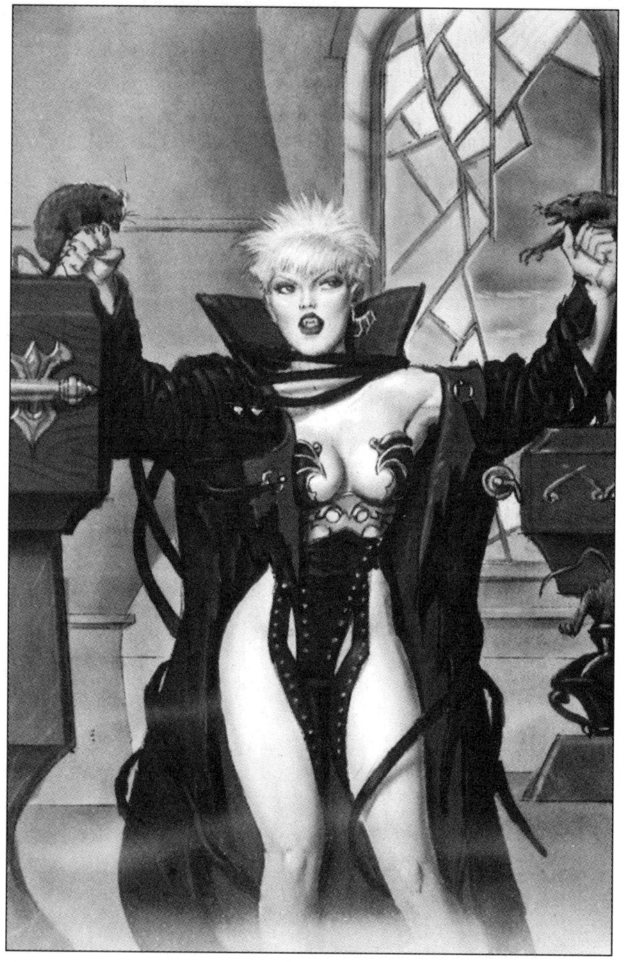

Clockwise from top left:

Proposed cover ideas for **666: Mark of the Beast**

Color study of same

Pencils to **666** #1

Following page: Alternate version of a color study for **Time Killers** #1

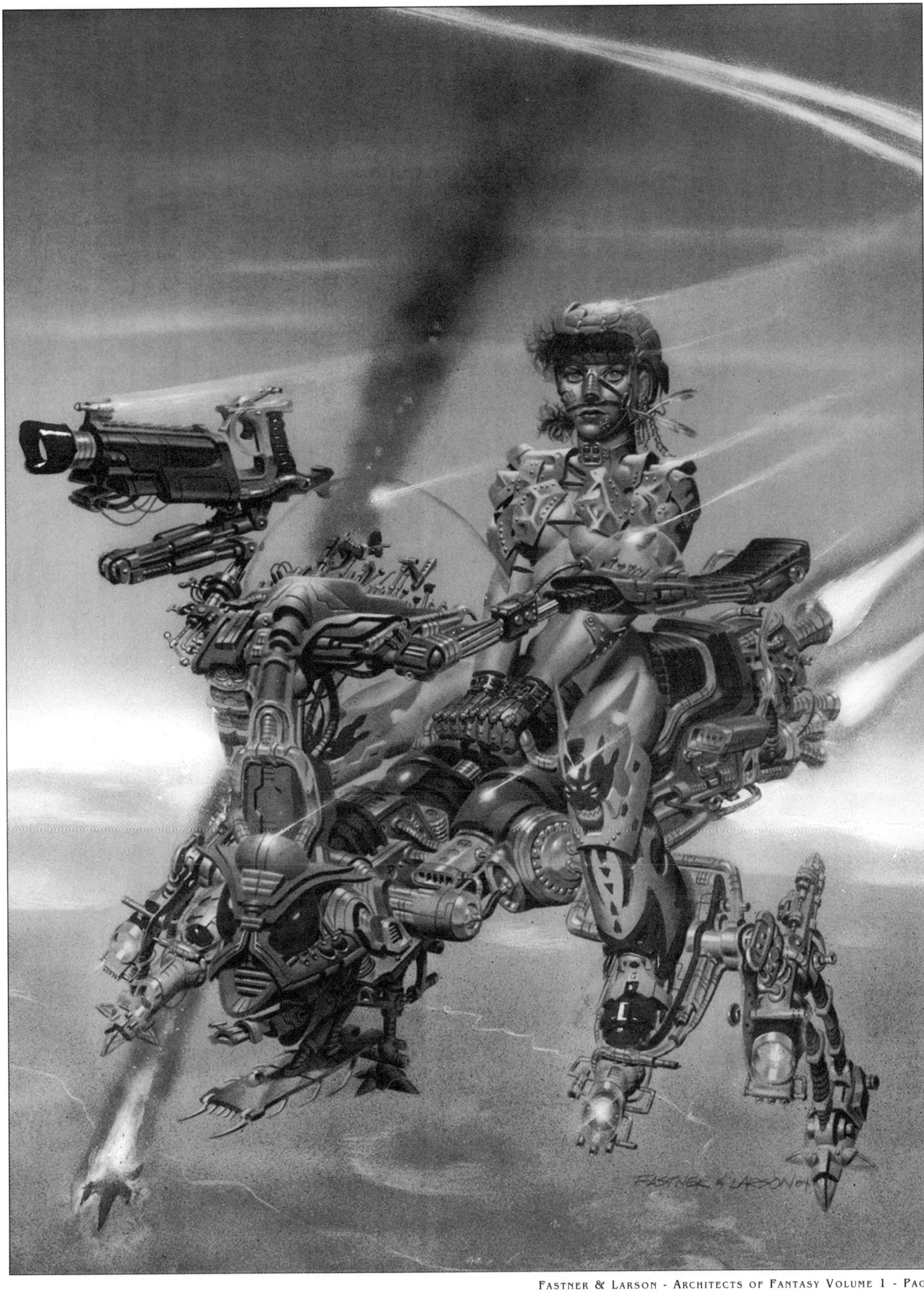
FASTNER & LARSON

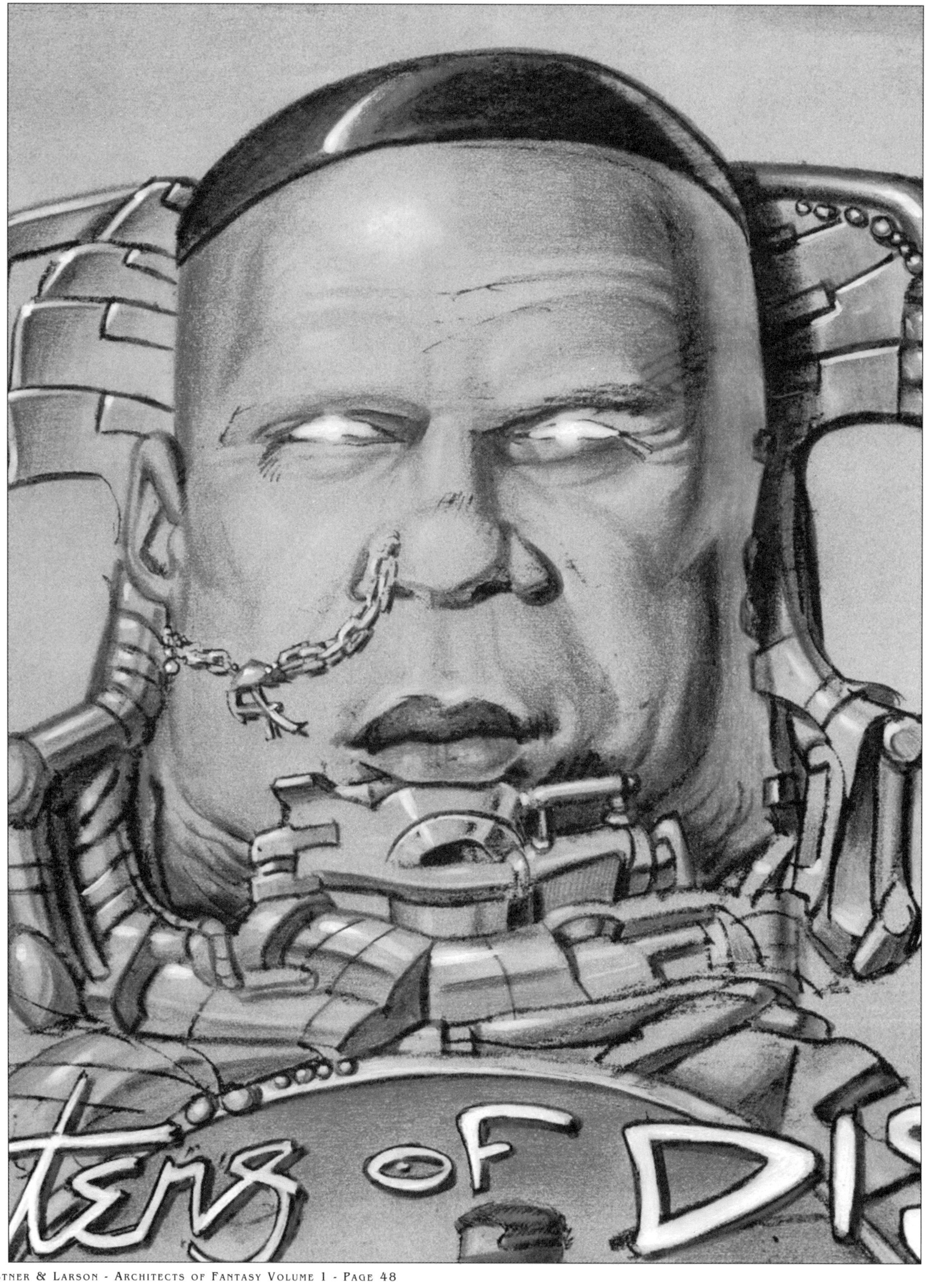
ters of DIS

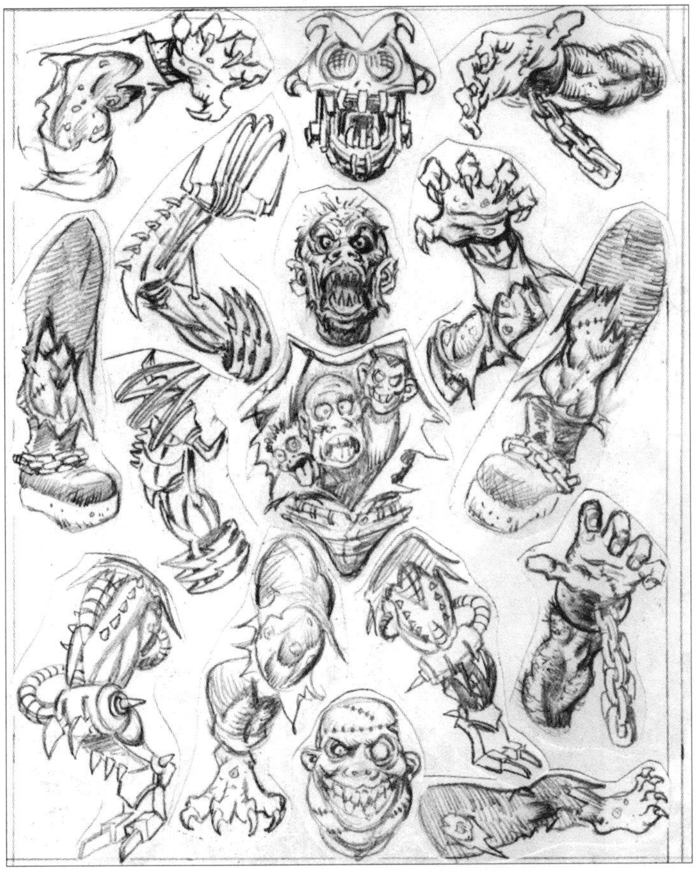

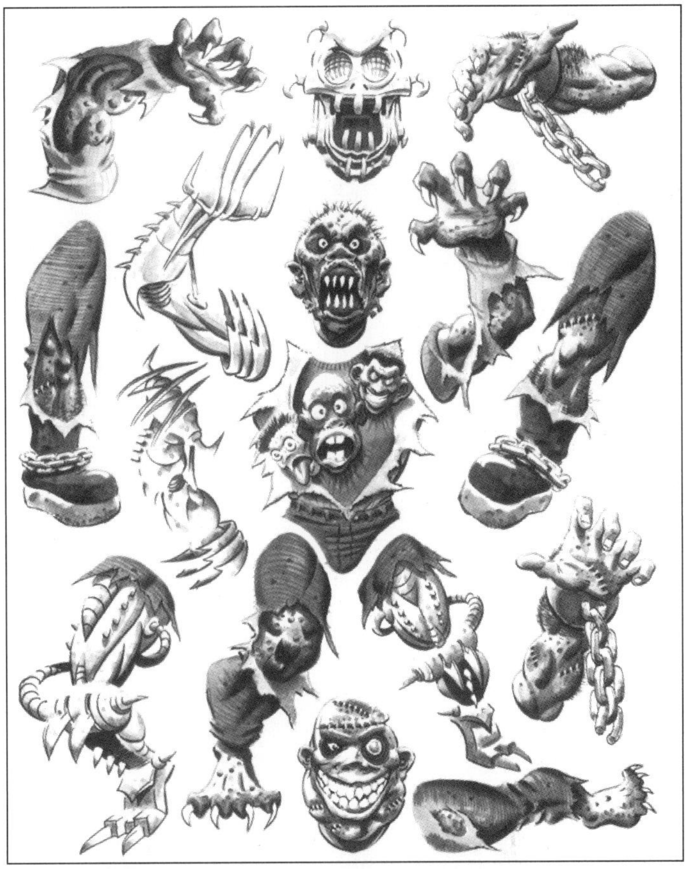

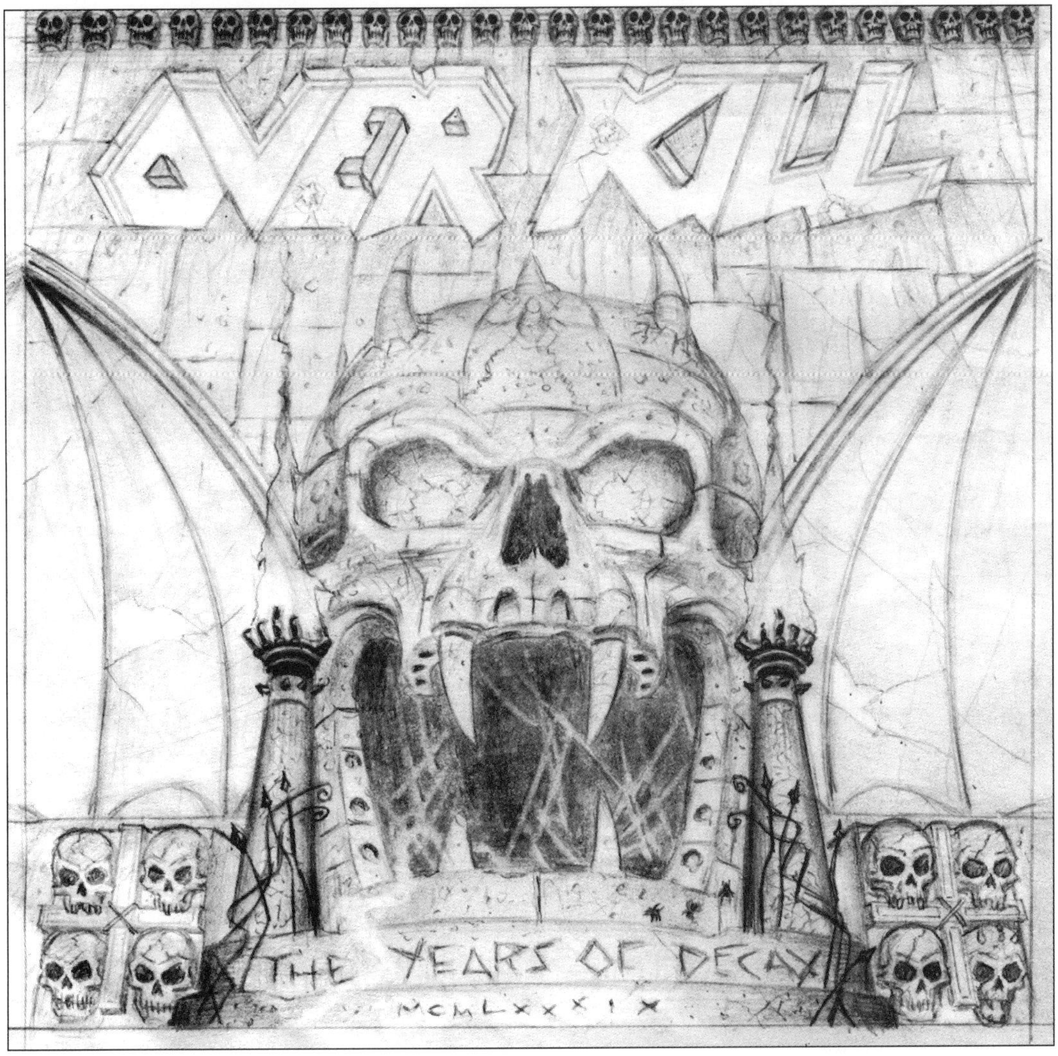


Opposite page:
Early color study of Godballah, from **Daughters of the Disk**

This page, clockwise from top left:

Pencils for a Monster Peel & Stick Toy Project

Finished art of same

Pencils from **Overkill's** "The Years of Decay"

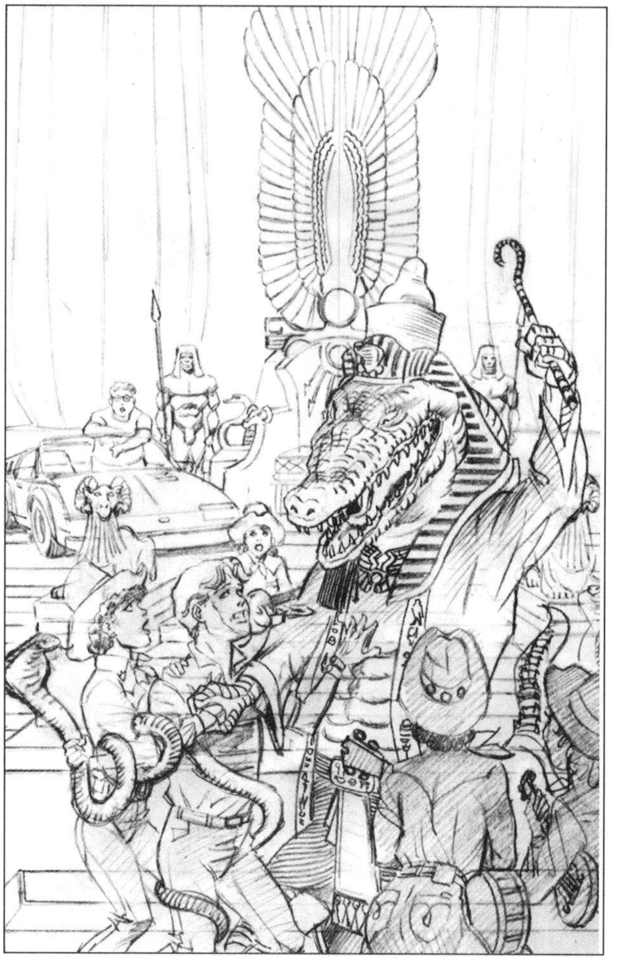

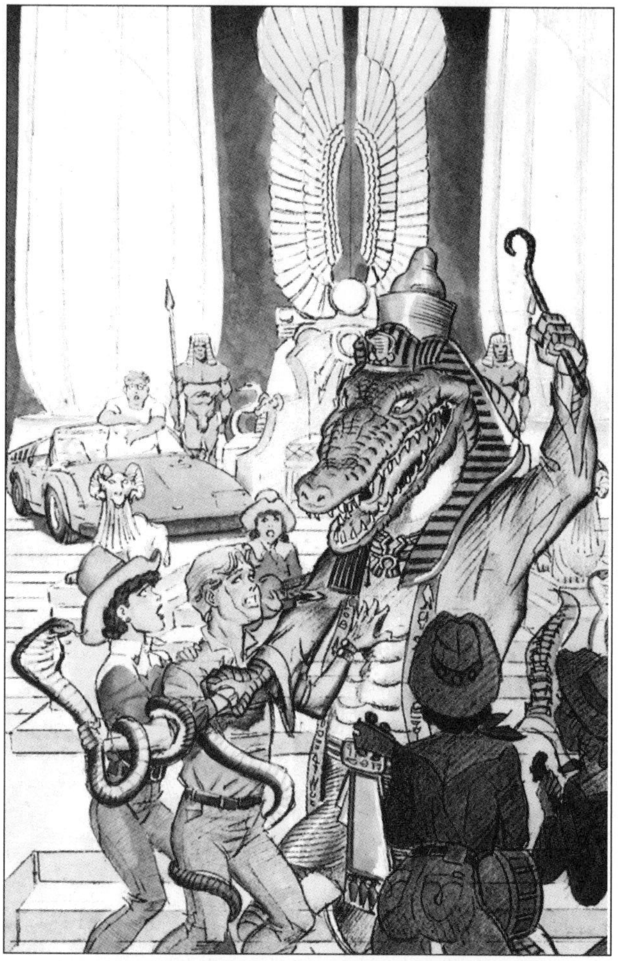

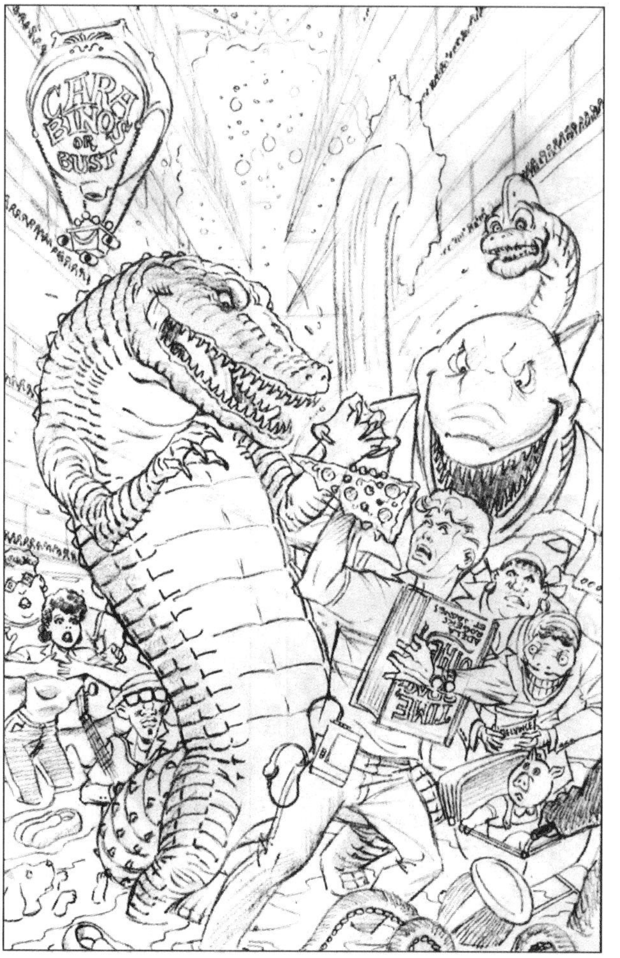

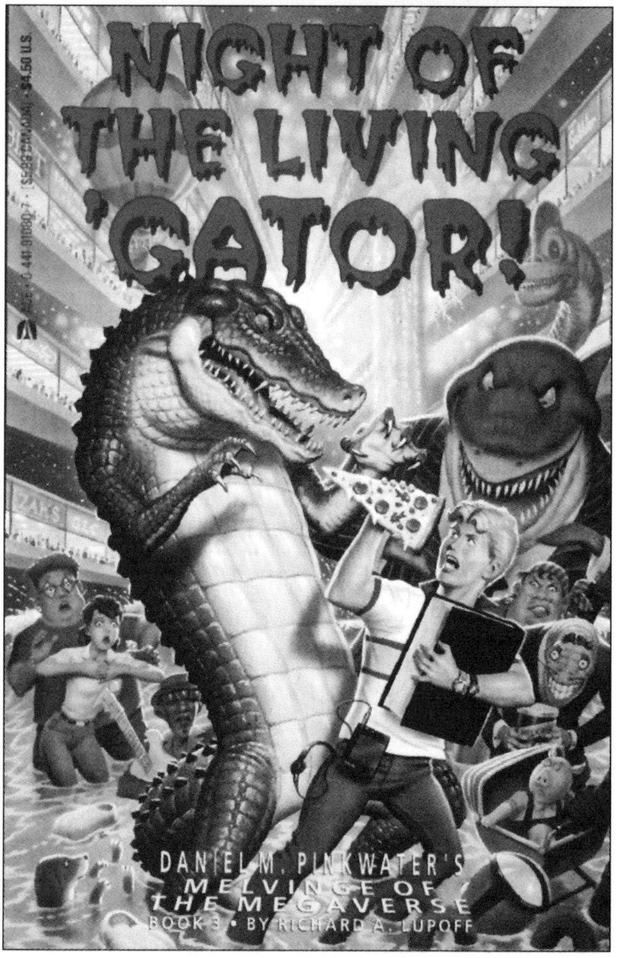


Clockwise from top left:

Alternate idea for "Night Of The Living Gator" Paperback

Color study for alternate design

Finished cover art with logo

Pencils for approved cover art

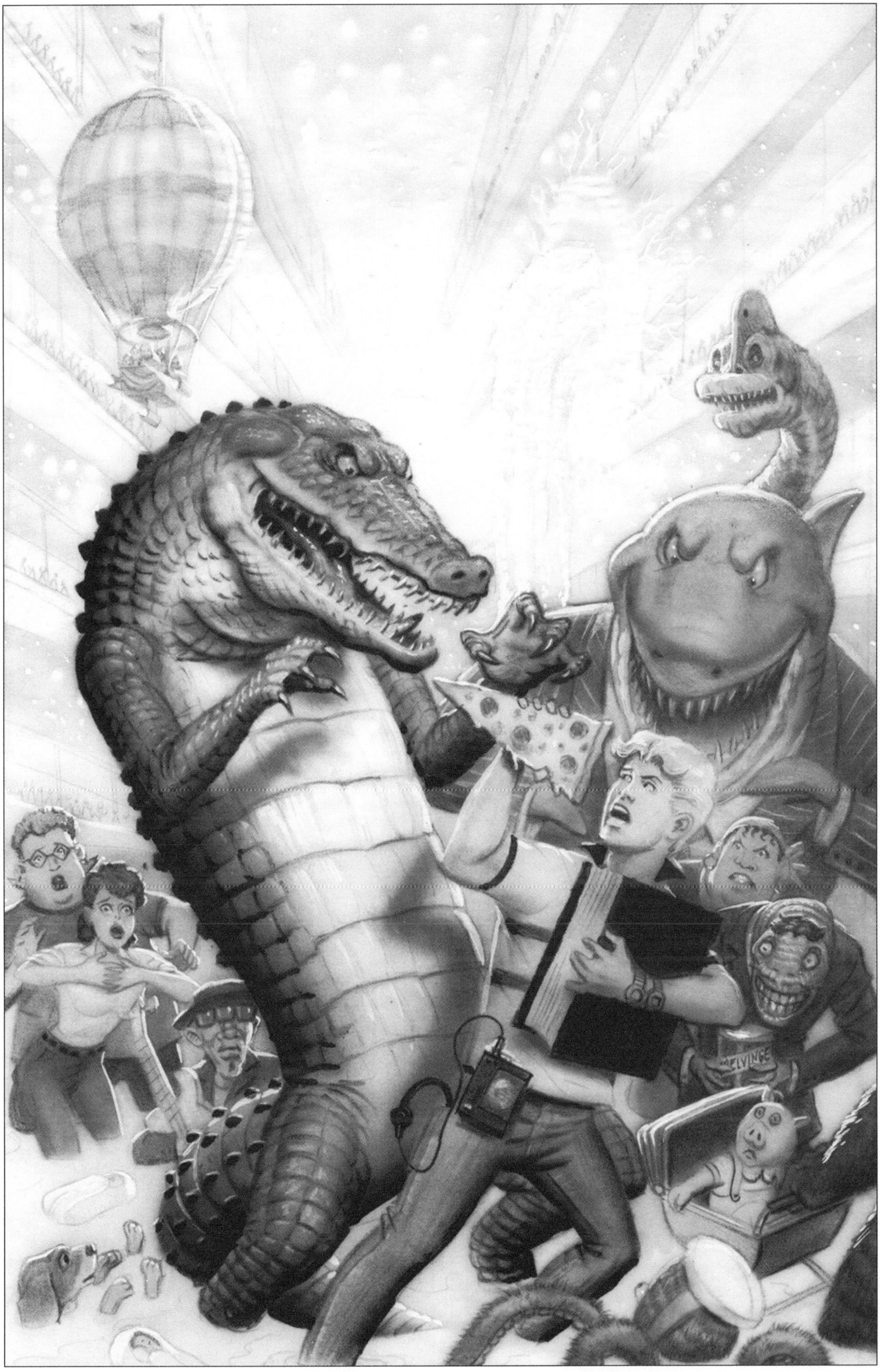

**STEVE:**

*"This cover won a prestigious 'Best Use As A Weapon' award from the American Pizza Association."*

Finished color study for "Night Of The Living Gator" cover art

**STEVE:**

*"Most of my finished art is marker and airbrush over xeroxes of Rich's pencils on ordinary 20 lb. stock. I've yet to fold, spindle, or mutilate a painting."*

**RICH:**

*"We've let the overnight couriers do that."*

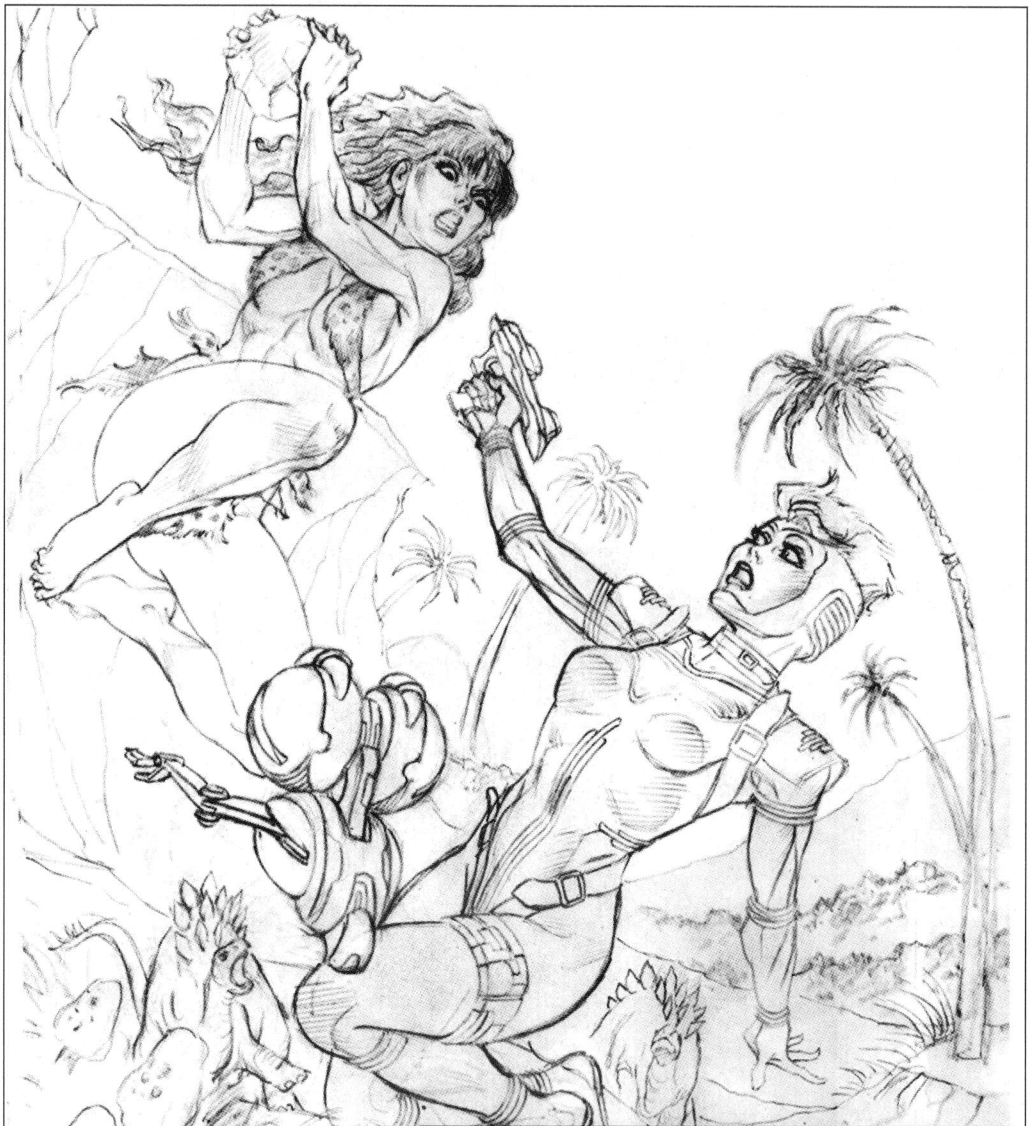

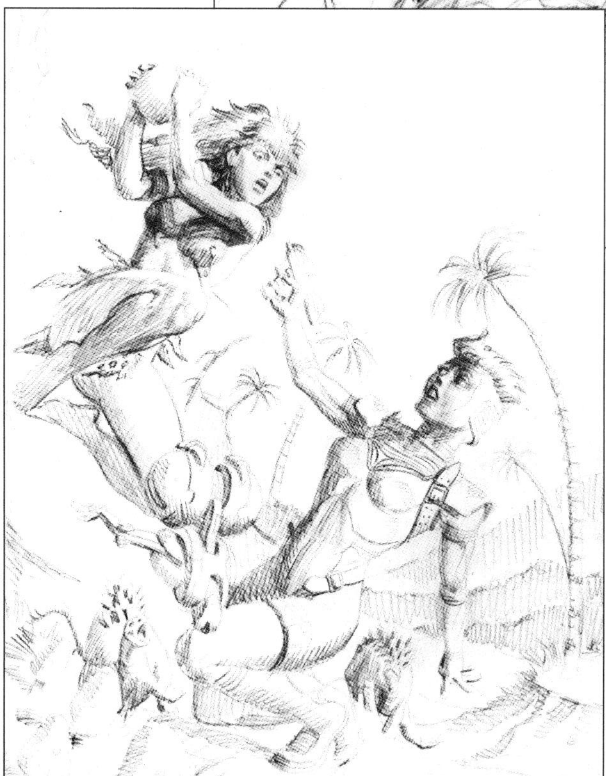

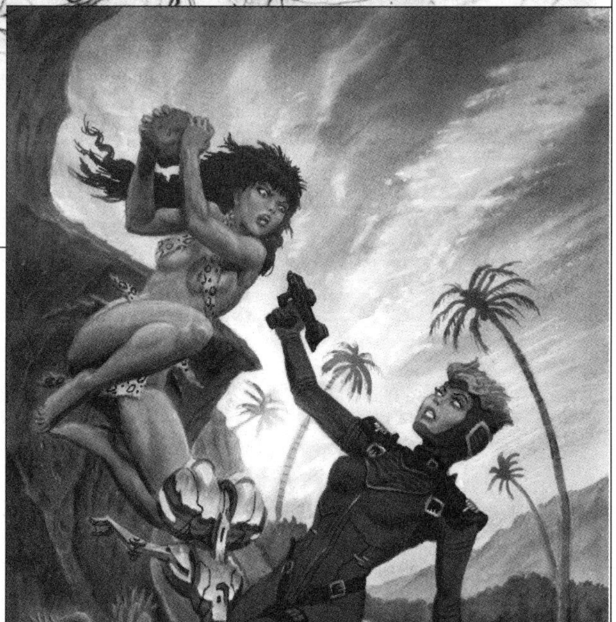

Clockwise from top:

Pencils for the cover of **Time Killers** #3

Final color study before finished art

Lighting study for same

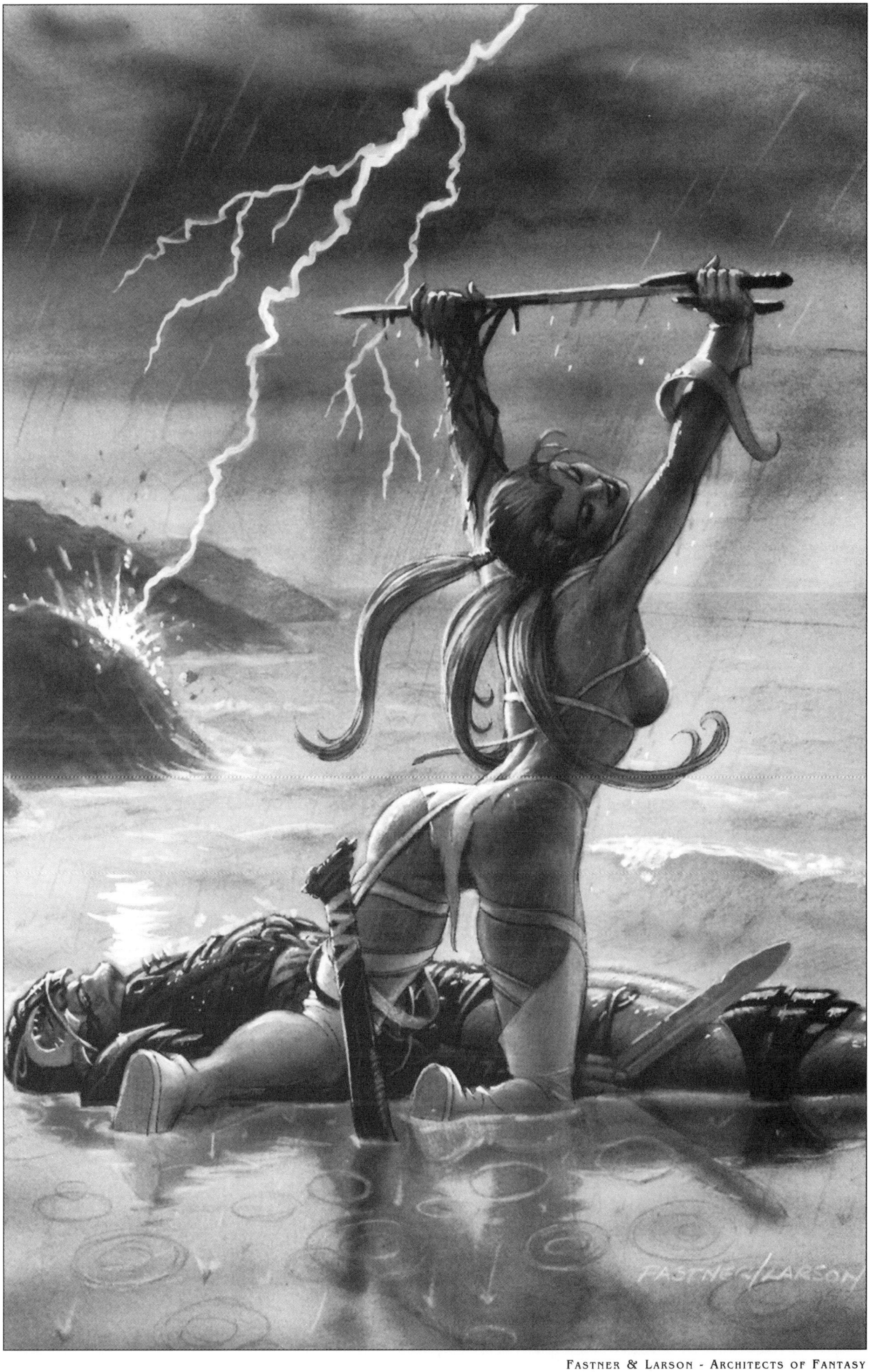

Tone study for plate in **Seven of Swords** Portfolio

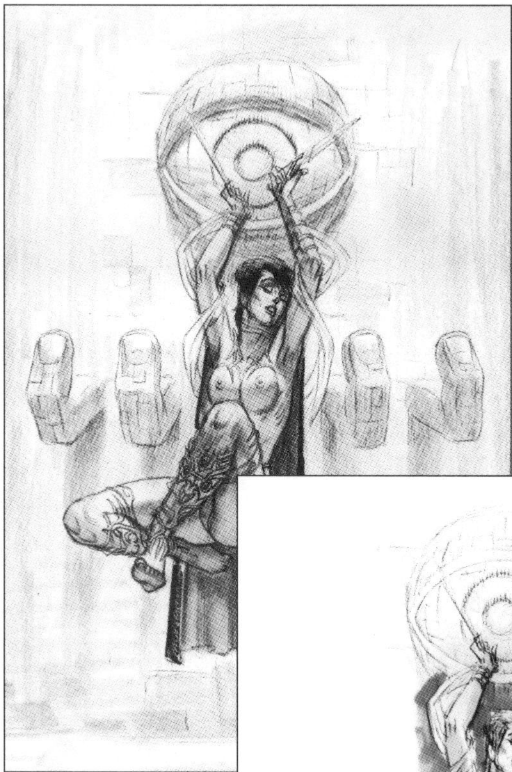

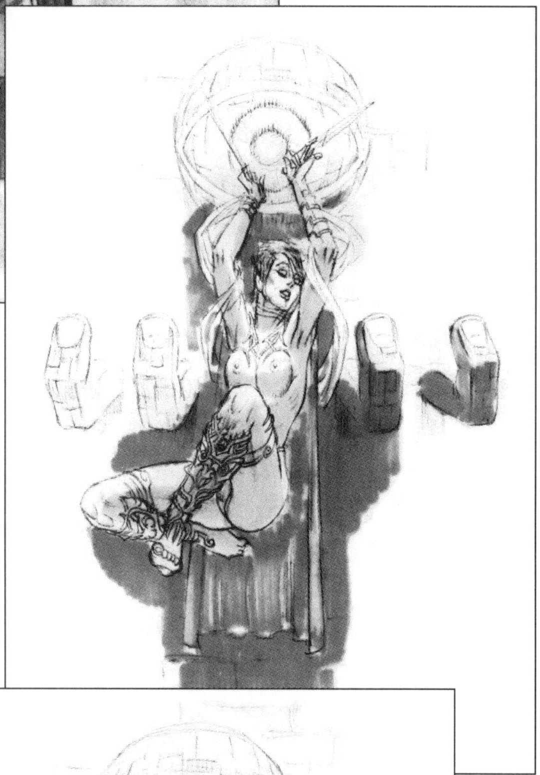

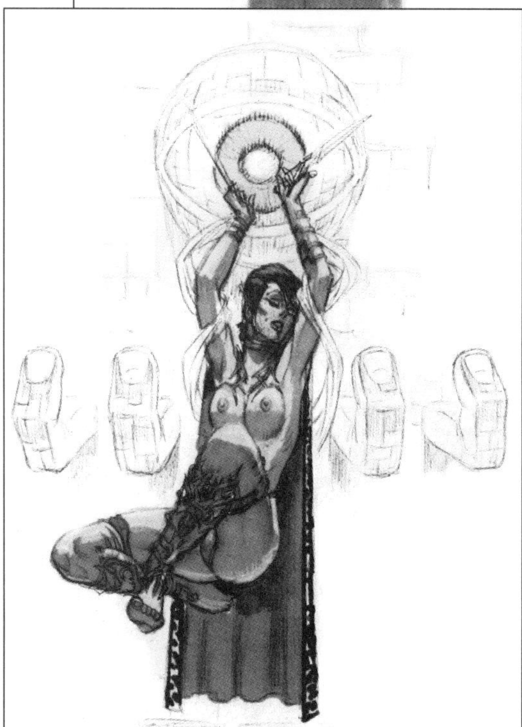

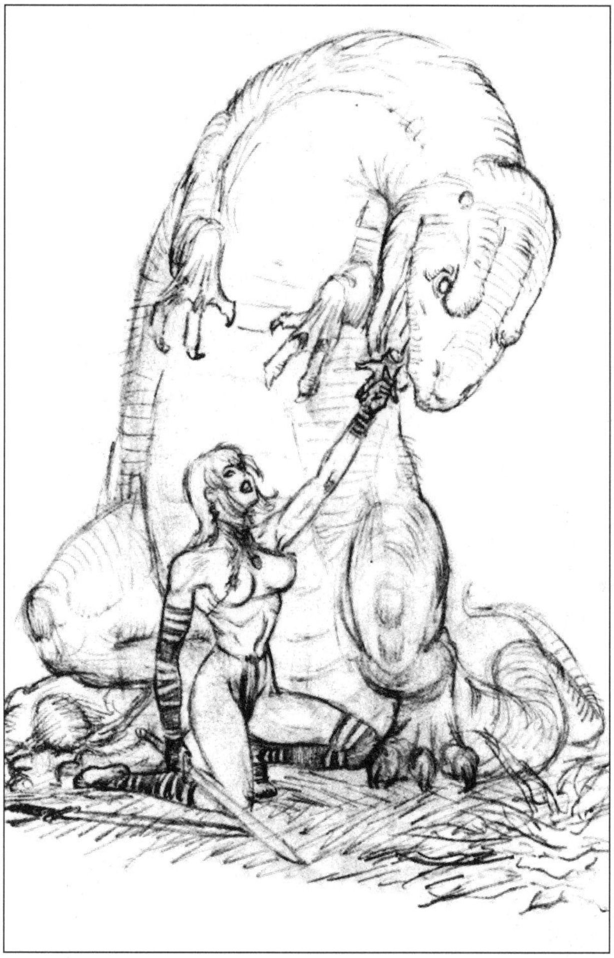

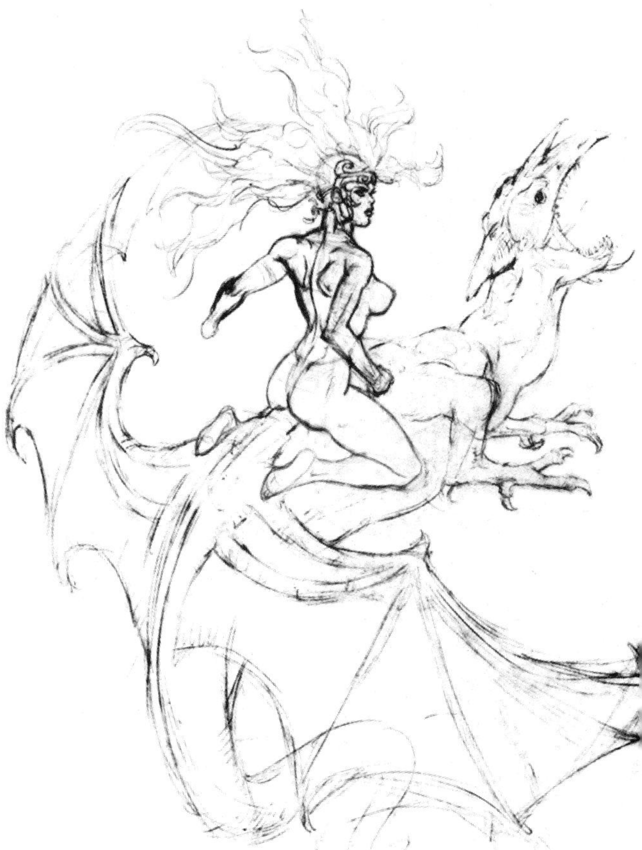

Various designs and ideas for the portfolio **Petz: Beauties and their Beasts**

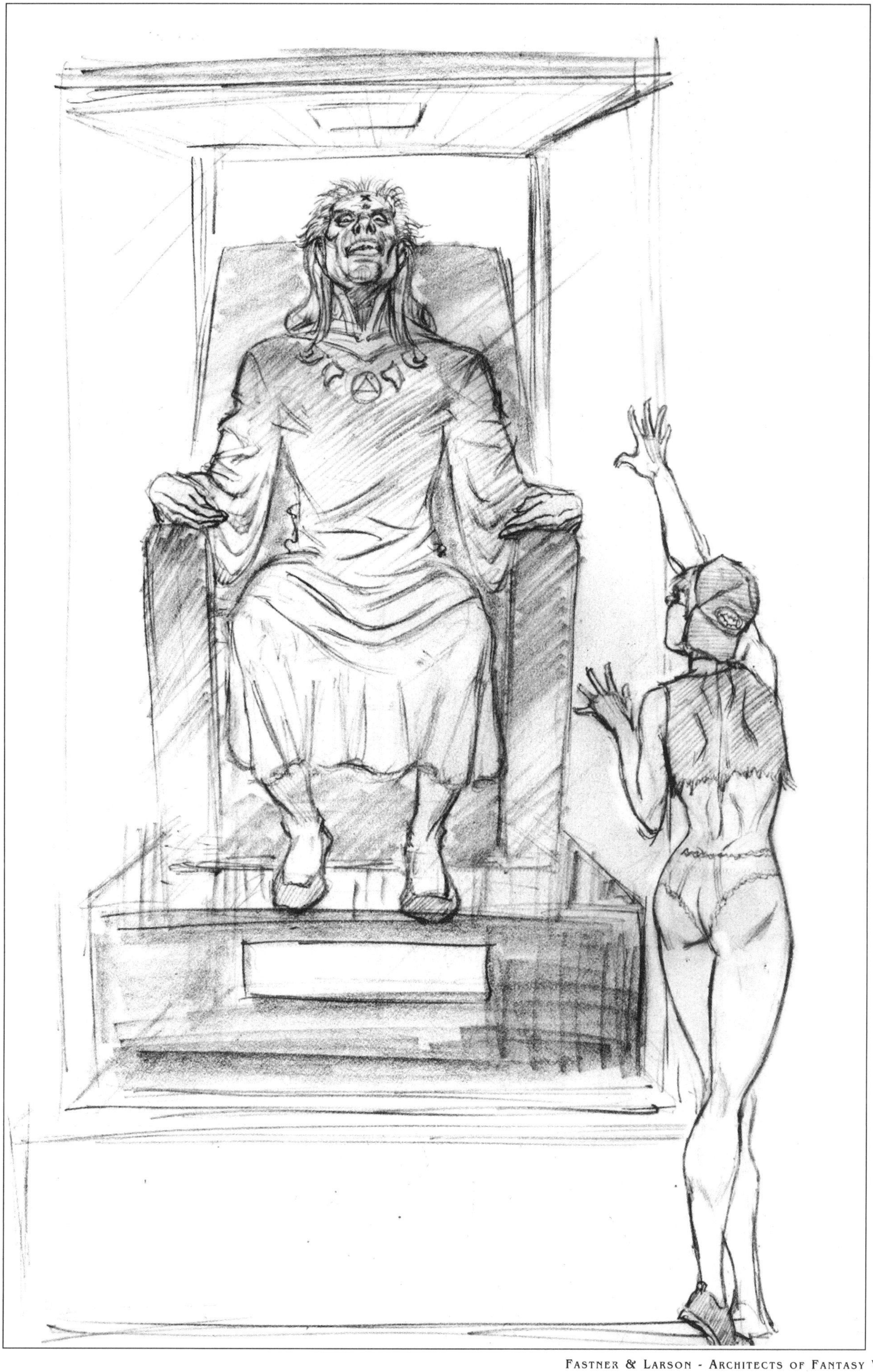

From the "Demon Baby" project:

The wizard Maalech

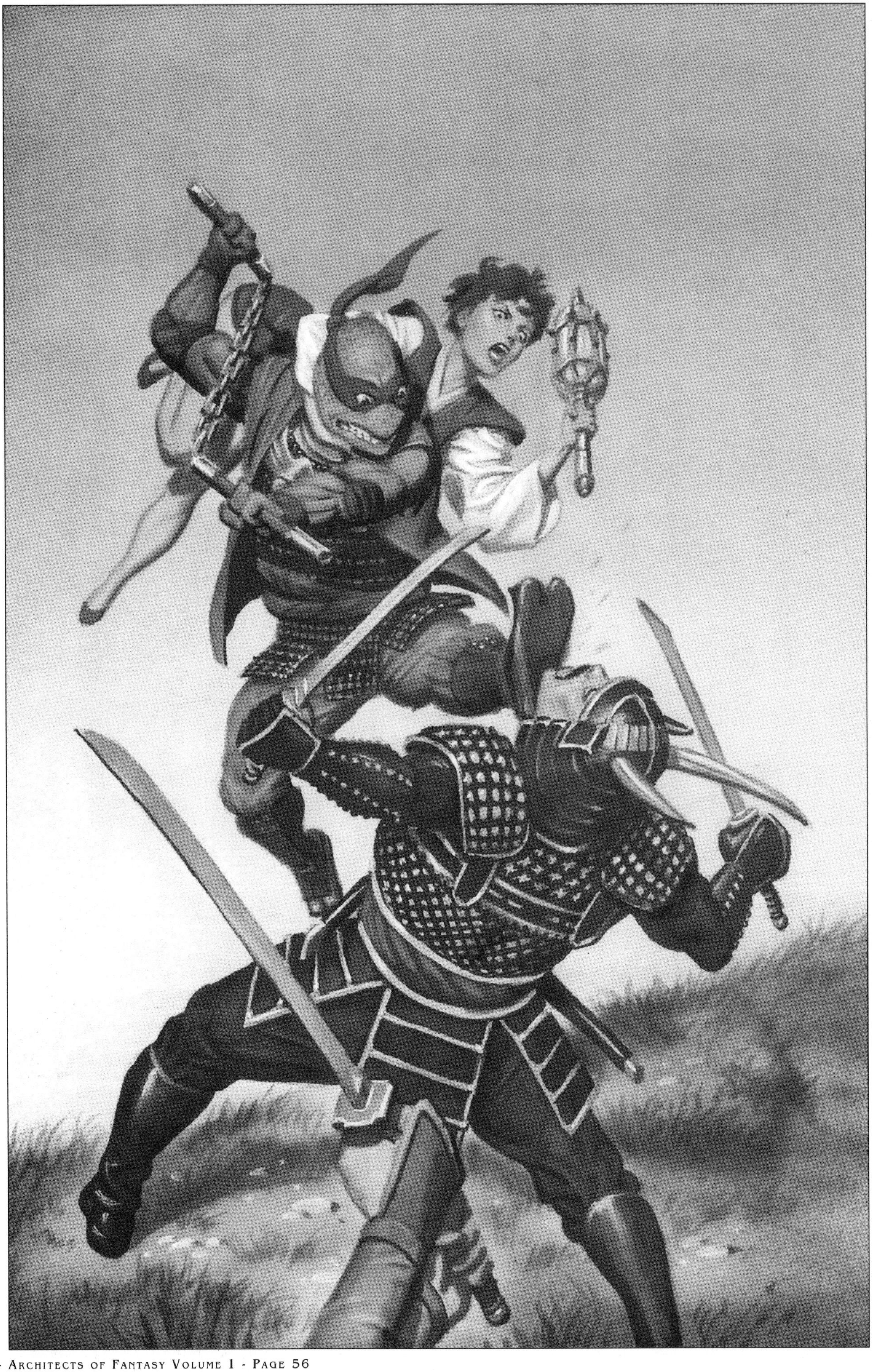

Color study for **Teenage Mutant Ninja Turtle** collector cards

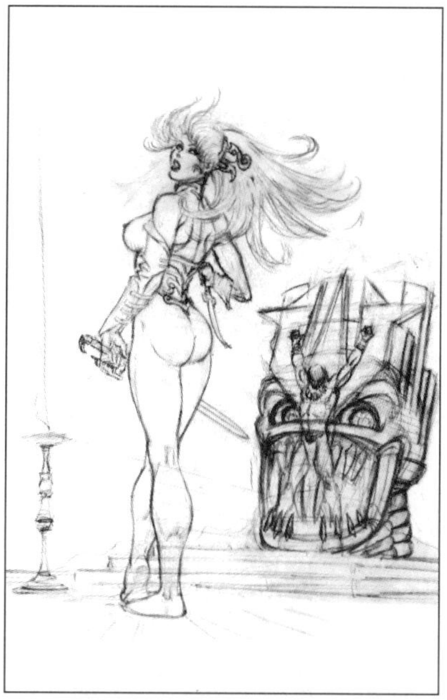

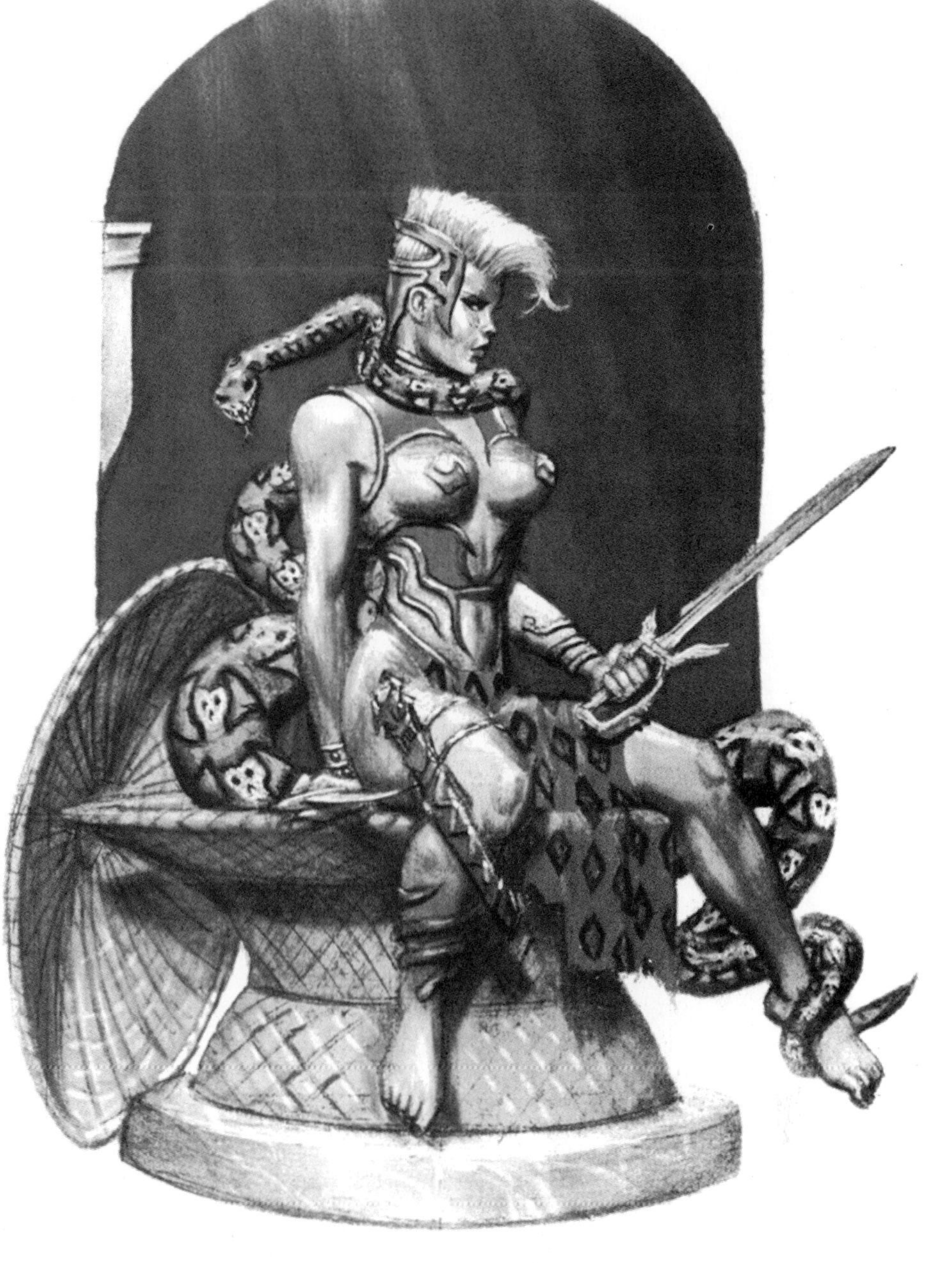

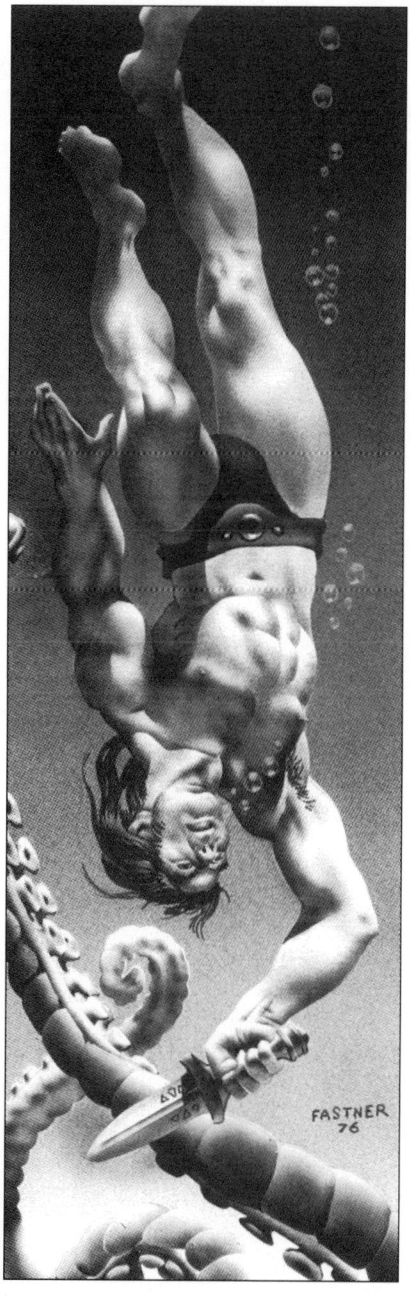


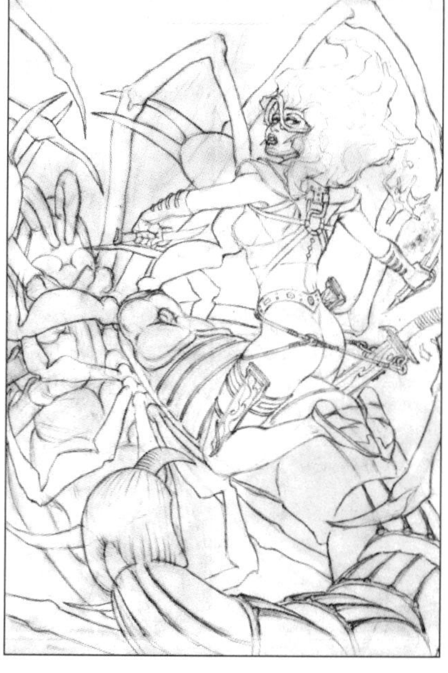

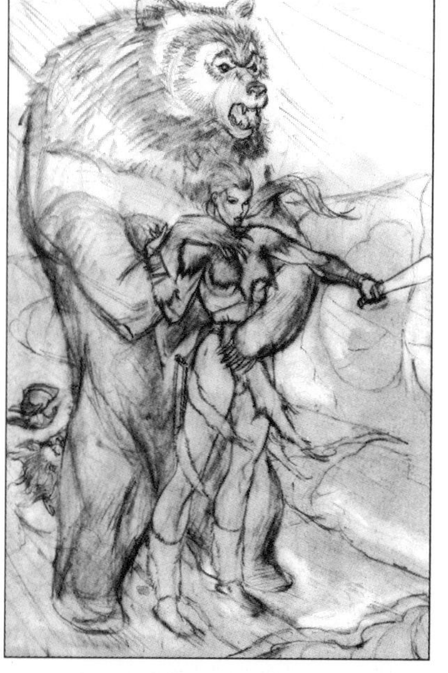

CLOCKWISE FROM TOP LEFT:

PRELIMINARY SKETCH FOR **FLESH & BLOOD** PORTFOLIO **SET 2**

COLOR STUDY FOR ANOTHER PLATE FROM **FLESH & BLOOD 2**

ALTERNATE DESIGN FOR POLAR BEAR AND FRIEND FROM **NIGHT SLAYERS** PORTFOLIO

PENCIL TO PLATE FROM **NIGHT SLAYERS**

FANZINE ILLUSTRATION BY STEVE IN THE MID-SEVENTIES.

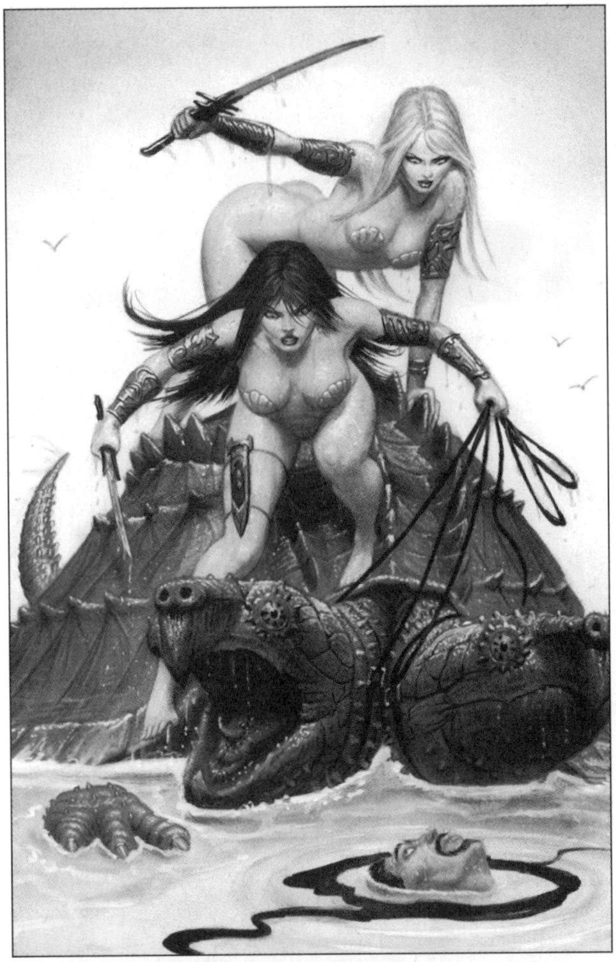

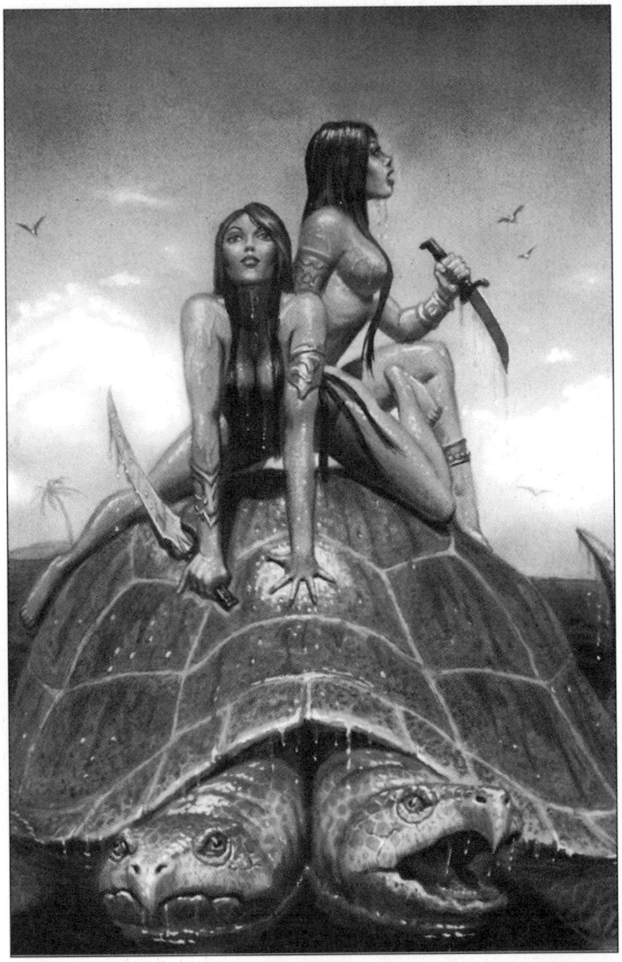

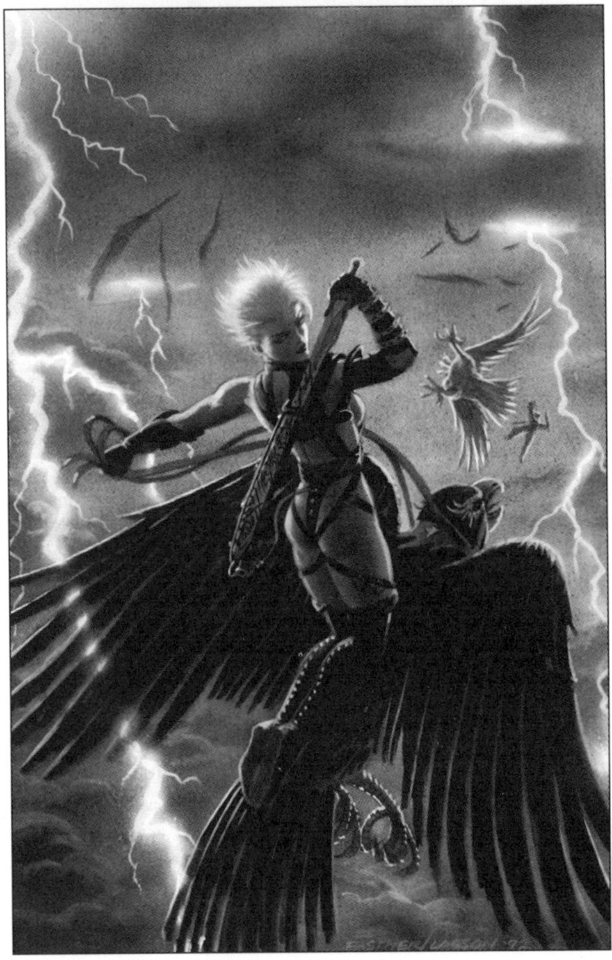

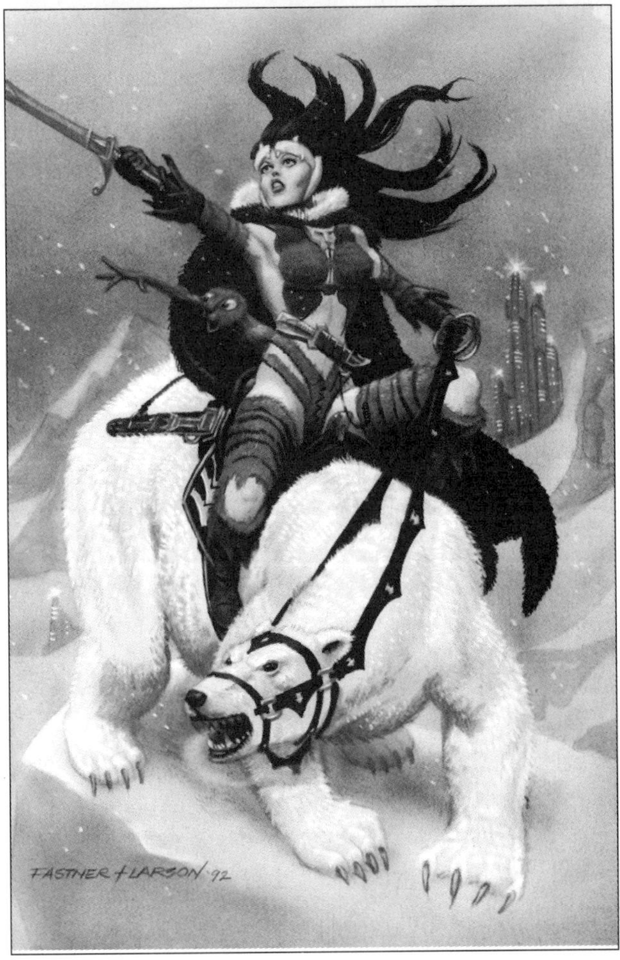


Artwork from **Night Slayers** Portfolio

Clockwise from top left:

Tone study for plate

Alternate design for 2-headed turtle piece

Tone study of final art for Polar Bear plate

Tone study

Following Page: Proposed cover for **Time Killers**

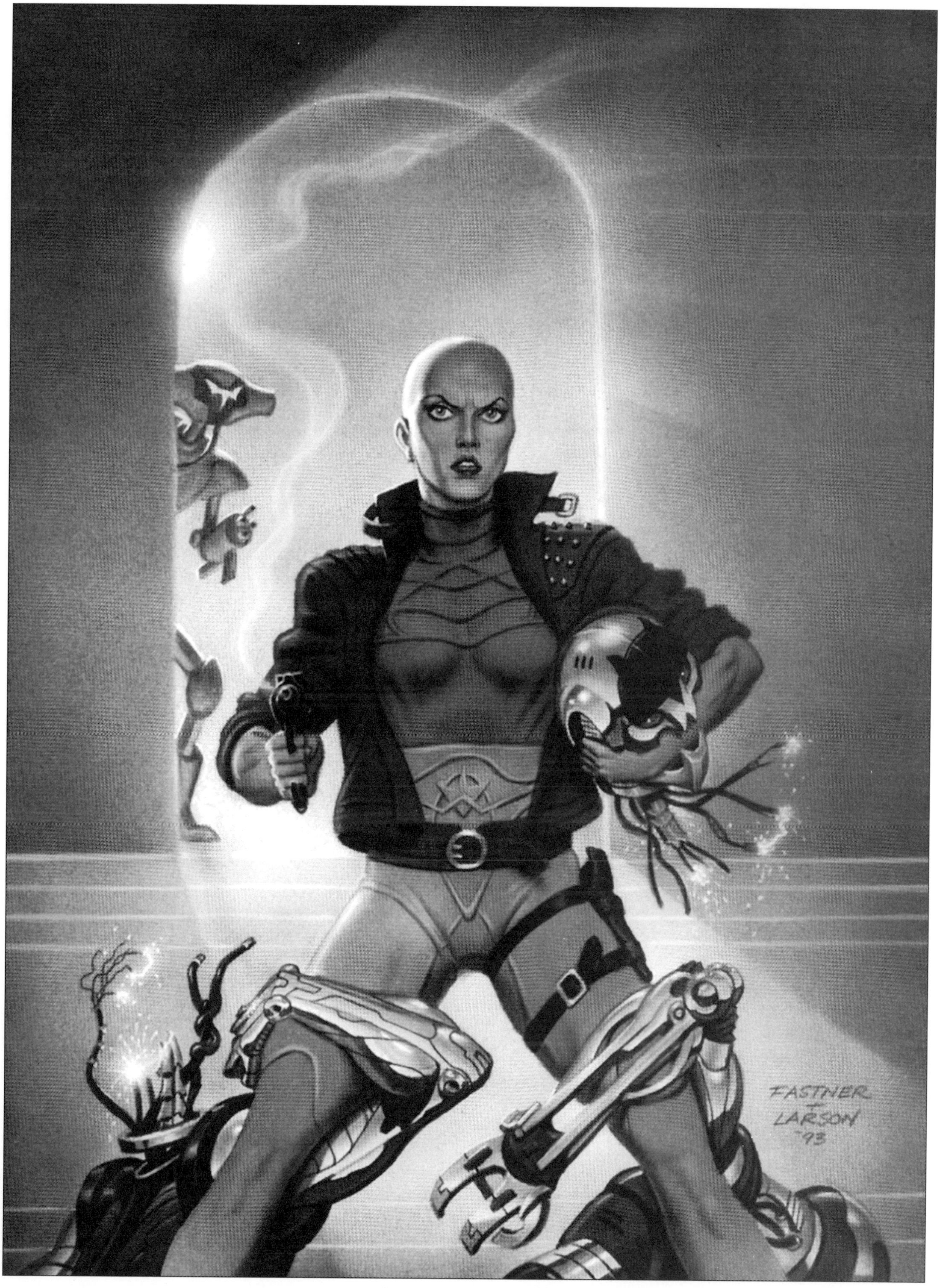
FASTNER
+
LARSON
'93

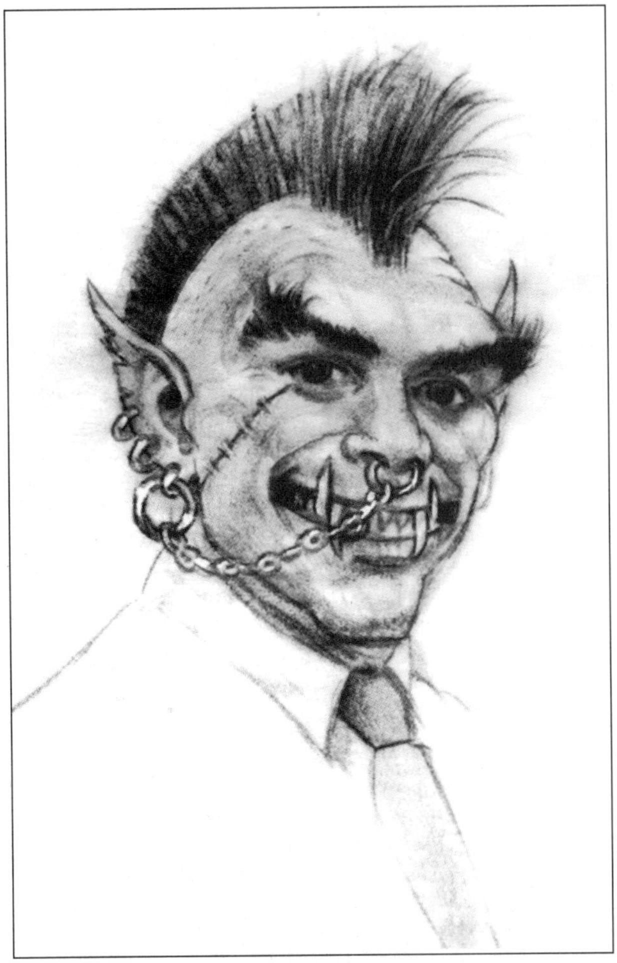

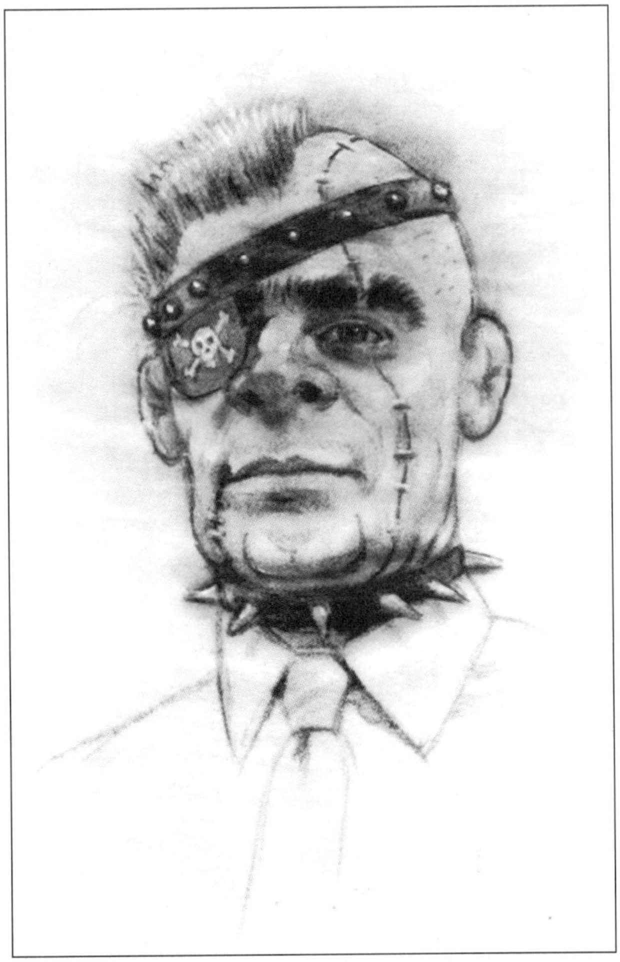

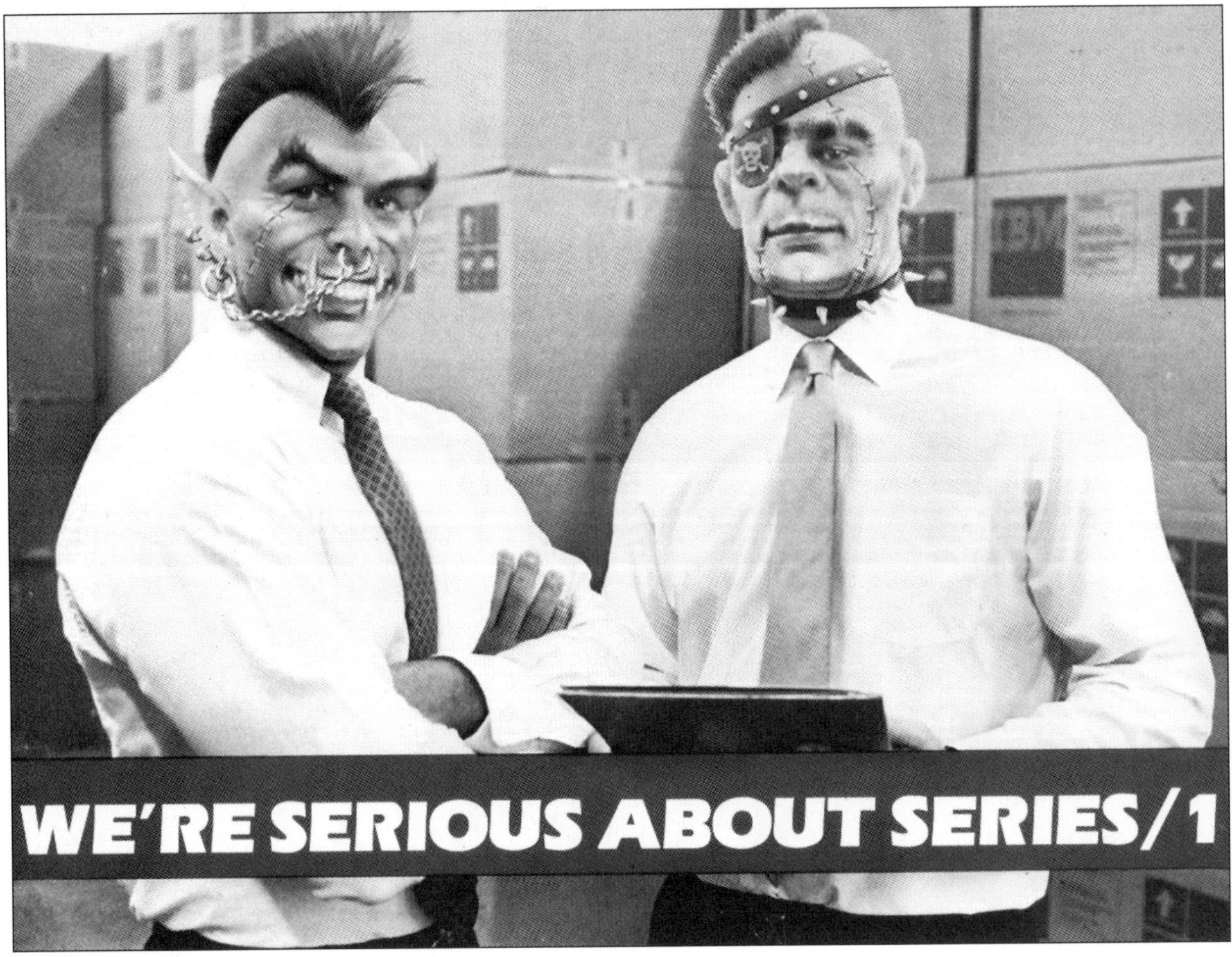


TOP: ADVERTISING ASSIGNMENT REQUIRED STEVE TO TURN NICE BUSINESSMEN INTO HORRIFYING MONSTERS

BOTTOM: HORRIFYING BUSINESSMEN!

FOLLOWING PAGE: PENCILS TO **X-MEN** PORTFOLIO FEATURING **WOLVERINE**

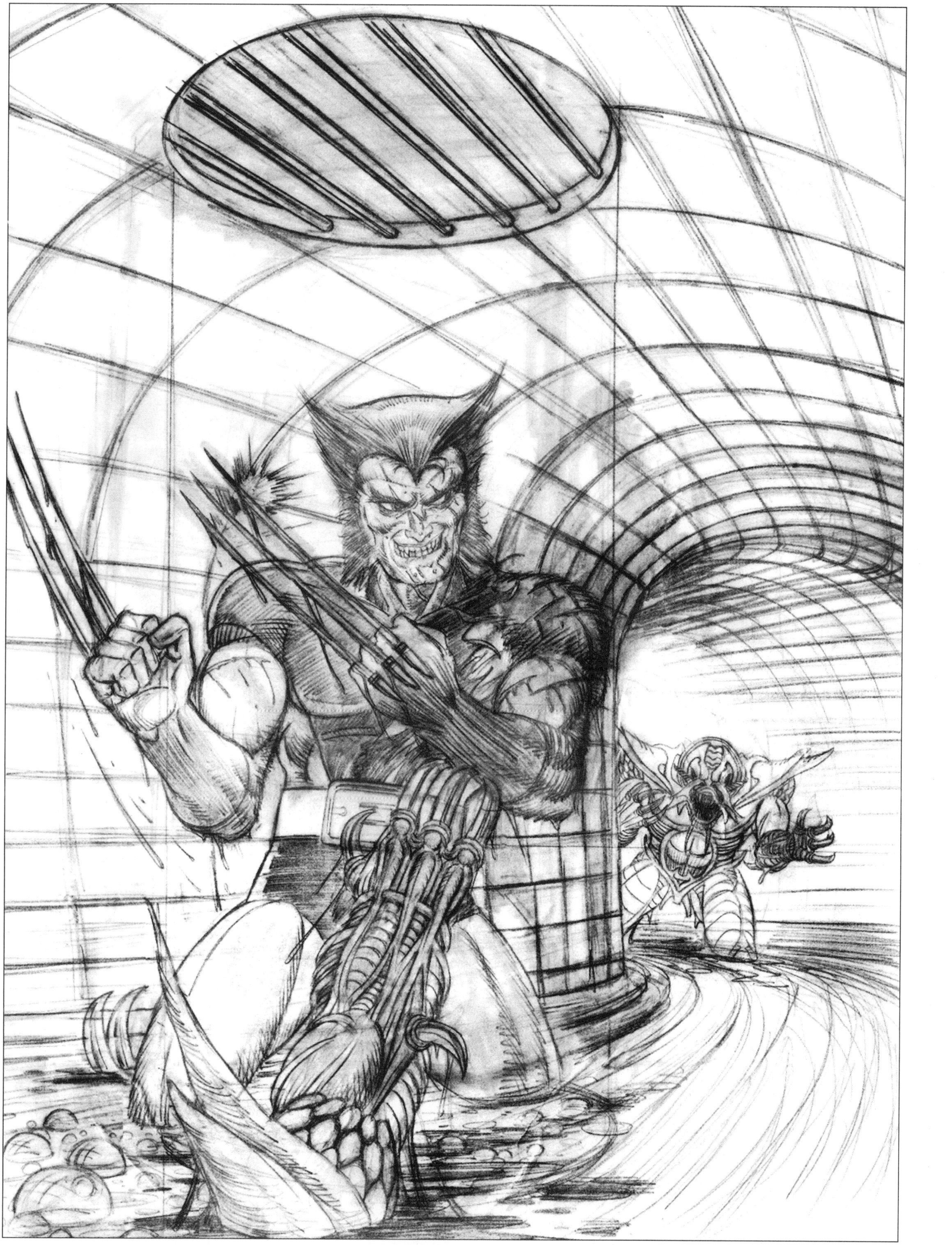

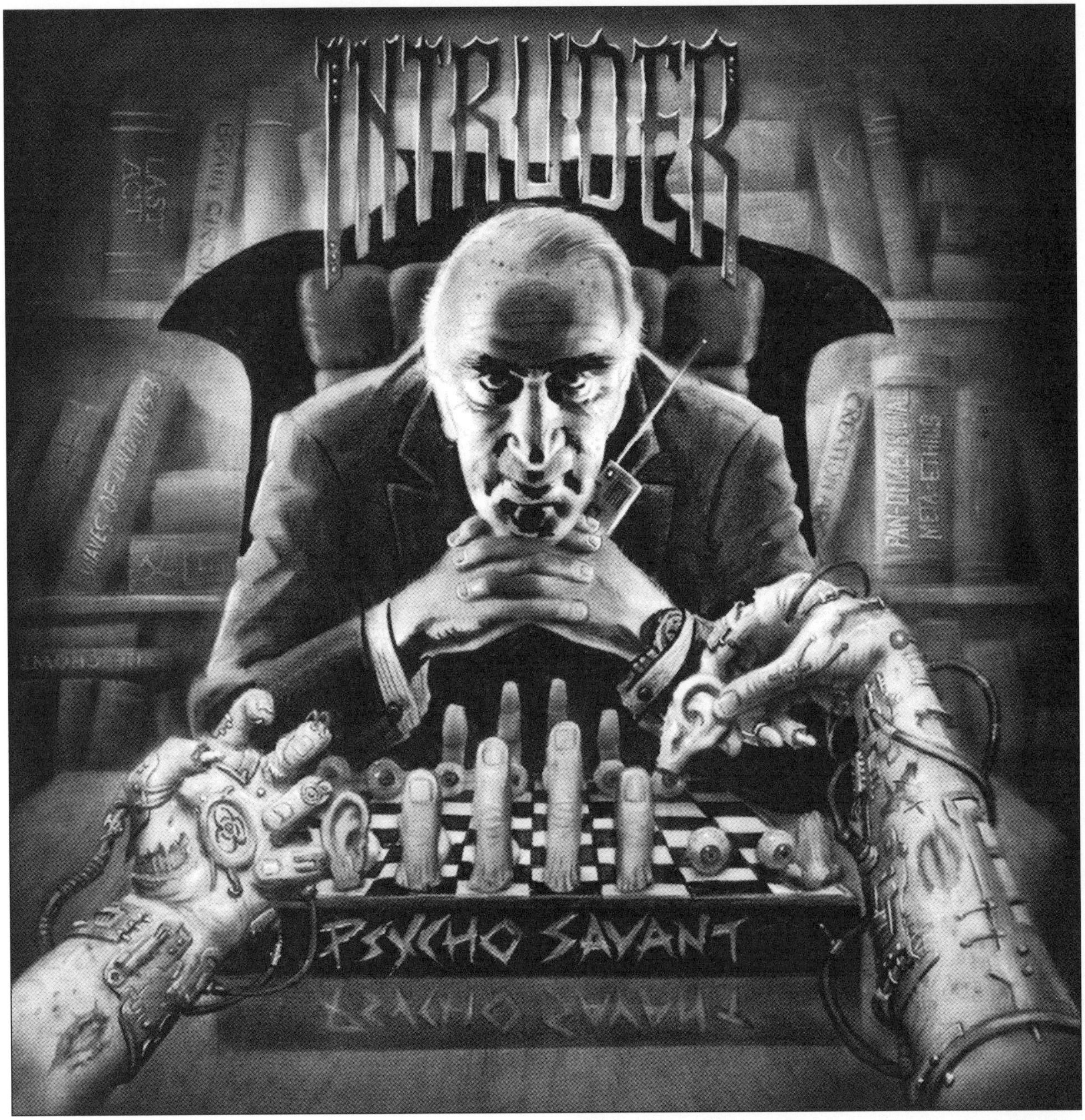


Clockwise from top:

For the band **Intruder**, "Psycho Savant" tone study.

Full size color study

Tight pencils of same

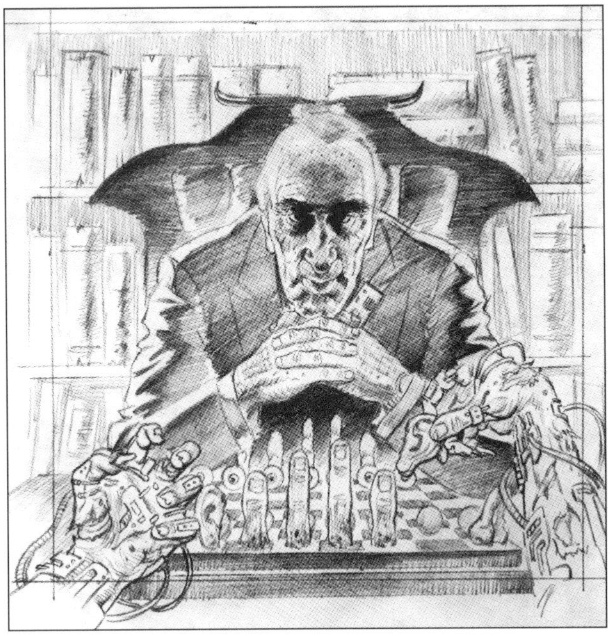

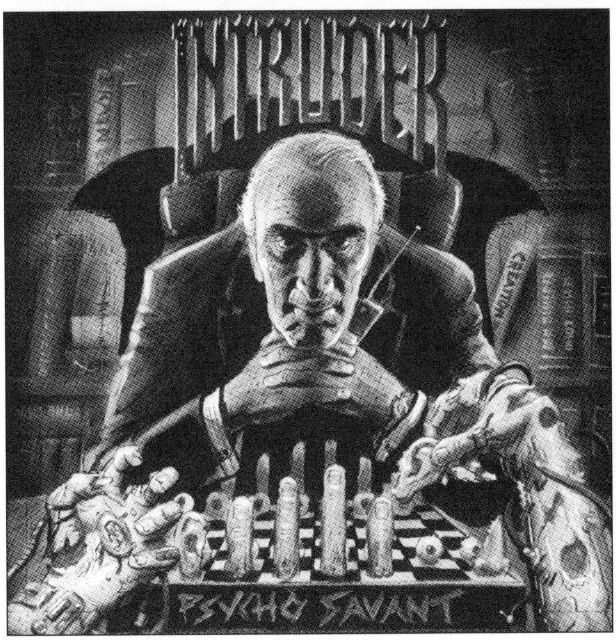

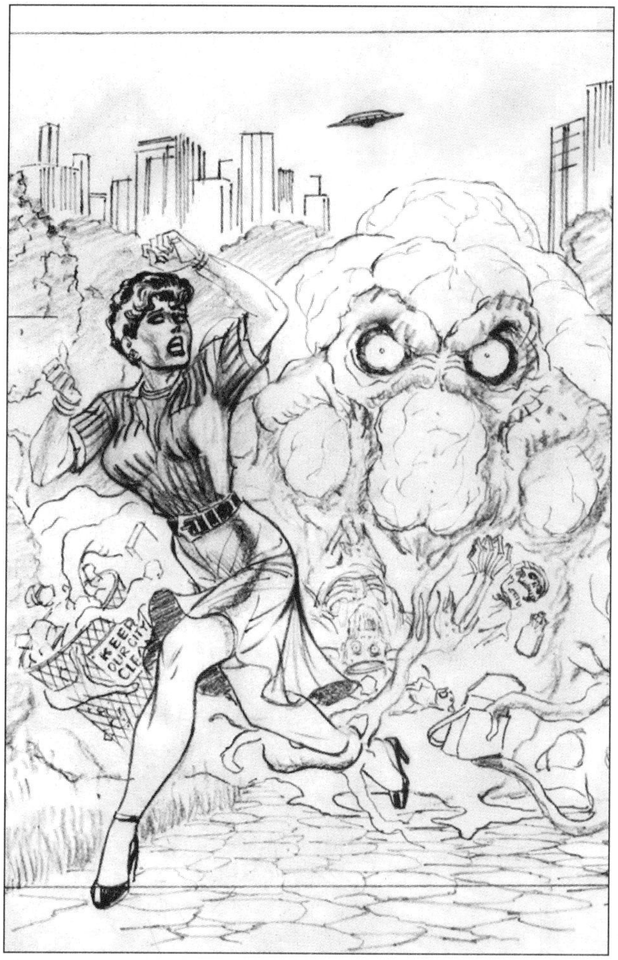

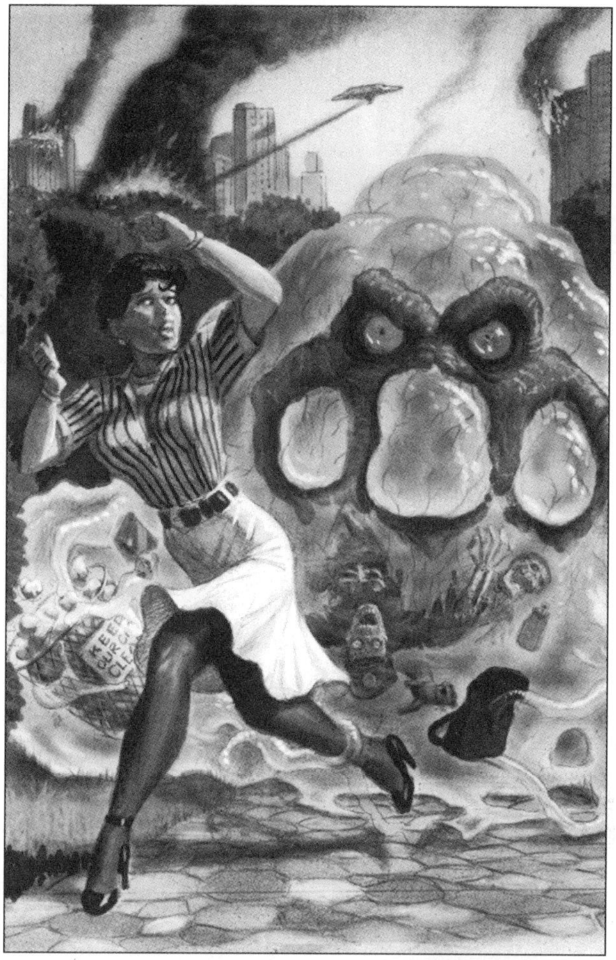

*"Plasmos, Tyrant from the Tenth Planet, cleans up NYC once and for all"*

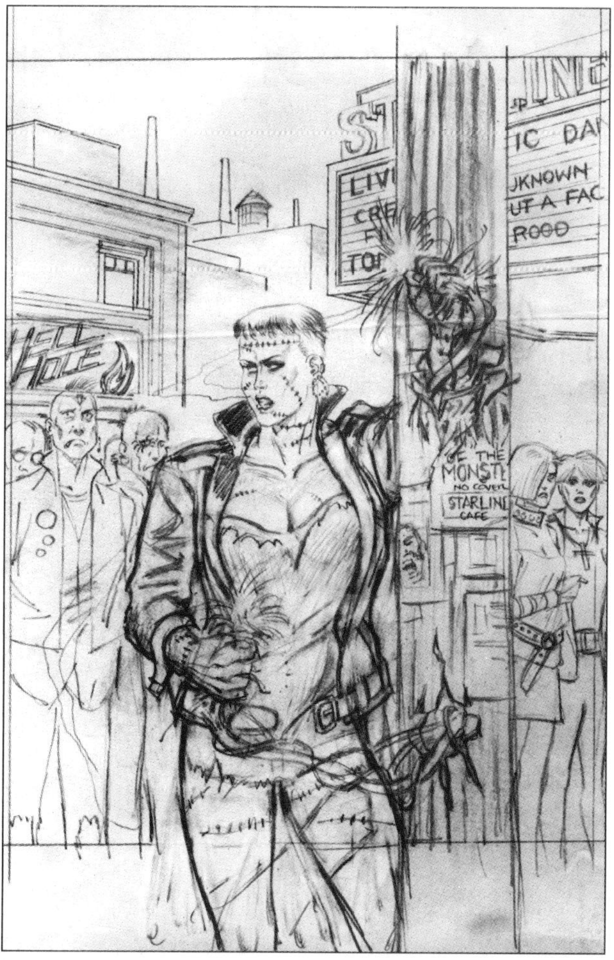


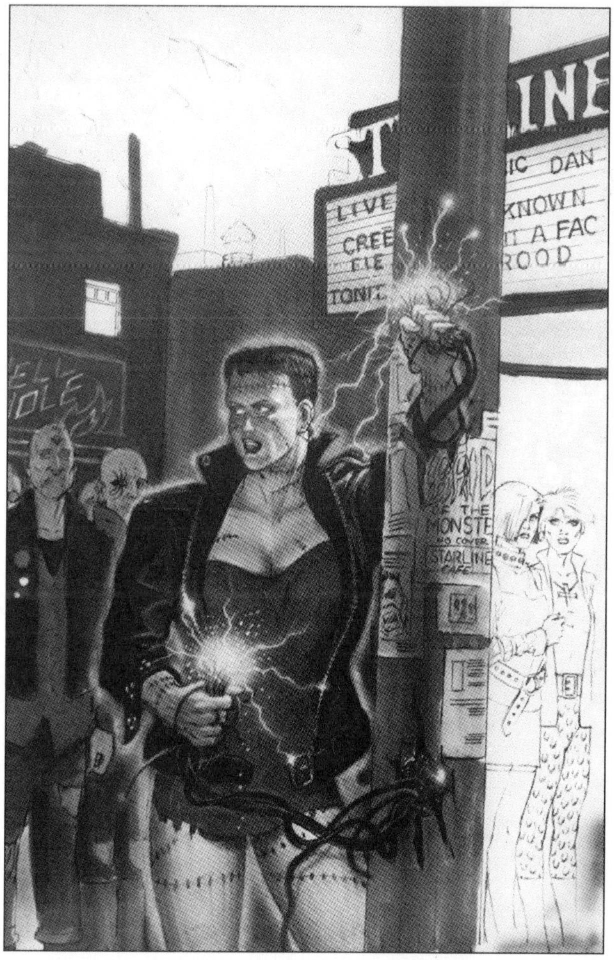


Clockwise from top left:

Pencils to the cover of **666** #6 - ode to a Blob!

Finished color study of same

**666** #5, featuring a punked-out Frankenbabe getting juiced in Greenwich Village!

Pencils to same

Following page: **Clawdia**, design for a T-shirt

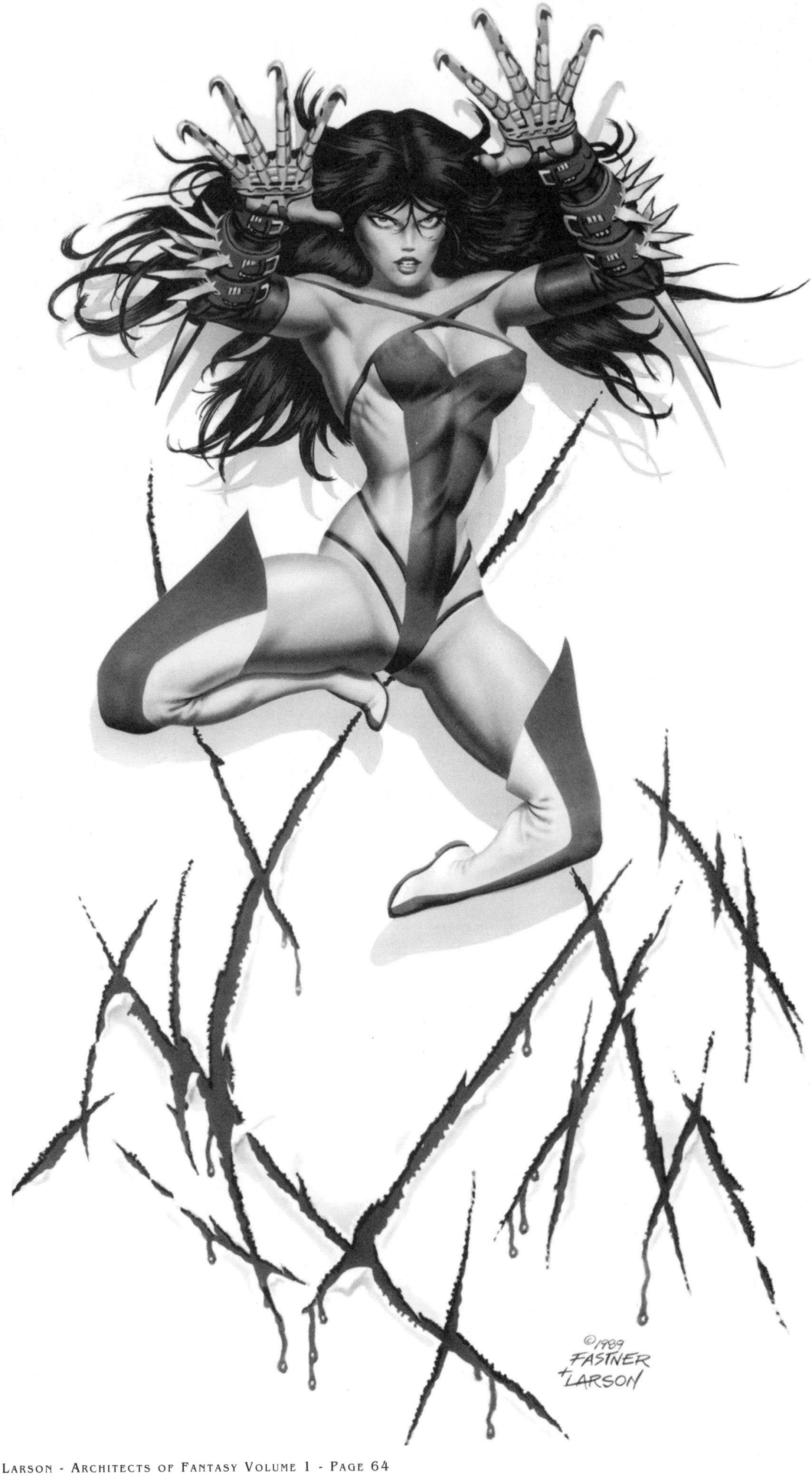
©1989
FASTNER
+LARSON